The Nineteenth-Century Wind Band and Wind Ensemble

Books by David Whitwell

Philosophic Foundations of Education
Foundations of Music Education
Music Education of the Future
The Sousa Oral History Project
The Art of Musical Conducting
The Longy Club: 1900–1917
A Concise History of the Wind Band
Wagner on Bands
Berlioz on Bands
Aesthetics of Music in Ancient Civilizations
Aesthetics of Music in the Middle Ages

The History and Literature of the Wind Band and Wind Ensemble Series

Volume 1 The Wind Band and Wind Ensemble Before 1500
Volume 2 The Renaissance Wind Band and Wind Ensemble
Volume 3 The Baroque Wind Band and Wind Ensemble
Volume 4 The Wind Band and Wind Ensemble of the Classical Period (1750–1800)
Volume 5 The Nineteenth-Century Wind Band and Wind Ensemble
Volume 6 A Catalog of Multi-Part Repertoire for Wind Instruments or for Undesignated Instrumentation before 1600
Volume 7 Baroque Wind Band and Wind Ensemble Repertoire
Volume 8 Classic Period Wind Band and Wind Ensemble Repertoire
Volume 9 Nineteenth-Century Wind Band and Wind Ensemble Repertoire
Volume 10 A Supplementary Catalog of Wind Band and Wind Ensemble Repertoire
Volume 11 A Catalog of Wind Repertoire before the Twentieth Century for One to Five Players
Volume 12 A Second Supplementary Catalog of Early Wind Band and Wind Ensemble Repertoire
Volume 13 Name Index, Volumes 1–12, The History and Literature of the Wind Band and Wind Ensemble

David Whitwell

The Nineteenth-Century Wind Band and Wind Ensemble

THE HISTORY AND LITERATURE OF THE WIND BAND AND WIND ENSEMBLE, VOLUME 5

EDITED BY CRAIG DABELSTEIN

WHITWELL PUBLISHING • AUSTIN, TEXAS, USA

Whitwell Publishing, Austin 78701
www.whitwellbooks.com

© 1984, 2012 by David Whitwell
All rights reserved. First edition 1984.
Second edition 2012

Printed in the United States of America

PAPERBACK
ISBN-13: 978-1-936512-33-1
ISBN-10: 1936512335

All images used in this book are in the public domain except where otherwise noted.

Composed in Bembo Book

Contents

Foreword		vii
Acknowledgements		ix

PART 1 MILITARY BANDS … 1

  1 Military Bands in Germany … 9
      Military Bands during the Napoleonic Period
        Infantry Bands
        Cavalry Bands
        Music of the Jäger Battalions
        Military Music Education
        The Arméemarsche Collection, 1817–1859
        The Nineteenth Century Zapfenstreich
      Infantry Bands, 1820–1838
      Cavalry Bands, 1820–1829
      Jäger Bands
      The Wilhelm Wieprecht Era
      Prussian Military Bands during the 'Golden Age'
        Wieprecht's Unified System
      Military Bands of the other German States

  2 Military Bands in Austria … 41
      Infantry Bands before Mid-Century
      Cavalry and Jäger Bands before Mid-Century
      Military Bands during the 'Golden Age'
      Music Schools
      The Birth of the Modern March

  3 Military Bands in France … 57
      The Napoleonic Period
      The Period of Sax

  4 Military Bands in England … 77
      Military Bands during the Napoleonic Period
      Post-Napoleonic Growth and Experimentation
      The Golden Age

  5 Military Bands in Russia … 85
  6 Military Bands in Italy … 87

PART 2 CIVIC WIND BANDS

    7   Military Bands in Public Concerts   97
          The 1867 World Band Competition in Paris
          Military Bands and Opera
          'Popularizing Orchestral' Music

    8   Civic Wind Bands in the German-Speaking Countries   125
          Civic Wind Bands before 1848
          Civic Wind Bands after Mid-Century

    9   Civic Wind Bands in France   143
          Civic Wind Bands after Mid-Century

    10   Civic Wind Bands in Italy   155
    11   Civic Wind Bands in England   161
          The Birth of the Brass Bands
          Early Brass Band Contests
          The First 'National' Contests
          Brass Bands after 1860

PART 3 COURT WIND BANDS

    12   Court Wind Bands in Austria   177
          The Liechtenstein Harmoniemusik
          The Imperial Harmoniemusik

    13   Court Wind Bands in Germany   185
          Court Wind Bands after the Harmoniemusik Period

    14   Court Wind Bands in Italy   195
    15   Court Wind Bands in France   197
    16   Court Wind Bands in England   201

PART 3 WIND BANDS IN THE CHURCH   207

Bibliography   221
Index   227
About The Author   235

Foreword

This volume is the fifth of several which together attempt a general History and Literature of the Wind Band and Wind Ensemble. At the time these volumes were first written there was no comprehensive history of the wind band. In addition these volumes together provide library identification and shelf-marks for more than 30,000 wind band manuscripts and early prints before 1900 found in more than 450 libraries. Over several decades it was my practice when conducting in Europe to add some weeks to my trip to visit libraries and examine early works for wind band and many of these scores I worked into the repertoire of my own concerts.

In the nineteenth century it was the military band, in particular, which not only grew in size, due to vast manufacturing activity following in the shadow of the Industrial Revolution, but became identified with the highest levels of society.

Civic bands, which on the continent were little heard from during the Napoleonic years, had a new birth of activity after the Napoleonic Period and the civic bands formed at that time are in many cases still very active today. In addition the organization of civic choral organizations at the same time led to a very large repertoire of compositions for voices and winds, including full band, especially commissioned by these organizations from virtually every great composer of the nineteenth century.

Court and Church bands are rarely found in the nineteenth century as independent organizations, however, there is a vast extant repertoire of original music written by the greatest composers for separate occasions being celebrated in the life of the court and church. In the Catholic areas there was an annual Sunday set aside for the blessing of the military and on those occasions there were sometimes commissioned full masses for military band and chorus.

The real purpose in writing these volumes has been an attempt to demonstrate to band directors everywhere that they represent a medium that has performed at the highest levels of society over a very great span of time and that while all musicians take their turn at functional music wind bands also performed music to be listened to. It is a very great mistake for any band director to assume that his role is limited to only entertaining the public.

> David Whitwell
> Austin, Texas

Acknowledgments

This new edition would not have been possible without the encouragement and help of Craig Dabelstein of Brisbane, Australia. His experience as a musician and educator himself has contributed greatly to his expertise as editor of this volume.

>David Whitwell
>Austin, 2012

PART I
Military Bands

Military Bands

NEVER DURING MODERN HISTORY has there been a century when the prestige of the military was so high as it was during the nineteenth century. Looking at nineteenth century iconography, one would think the governments and the military were one, for even kings and emperors regularly wore military uniforms.[1] It was the last century in which war could be a grand adventure.

This close connection between the military and society in general during the nineteenth century extends, of course, to military bands. Consequently, one cannot speak of nineteenth-century court music without speaking of musicians in military uniforms, and the same can be said for church and civic affairs. Accordingly, in the following section I will discuss only the development of the military band as a medium and its appearances in the military environment. The appearances of military bands which were civic, court, or religious in character will be discussed later, together with the other music of those environments. It is very appropriate to think of nineteenth-century music in this way, for there was a strong circle of influence from the military to civic music and back again to military music. As Sehnal points out,[2] during the Napoleonic Wars troops were often stationed for long periods in a single town. The military musicians were eager to take part in court and civic musical activities and often their participation made possible larger musical productions.[3] Thus, while the military was supporting civic music, at the same time civic needs were moving the military musical organizations away from purely functional activities and toward aesthetic (concert) activities.

For discussion of the development of the medium itself, it seems to me there are three rather natural periods for nineteenth-century military bands. First, there is the period from the beginning of the century through the Napoleonic Wars, when the military bands in most countries seem only to continue the fundamental *Harmoniemusik* approach of the eighteenth century. Second, beginning about 1820–1825, is a period of extraordinary developments in individual wind instruments,

[1] The American Presidents were a rare exception.

[2] Jiri Sehnal, 'Die Musikkapelle. des Olmützer Erzbischofs Anton Theodor Colloredo-Waldsee 1777–1811,' *Das Haydn Jahrbuch*, vol. 10 (Wien, 1978), 138.

[3] One sometimes sees icons of nineteenth-century orchestras in which the string players are in white tie and tails while the wind players are in military uniforms, as for example a woodcut of a concert given in Covent Garden, published in *The Illustrated London News* (London, 1846), IX, 289. Berlioz, in *Memoirs of Hector Berlioz* (New York: A. A. Knopf, 1932), 222, describes the rehearsals for his *Carnaval Romain* in 1838:

> Habeneck had heard that we had rehearsed it in the morning without the wind instruments, part of the band having been called off for the National Guard. 'Good!' said he to himself. 'There will certainly be a catastrophe at his [Berlioz's] concert this evening. I must be there.' On my arrival, indeed, I was surrounded [off stage] by all the wind players, who were in terror at the idea of having to play an overture of which they did not know a note.

Indeed, this tradition is not yet dead in the twentieth century, as I discovered once during an appearance with the National Orchestra of Bolivia. At the first rehearsal all the winds were missing, but I was reassured not to worry—'the band will be here later.' And, indeed, they appeared an hour later, and all in uniform!

both old and new, and a corresponding growth in the size and instrumentation of military bands everywhere. Finally, this leads, by mid-century, to the 'Golden Age' of military bands.

While it is not necessary here to duplicate the wealth of information now available on the amazing developments in the manufacture of wind instruments during the nineteenth century, perhaps it would be helpful to the reader of the following pages to summarize briefly the major accomplishments of this period. The historic step forward for the brass instruments of the nineteenth century was, of course, the invention of the valve. The fact that we do not know today whom to credit with its invention, probably only reflects the fact that so many persons were searching along the same lines. There is the often mentioned patent of Charles Clagget in London, which describes some sort of valve prototype in 1788.[4] A valve trumpet dated 1806, made by A. and I. Kerner, in the Tölzer Museum represents another early example.[5] An article titled, 'New Discovery,' in the *Allgemeine Musikalische Zeitung* (May, 1815) credits one, Heinrich Stölzel, of Ples, with the invention of something which sounds like the modern valve in principle. Wilhelm Wieprecht (1802–1872), who would become the head of all Prussian military bands, wrote in 1845[6] that when Stölzel's patent expired in 1828, another musician, named Blühmel, came forward with documents to suggest that he had sold his invention to Stölzel ten years earlier. Wieprecht, although he knew them both personally, was unable to determine who had the greater claim.

In any case, the valve had arrived and it opened the door to effective chromatic playing for the first time, replacing the various attempts at keyed brass instruments. The valved trumpet appeared in the Prussian military music by about 1826,[7] and soon thereafter in Russia (1830) and England (1831), where it was first known as the 'Russian Valve Trumpet.'[8]

A new instrument appeared, the *cornet à pistons*, which, being conical was first thought of as more related to the horn family and hence first played by horn players. It soon became very popular, especially in France and England, where its association with light popular music has ruined its reputation[9] even to the present day.

[4] The patent, as quoted in Adam Carse, *Musical Wind Instruments* (New York: Da Capo Press, 1965), 63ff., read,

> My Sixth new improvement on musical instruments relates to the french horns or trumpets, and consists in uniting together two french horns or trumpets in such a manner that the same mouthpiece may be applied to either of them instantaneously during the time of performance, as the music may require. In the cover of this box, what is commonly called the mouthpiece is fixed by means of a joint, by means of a elastic, gum, or leather, or otherwise so that the point of the mouthpiece may be directed to the opening of either of the horns or trumpets at pleasure, at the same time that another piece of elastic stops the aperture of the horn or trumpet which is not in use.

No one knows what happened to this device, or if it ever existed. A contemporary, Busby, in *Concert Room and Orchestra Anecdotes* (London: Clementi, 1825), described Clagget as one, 'the misfortune of whose life it was, to have ideas theoretically sublime, but deficient in practical utility.'

[5] Johannes Reschke, *Studie zur Geschichte der brandenburgischpreussischen Herresmusik* (Berlin: VDI-Verlag, 1936), 38.

[6] In the *Berliner Musikalische Zeitung*.

[7] Reschke, *Studie zur Geschichte … Herresmusik*.

[8] Carse, *Musical Wind Instruments*, 239.

The adaptation of valves to the horn[10] and trombone[11] was tried immediately, but in both cases the prejudices of the players somewhat retarded final acceptance.

The story of nineteenth-century low 'brass' begins with the ancient serpent, which now began to take on as many as fourteen keys. 'Frigid and abominable blaring ... essentially barbarous,' Berlioz called it.[12] Nevertheless it is found in his scores, as well as in those by Mendelssohn and Wagner. The instrument developed from it, the bass horn, was little better—Berlioz observing that it 'might be withdrawn from the family of wind instruments without the slightest injury to Art.'[13] The ophicleide appeared first in 1821 in France and soon found its way into the scores of Mendelssohn, Meyerbeer, Schumann, Berlioz, Verdi, Wagner, etc., not to mention wind band scores. It was much superior to either the serpent or the bass horn, but it came too late for soon they and all their relatives[14] were replaced by the tuba,[15] which was patented in Berlin in 1835 by Wieprecht.[16]

No less important were the rapid improvements in woodwind manufacture. Consider some of these significant developments: perforated key-covers (1810–1850), horizontal rod-axles (1832, and with multiple action in 1838), rollers (on the clarinet by 1823), and the appearance of ring keys (1840) and German silver (1823).

The result of these developments[17] was an astonishing production of almost countless varieties of the principal woodwind instruments, each instrument differing dramatically from maker to maker and from country to country. Consider, for example, a single advertisement (Lafleur) for oboes from 1870 London.

> The Oboe, the most delicate of all the Musical Instruments, has been greatly improved of late years, owing to the constant labours and ability of the world renowned maker Mons. Triébert, who may be called the Stradivarius of Oboe makers ... The instruments are all most carefully tested by the celebrated Oboe player Mons. Barret, now retired from the leading situations he occupied at the Opera and societies in London.
>
> Triébert's Oboe, rosewood, 12 keys, German silver or real silver mounted
>
> > 15 keys, with metal-lined joints
> > The same with plate for top D and double use of E flat

---

9 In England, George Bernard Shaw was especially critical of the cornet. See, Corno di Bassetto [George Bernard Shaw], *London Music* (London, 1937), 75 ('The vulgarity of the cornet is incurable.'), 127, and 211. But Shaw was wrong, for the instrument was not bad—just how it was played and what it played. As Carse observed (*Musical Wind Instruments*, 250), the trumpet, which Shaw favored, can also be made to sound less than noble.

> The dance bands of the present century have proved in a most convincing manner that the trumpet can be played in a style which is infinitely more vulgar and degrading than the very worst style of cornet-playing.

10 Some horn players seem to have misunderstood the principle of the valve, believing it only to be a wonderful replacement for the 'bag of crooks,' but not realizing at first that it was possible to 'finger' the various notes in the manner of woodwind instruments and in the manner modern valve brass instruments are taught. One must remember, to be fair, that while the fingering principle of a flute is visually self-explanatory, the same can not be said for the valve. (For further discussion of this misunderstanding, see my '19th Century Russian Composers—Their Music for Winds,' *The Instrumentalist* [February, 1968]). Since it was thus not immediately clear that the new valve would be accepted, some nineteenth-century composers, among them Wagner and Schumann, scored for both valved and natural horns, as if they wanted to make sure their works could be played by whichever instrument should win out.

17 keys, with C plate and Bb for left thumb
  The same, with shake for C#, down to low Bb

Triébert's Oboe with octave keys at double employ
  The same with Barret celebrated system
  The same with Boehm system for the right hand
  Ditto, down to A, etc.

Pastoral Oboe in G or Ab acute, maple, 4 brass keys
  The same, Boehm system, in G, rosewood
  The same, 10 keys, rosewood Military Oboe

Our own make Oboes
  Boehm system, cocoa; 15 keys
    The same 12 keys
  13 keys and two rings, ordinary make (capital for beginners), boxwood

Corno Inglese, Triébert's make

Baritone Oboe, rosewood, G.S. mounts, Triébert's make

Superior Morton's English make Cor Anglais, 13 keys, down to Bb

Musette (reed included)—Pastoral Instrument to imitate the Swiss Pipe
  Trébert's make, cocoa, 8 keys
  The same, boxwood, brass-mounted

It was during the nineteenth century that the oboe took on most of its chromatic keys. Beethoven and Weber would have known the two-key instrument, an instrument which would have been quite old-fashioned by mid-century.[18]

No less dramatic were the changes in the flute, led, of course, by Theobald Boehm (1794–1881). His first period of work, after 1831, concentrated on the improvement of the mechanism and the arrangement of keys with respect to fingering. After 1846 he began to concentrate on the bore and produced the cylindrical design which brought to an end one hundred and fifty years of the conical flute.

The clarinet began the nineteenth century with at most six keys and by the end of the century some models had nineteen! The French and German preferences were increasingly distinct, the French developing the so-called 'Boehm system clarinet' near mid-century.[19] The French and German bassoons also differed greatly; the French sought individuality, the Germans the capacity to blend.

---

[11] The valved trombone with the bell facing backwards never found the approval in Prussia which it had in Hungary (1820), The Netherlands (1825), Belgium (1831), or the United States (Civil War period). See Reschke, *Studie zur Geschichte der brandenburgischpreussischen Herresmusik*, 39.

[12] Quoted in Carse, *Musical Wind Instruments*, 276. In his *Treatise on Instrumentation* (New York: Kalmus, 1948), 348, Berlioz adds, 'The truly barbaric tone of this instrument would be much better suited for the bloody cult of the Druids.'

[13] Berlioz, *Treatise on Instrumentation*.

[14] Berlioz, ibid., 338, mentions a 'Double-bass Ophicleide,' which he says,

> up to the present nobody in Paris has been willing to play because of the volume of breath required. This surpasses the lung power of even the strongest man.

[15] In some places it took a while. At the first brass band festival to be held in the Crystal Palace in London, in 1860, there were present 157 tubas, but still 133 ophicleides. (Carse, *Musical Wind Instruments*, 304)

[16] The instrument which has survived is the 'bass tuba' of an original family of at least five members made by Wieprecht. One of his arrangements of the music of Meyerbeer in fact uses all five. Berlioz described (*Treatise on Instrumentation*, 339) the 'bass tuba' as a 'kind of bombardon,' adding, 'The effect of a great number of bass tubas in a large military band is beyond imagination.'

[17] Carse, *Musical Wind Instruments*, 46ff.

[18] Ibid., 137ff.

There were entirely new woodwinds, including a nine-member sarrusophone family and, of course, the saxophone family. Berlioz,[20] like a proud God-father, gave his prediction for the aesthetic future of this new instrument.

> Naturally, this instrument will never be suitable for rapid passages, or complicated arpeggios, but ... instead of complaining, we must rejoice that it is impossible to misuse the Saxophone and thus to destroy its majestic nature by forcing it to render mere musical futilities.

Fueled not only by the immediate market of military bands, which were growing both larger in size and in number everywhere, but, of course, by the industrial energy initiated at the beginning of the century by the so-called 'Industrial Revolution,' instrument makers brought forth a virtual flood of new, or newly designed, instruments. Rimsky-Korsakov, upon being appointed Inspector of Naval Bands in Russia in 1873, attempted to write a treatise which would sort out this multiplicity of wind instruments. One can sense the severity of the problem through the frustration expressed in his description of it.

> The woodwinds, in particular, proved to include untold multitudes of makes; in reality each maker or each factory has an individual system. By adding an extra valve or key, the maker either adds a new trill on his instrument or makes easier some run that presents difficulties on instruments of other makes. There was absolutely no possibility of finding one's way through all this maze. In the group of brass instruments I found some with three, four, and five valves; the construction of these valves is not always the same on the instruments of the various firms. To describe all this was absolutely beyond my power.[21]

The developmental work on so many instruments in so brief a time must, we may be sure, have rendered some instruments more successful than others. 'It splits your head to hear these hundreds of wretched machines, each more out of tune than the next,' said Berlioz, after judging musical instruments at an exhibition in London in 1851.[22]

One consequence of this multiplicity of invention and design was that local military bands tended to use the instruments of local manufacturers, resulting in military bands which differed in instrumentation according to national or

[19] It was perfected by the player Klosé together with the French maker Auguste Buffet.

[20] Hector Berlioz, *Journal des Debats*, June 12, 1842.

[21] Nikolay Rimsky-Korsakov, *My Musical Life* (New York: Tudor Pub., 1936), 117.

[22] Quoted in Jacques Barzun, *Berlioz and the Romantic Century* (Boston: Little, Brown, 1950), 2:33.

local tastes—in contrast with the symphony orchestra, whose instrumentation was more international in character. Whether this is to be viewed as a hindrance to the international development of literature, or as a positive cultural characteristic at the national level, depends on one's perspective.

1   *Military Bands in Germany*

WHILE I WILL ATTEMPT TO PROVIDE some important information about all the major states of nineteenth-century Germany, the focus of this chapter must be on Prussia. This is necessary not only because of the political dominance which Prussia exercised in German affairs during the eighteenth and nineteenth centuries, but because nearly all important innovations in German military music had their origin there.

GERMAN MILITARY BANDS DURING THE NAPOLEONIC PERIOD

Infantry Bands

For Prussia, the new century began poorly. Frederick William III, reigning 1797–1840, the next major Prussian King after Frederick the Great,[1] was a good man and not a bad leader.[2] In view of the army and government he inherited, not to mention the overwhelming initial success of Napoleon over nearly everyone, perhaps it is better to remember his achievement in the rebuilding of Prussia than his relationship to its collapse in 1805–1807. Frederick William's first encounter with Napoleon resulted in defeat and the compromising Peace of 1805–1806, through which Prussia lost Neuchâtel, Cleves, and Ansbach to France. Things became much worse with the annihilation of the Prussians and Saxons at Jena and Auerstedt on 14 October 1806. Now Napoleon (sitting in the King's chambers in Berlin!) directed the 1807 Peace of Tilsit, through which Prussia lost forty-nine percent of her former terrain and more than half of her former population.[3]

    The complete absence of official government documents which mention details of Prussian military bands during this period makes it difficult to speak with authority, but the depressed economic situation, the limits of a forty-five thousand man military imposed by the Peace of Tilsit, and some

[1] Between them was Frederick William II, reigning 1786–1797, who, despite his acquisition of large parts of Poland, allowed the mighty military discipline established by his uncle, Frederick the Great, to decay.

[2] As with the other members of this Prussian family, he also tried his hand in composition. There are at least two extant autographs in Berlin, Deutsche Staatsbibliothek, of his own *Pfeifenmärsche*. His beautiful young wife, Louise of Mecklenburg-Strelitz (1776–1810), was the idol of everyone. Her hold on the minds of the German people can be measured in a small way by the appearance, sixty years after her death, of a *Prelude & Fugue* for military band by Buchholz (an uncataloged manuscript in Graz, Hochschule für Musik), marking the one hundredth anniversary of her birth.

[3] Will & Ariel Durant, *The Age of Napoleon* (New York: Simon and Schuster, 1975), 596.

additional evidence seem to suggest that little development beyond the practice of the late eighteenth century occurred during this period.

While no official policy for the instrumentation of Prussian infantry bands seems to have been made during the eighteenth century,[4] one might suppose a typical infantry band at the end of the century consisted of pairs of oboes, clarinets, and bassoons with a trumpet, if one can judge by the extant music of the Hausbibliothek collection in Berlin.[5] This seems entirely consistent with an advertisement in the *Berlinische Musikalische Zeitung* for 1805, which offered music, 'for the customary combination of the Regimental bands of the Prussian Infantry,' scored for pairs of oboes, clarinets, horns, and trumpet.[6]

This instrumentation falls within the general categorization known as *Harmoniemusik* (usually six or eight players of pairs of oboes, clarinets, horns, and bassoons). I have outlined, in volumes three and four of this series, the development of this medium, from the seventeenth-century *Les Grands Hautbois*, into the Baroque German court and military *Hautboisten*, and finally, with the arrival of the Bohemian influence, into the Classical court *Harmoniemusik* and the military *Hoboisten*. It is important for the reader to remember, therefore, that this is not merely a term invented by later musicologists, but was, by the beginning of the nineteenth century, an established medium known to all musicians

Players being traditionally conservative, due to their many years devoted to learning one specific skill, one can understand that there was a certain sense of protection of this tradition on the part of the established wind players. Thus the name 'Harmonie,' or 'Hoboisten,' remains associated with military bands long after there is any real resemblance to the old tradition itself. One can see this in the titles of many nineteenth-century military band works which seem to point to a nucleus of *Harmoniemusik*, with everything else described as only an appendix of sorts. I might offer as examples the Maschek *Die Schlacht bei Leipzig* (1813) for 'Harmoniemusik und Türkische musik' or the well-known Spohr work, the *Notturno* (1817), for 'Harmonie- und Janitscharenmusik.' Exactly the same tradition is reflected in the nineteenth-century Austrian military custom of distinguishing (in uniform and sometimes in pay) between the 'Hoboisten' and 'Bandisten' within a single band.

[4] One often reads, although no writer ever gives his source, of such a policy laid down in 1763 by Frederick the Great. I have discussed this in the fourth volume of this series, where I mention that Roger Hellyer, in 'Harmoniemusik,' (dissertation, Oxford, 1972), 47, has studied this question in depth and concluded that no such order ever existed.

[5] Reschke, *Studie zur Geschichte der brandenburgischpreussischen Herresmusik*, 38, who had the opportunity to study this collection before a large part of it was destroyed during World War II, suggests a somewhat broader choice of 'typical' instrumentations: pairs of oboes, clarinets, and bassoons; or pairs of oboes and clarinets, with a bassoon and trumpet; or pairs of clarinets, horns, and bassoons.

[6] Quoted in Hellyer, 'Harmoniemusik,' 227, who points out that the missing bassoons here is almost surely an error. A. Kalkbrenner, in *Wilhelm Wieprecht* (Berlin: E. Prager, 1882), 34, suggests, without source, that a typical infantry instrumentation until 1805 was pairs of large flutes, oboes, clarinets, bassoons, invention-horns, invention-trumpets, and bass trombones, to which were added in 1806, E♭ clarinet, serpent, contrabassoon, two trombones and percussion.

This sense of protection of the *Harmoniemusik* medium by the players was of course strongest felt at the beginning of the nineteenth century when they no doubt associated some sense of security to the medium itself, in view of the history of its role in the court music of the end of the eighteenth century. One sees an example of this in an extraordinary public appeal, made through the *Allgemeine Musik Zeitung*, of August 1804, by eight members of the theater orchestra in Nürnberg. Their sole apparent concern seems to have been to prevent the intrusion of the flute into the instrumentation of the military band as they knew it.

> Mr. Mainberger, Kapellmeister in Nürnberg and who is also in charge of the theater personnel, has ordered for the military music, along with the two oboes, two horns, two bassoons, and all the noisy percussion instruments, two flutes instead of the clarinets and piccolos which are necessary for this music. He orders this, meeting informed and expert tradition with spite and insults. Thus musicians working in this orchestra could put up with this purposeless institution [the addition of two flutes], if they did not have to hear the accusations from persons visiting the theater that one can hear no worse military music in Nürnberg than that which is heard in the theater.
>
> In order to counter these opinions attacking the honor of the orchestra, the undersigned see themselves moved to request the honorable Kapellmeister Mainberger to defend himself against the following criticism of his musical orders in a newspaper dedicated to the arts:
>
> > The flute, because of its delicate tone, can not be used as an instrument for military music. Even the non-musician must understand this, if he is made to notice that along with the even much louder bassoon, one needs the so-called serpent; in order to help the too delicately sounding horns, one must include the trumpets; and along with the oboes and clarinets, one has the piccolo yes even the *Duodezflötchen*.
>
> The above-mentioned orders of the town Kapellmeister, because he chooses the most delicate instrument for military music, goes therefore not only against all tradition, but against the nature of the musical instruments and produces a vague and repulsive clamor and noise.
>
> The senders of this criticism are not afraid to sign their names, because we are not subordinates following the orders of a commander, but rather artists under an artist, free to criticize, as they are in a relationship equal to him.[7]

Given the strength of this tradition, therefore, one can understand that in general the growth of German military bands during the nineteenth century began with only the expansion of the Harmoniemusik nucleus, not in the addition of new instruments to it. The first step, following the French taste, was the expansion in the number of clarinet players. In Bavaria, for example, an order in 1790 had established all infantry regiment bands at four clarinets, with pairs of bassoons and horns. The Elector, and later King, Max Josef, increased the numbers first to ten, then twelve, and finally in 1811 to thirteen regular members, in addition to percussion.[8] Kastner wrote that the

---

[7] The original text:

> Der Herr Kapellmeister Minberger in Nürnberg, dem die Besetzung der Musik in dem dasigen Theater übertragen ist, stellt bey militairischen Musiken zu 2 Oboen, 2 Hörnern, 2 Fagotten und allen zur türkischen Musik gehorigen rauschenden Instrumenten, statt der dabey unentbehrlichen Klarinetten und der hell tönenden Flauti piccoli 2 Floten an, und zwingt, bescheidene Erinnerungen verachtend und mit Beleidigungen zurückweisend, die ihm untergebenen Musiker durch sein amtliches Ausehn, dieser Anordnung Folge zu leisten. Die bey dem Orchester angestellten Musiker könnten sich diese zweckwidrige Einrichtung gefallen lassen, wenn sie nicht täglich von Personen, die das Theater besuchen, den Vorwurf hören müssten, dass man in Nürnberg keine schlechtere Kriegsmusik hören könne, als diejenige, die auf dem Theater vorkame.
>
> Diesen die Ehre des Orchesters angreifenden Urtheilen zu begegnen, sehen sich die Unterzeichneten bewogen, den Herrn Kapellmeister Mainberger zu bitten, sich gegen die folgende Kritik seiner musikalischen Anordnung in einem den Künsten gewidmeten Blatte zu erklären.
>
>> Die Flöte kann ihres zarten Tones wegen kein Instrument zu Kriegsmusiken abgeben. Dieses muss auch der Nichtmusiker einsehen, wenn man ihn darauf aufmerksam macht, dass man sogar neben dem doch viel stärker tonenden Fagotte den sogenannten Serpent braucht, dass man, um den gleichfalls zu sanft tönenden Hörnern aufzuhelfen, die Trompete beysetzt, den Oboen und Klarinetten aber die Flauti piccoli (Oktavflöten) ja sogar Duodezflötchen beygiebt.
>
> Die obengenannte Ordnung des Herrn Kapellmeisters, vermöge welcher er das zarteste Blasinstrument zur Kriegsmusik wählt, läuft daher nicht nur gegen alle Gewohnheit, sondern auch gegen die Natur der musikalischen Instrumente an, und verursacht ein unbestimmtes widerliches Geräusch und Gepolter. Die Einsender dieser Kritik scheuen sich nicht ihre Namen zu unterzeichnen, da sie es hier nicht als Untergebene mit ihrem Obern, sondern als Künstler mit dem Künstler zu thun haben, dessen Anordnungen sie in dieser Eigenschaft, folglich in einem mit ihm gleichen Verhähtnisse, beurtheilen dürfen.
>
>> Nurnberg den 4. August 1804.
>> Heinrich Backofen,
>> Ernst Backofen,
>> Gottfried Backofen,
>> Siegmund Huzler,
>> Ludwig Huzler,
>> Birckmann,
>> Hartung jun.
>> Molique.

In his answer, published the following month, Herr Mainberger observed that he was only following the model of the 'marches from the new collection published in Offenbach, scored for flutes instead of clarinets, with oboes, bassoons and horns,' and that perhaps it was best to leave the question of instrumentation to composers and publishers, rather than players. He adds that the piccolos, which the players refer to as indispensable, he could recall hearing as part of a military band only on the most rare occasions. 'Incidentally,' he writes in closing, he will not, 'come what may, answer anything else in public.'

[8] According to Peter Panoff, *Militärmusik in Geschichte und Gegenwart* (Berlin: K. Siegismund, 1938), 170. Panoff gives for 1811: piccolo, six clarinets, pairs of horns and bassoons, trumpet, trombone, and 'türkische Musik' of Schellenbaum, large and small drum, with two pair of cymbals.

German bands were excellent, though smaller than the French ones, with those of Darmstadt and Cassel having from seven to ten players.[9] Württemberg, he points out, even as late as 1819 consisted of only a 'simple musique d'harmonie.'[10] Finally, for these years, Kastner gives as the typical regimental instrumentation for Prussia, Hanover, Saxony, (and Austria), two or four clarinets, pairs of flutes, oboes, bassoons, horns, with trumpets, trombones, contrabassoon or serpent, and percussion.[11]

Panoff and Degele disagree in their estimate of the size of a regular Prussian infantry regiment band in 1807, the former suggesting ten members[12] and the latter, fifteen members.[13] Both, however, agree that by 1807 the (Headquarters) Guard Regiment had twenty-four regular members. If there were indeed individual military bands of this size by 1807 in Prussia, I would tend to believe that the larger numbers reflect the hiring of extra players by the officers of the regiment and not official government policy.[14]

The earliest extant Prussian government document[15] which sets official policy for instrumentation mentions the possibility of a regiment having up to twelve of the extra hired musicians (*Hilfsmusiker*), while also setting the regular, maintained limit at twelve.[16] At this time both the Berlin Guard Infantry Regiment[17] and the Berlin Guard Artillery Brigade[18] took advantage of the extra twelve players. This first extant document of the nineteenth century, issued by Fredrick William III, is very interesting in its detailed description of not only the instrumentation specified for the infantry regiments, but also the costs of the instruments.

> I am sending … this order on how to divide the ten bandsmen of a regiment. Each regiment can also have two men extra for *Janitscharen-Musik* [percussion], but these two will not have the advantages of the other ten. The Second Regiment and the *Füsilierbataillion* should not have special bands, at least not when I see them. The *Hoboisten-* [band] and *Janitscharen-Chor* should be the only music ensemble of a regiment.
>
> Orders on how to Divide the Ten Hoboisten of a Regiment
>
> The instrumentation should be: two clarinets in C, clarinet in F, two Inventionshorner, piccolo, two bassoons, bass trombone, and trumpet.[19]

[9] Georges Kastner, *Manuel Général de Musique Militaire* (Paris: F. Didot frères, 1848), 173.

[10] Ibid., citing an article on the reorganization of military music in Württemberg in the *Neue oestreischische militaerische Zeitschrift* (Wien, 1819).

[11] Ibid.

[12] Panoff, *Militärmusik in Geschichte und Gegenwart,* 168–169, without giving a specific instrumentation.

[13] Ludwig Degele, *Die Militärmusik* (Wolfenbuttel, 1937), 114–115, who suggests an instrumentation of pairs of large flutes, oboes, clarinets, bassoons, trumpets, and horns, with a bass trombone, serpent, and bass drum.

[14] Charles Burney, *The Present State of Music in Germany, The Netherlands, and United Provinces* (New York, London: Oxford University Press, 1959), 1:17–18, reports on this practice of the Prussians hiring extra players already in 1775. Citing a Prussian garrison in Ghent, Burney speaks of two bands, one an ensemble of hired non-military musicians, whose purpose was perhaps to imitate the local court Harmoniemusik, and the other consisting of real soldier-musicians.

> There were two bands attending every morning and evening, on the *Place d'Armes*, or parade. The one was an extra-band of professed musicians, consisting of two hautbois, two clarinets, two bassoons, and two French horns; the other were enlisted men and boys, belonging to the regiments; the number of these amounted to twenty. There were four trumpets, three fifes, two hautbois, two clarinets, two tambours de basque, two French horns, one crotolo, or cymbal, three side-drums, and one great kettledrum.

The only other early nineteenth century regimental bands which had 'Hoboisten,' that is to say an ensemble of mixed brass and woodwind instruments, were those of the artillery. According to Panoff, these averaged eight Hoboisten, with two signal trumpets, by the end of the eighteenth century and ten Hoboisten by 1807.[20] Larger bands were found in the Berlin Guard Artillery Brigade (twenty-four members in 1816)[21] and in Bavaria, where one found a band of eighteen Hoboisten with a conductor in 1817.[22]

When the infantry and artillery regiments appeared in the field, there was still a vital need for the so-called 'Spielleute,' those who provided the signals for troop movement.[23] Every mounted infantry battalion had four fifes during the first two decades;[24] after 1831 one probably would have found them replaced by some type of signal horn. The drum used for signal purposes was still the old large wooden instrument.[25] These signal-musicians also provided the 'music' to march by, which in the Ordinaire of 1812 was a pace of MM.75 There was a 'fast march' pace of MM.108 and a double time of MM.165–170.[26]

Cavalry Bands

It is, however, the mounted brass of the Cavalry, often called 'Trompetenmusik,' that one usually associates with early nineteenth century Prussian military signals. The number of players and the nature of the instrumentation of this 'Trompetenmusik' seems to have varied somewhat, but an average number up until the 1806–1807 wars seems to have been approximately twelve players.[27] Degele, without giving a source, lists for 1805: ten trumpets (four in G, four in F, and two in low C), with three trombones.[28] This, in numbers of instruments if not in keys, reminds me of an interesting work published ca. 1820–1830 (?) by Schott, the *Musique Militaire pour Cavallerie*, op. 11, by C. Fischer, which is scored for two 'Cors de Signal a Clefs,' two trumpets in B♭, one in A♭, two in E♭, two 'Principales,' and three trombones. The keyed signal horns here are most likely the Kenthorns, which were in use in the Prussian Cavalry by 1818,[29] or one of the other more experimental models being offered the army by Berlin instrument makers from about 1811.[30]

[15] Berlin, Allerhöchste Kabinetts-Order, for March 13, 1816.

[16] Max Thomas, 'Heinrich August Neithardt' (dissertation, Freien Universität, Berlin, 1959), 22.

[17] Allerhöchste Kabinetts-Order, March 13, 1816.

[18] Allerhöchste Kabinetts-Order, May 14, 1816.

[19] Allerhöchste Kabinetts-Order, March 13, 1816.

> Ich übermache Ihnen hierneben eine Nachweisung, wie die Instrumente unter den 10 Hoboisten eines Regiments zu vertheilen sind. Ausser diesen 10 Hoboisten können die Regimenter zur *Janitscharen-Musik* noch per Compagnie 1 mann also überhaupt 12 Mann nehmen, auf welche letztere aber nichts besonders gut gethan wird. Das 2. und das Füsilierbataillon eines Regiments sollen keine besondere Musik-Chöre haben; wenigstens wenn ich sie sehe, soll jedes Hoboisten- und Janitscharen-Chor das einzige Musik-Chor eines Regiments seine
> Nachweisung, wie die Instrumente unter den 10 Hoboisten eines Regiments zu vertheilen sind: 2 C-Klarinetten, 1 F-Klarinetten, 2 Inventionshörner. 1 Quart- oder Picol-Flöte, 2 Fag., 1 Quart-Bass-Posaune, 1 Trompete.

Later the same Allerhöchste Kabinetts-Order gives the relative costs of these instruments as: 19 Reichstaler for each regular clarinet and 12 Reichstaler for the small clarinet; 40 Reichstaler for each Inventionshorn; 2 Reichstaler, 16 Groschen for the piccolo; 24 Reichstaler for each bassoon; 25 Reichstaler for the bass trombone; and 18 Reichstaler for the trumpet, here identified as an *Inventionstrompete*.

The precise determination of the instrumentation of the cavalry Trompetenmusik during the early years of the century is impossible, not only because of the general lack of records dealing with military music, but also because many of the valuable silver trumpets were lost, stolen by the enemy, or melted down during the 1806–1807 war years. A few documents, beginning ca. 1810, reflect efforts at rebuilding the trumpet corps.[31]

In the *Musique Militaire pour Cavallerie*, mentioned above, the appearance of the 'Principal' style (the eighteenth-century low, improvisatory parts) reminds one that during the first years of the nineteenth century it was still the ancient, noble trumpet guilds who controlled the Prussian cavalry music. During the first decade of the nineteenth century, an aspiring trumpeter would typically spend five years in apprenticeship with a civic trumpeter, followed by two more years with a military staff trumpeter (*Stabstrompeter*). His final certification was only complete upon the signature of the staff trumpeter, that of the troop commander, and two witnesses, who were also trumpeters. This certification was supposed to include a payment to the staff trumpeter of 100 Reichstaler, as a reward for the successful training of a new trumpeter, although in practice the payment was usually 10 Reichstaler with another Reichstaler going to each witness.[32] King Friederick Wilhelm III, who had paid 50 Reichstaler for the trumpeter, Sandow, of the Guard Regiment, in 1805,[33] refused to pay for five new trumpeters in 1810 and issued the following order which brought the ancient trumpet guild system to an abrupt end in the Prussian military.

> His Royal Majesty wishes it known that the guild system which has up to now existed in the trumpets of the Cavalry regiments, in which every new incoming trumpeter must submit himself to a strict time of apprenticeship, and following which his formal reception as a member of the guild entails payment to the staff trumpeter, is disolved.[34]

Music of the Jäger Battalions

The music corps of the Jäger Batallions, and later the Engineer Batallions, were known as 'Waldhornmusik,' or 'Hornmusik.' The actual instrument, until after 1834, was a small half-moon shaped instrument, not the 'concert' instrument

---

[20] Panoff, *Militärmusik in Geschichte und Gegenwart*, 173.

[21] Allerhöchste Kabinetts-Order, May 14, 1816.

[22] Panoff, *Militärmusik in Geschichte und Gegenwart*.

[23] A brief history of the 'Spielleute' is provided by Degele, in *Die Militärmusik*, 120–121.

[24] Allerhöchste Kabinetts-Order, January 28, 1817.

[25] Reschke, *Studie zur Geschichte der brandenburgischpreussischen Herresmusik*, 42, where one can also find a lengthy discussion of the 'Spielleute' uniforms.

[26] *Exerzier-Reglement 1812*, III, 6.

[27] Reschke, *Studie zur Geschichte der brandenburgischpreussischen Herresmusik*, 38.

[28] Degele, *Die Militärmusik*, 143.

[29] Degele, ibid.

[30] Reschke, *Studie zur Geschichte der brandenburgischpreussischen Herresmusik*, 37.

[31] Reschke, ibid.

[32] Berlin, Secret State Archives, H.A.Rep.4.Z.D.109. Letter, dated November 1, 1810, from Major General von Beeren to Major General von Hake.

[33] Letter of the staff trumpeter, Weinau, of the Guard Regiment, dated September 30, 1810, quoted in Reschke, *Studie zur Geschichte der brandenburgischpreussischen Herresmusik*, 36.

[34] Allerhöchste Kabinetts-Order, November 8, 1810:

> Seine Kgl. Majestät pp wollen das unter den Trompetern der Cavallerie-Regimenter bisher bestandene Zunftwesen, vermöge desselben jeder neu eintretende Trompeter sich einer festgesetzten Lehrzeit und einer demnächstigen förmlichen Aufnahme als Mitglied der Zunft unterworfen, auch ein Lehrgeld für ihn an den Staabs-Trompeter bezahlt werden musste, von nun an völlig aufgehoben wissen.

of the same name at the same time.[35] In 1801 each company of Jäger-Foot-Troops had three of these instruments,[36] who in addition to signaling, played a repertoire of brief fanfares and field marches. By 1806 the typical instrumentation is given as trumpet, three horns, and bass trombone[37] and by 1817 an even larger ensemble of two trumpets, two Kenthorns, three horns, and two trombones (tenor and bass).[38] The major period of development of Jäger music begins with the arrival of Johann Gottfried Rode (1797–1857), in 1817, which will be discussed below.

Military Music Education

The old Prussian Army Music School in Potsdam, founded in 1724 by Friederick Wilhelm I, was forced to close in 1792 due to the financial restraints of the Napoleonic Wars. When it reopened in 1817 it was permitted to maintain thirty students, who pursued a three-year period of study.[39] The small size of the Potsdam school and the apparent hesitance of the government throughout the nineteenth century to provide broader training for the military musicians perhaps reflects a government attitude that since the bands usually recruited 'professional' musicians,[40] no further training was necessary.

The earliest document which addresses the formal recognition of a conductor of the army Hoboisten is dated 1817 and permits some Hoboisten to wear the sword tassel of the non-commissioned officer.[41] A following order permitted those who wore this sword tassel, and who functioned as leaders, to officially be given the title, 'Musikmeister.'[42] In Prussia this position seems to have been filled from the ranks, and by tradition seems to have usually been the first clarinet player, during the early years of the century.[43] The first evidence of governmental interest in the *musical* qualities[44] of this leader is found in a letter to Duke Karl von Mecklenburg-Strelitz, in which Friedrich Wilhelm III expressed an interest in finding a military band leader who was also a composer.[45]

As the municipal conservatories began to appear in Germany during the second quarter of the nineteenth century, they began to serve as institutions for training the band leaders. Nevertheless, by the second half of the century, Prussia was far behind England and France in the training of her military

---

[35] Carl Friedrich Gumtau, *Die Jäger und Schützen* (Berlin, 1834). The only actual music I have found which carries this name is the collection of twelve *Märsche* (Offenbach, André) for four 'Halbemondhörner' and trombone by Josef Küffner (1776–1856), a copy of which can be found in Einsiedeln, Kloster Einsiedeln, Musikbibliothek.

[36] Reschke, *Studie zur Geschichte ... Herresmusik*, 43.

[37] Reschke, ibid., 44; and Degele, *Die Militärmusik*, 136.

[38] Reschke, *Studie zur Geschichte ... Herresmusik*.

[39] Reschke, ibid., 27.

[40] Wilhelm Stephan, 'German Military Music: An Outline of its Development,' *Journal of Band Research* 9, no. 2 (1973): 16.

[41] Allerhöchste Kabinetts-Order, January 15, 1817.

[42] Allerhöchste Kabinetts-Order, January 14, 1823.

[43] Reschke, *Studie zur Geschichte ... Herresmusik*, 41.

[44] The first Hoboisten to be awarded the sword tassel was given this distinction on the basis of his bravery in the field, see Reschkes, ibid.

[45] Reschkes, ibid., citing the Berlin Secret State Archives, Acta betr. die Musikchöre der Regimenter, He.A.Rep.4.Z.D.469, I–II, where the possible employment of the well-known musician Franz Tausch was discussed.

musicians and their leaders. In 1853 Wieprecht complained bitterly to the King regarding the basic education of his musicians and requested that ten of them be sent at state expense to a private conservatory in Berlin (where he himself was on the faculty).[46] The King rejected this proposal, as well as another in 1858 by the civic music director of Zeitz, Carl Henning, for the creation of a university-level military music school. It was not until 1874 that such an institution, attached to the Hochschule für Berlin, was created.[47]

The Armeemärsche Collection, 1817–1859

To Friedrich Wilhelm III one must give credit for the idea of collecting and preserving the traditional and historical army marches of Prussia. The historical importance of this decision can be easily understood if one recalls that all of the Baroque and Classical Period marches of the trumpet corps were learned only on an aural basis, controlled by the quasi-secret aristocratic trumpet guilds. Therefore to help prevent the further loss of traditional marches, and perhaps as a vehicle to introduce into regular use some of his favorite Russian literature,[48] the King issued the following order in 1817:

> To help the regiments in the selection of good army marches, I have made possible a collection of approved music for every regiment. The troops will thus be in possession of good music and it is my will that in all parades and reviews, and especially when I am in attendance, that no other marches will be played.[49]

The original plan for the collection was impressive: one hundred and seventy-six marches for the foot troops and fifty-nine marches for the mounted troops. The collection was expanded during the period of Wieprecht and the music was printed, both in lots (usually twelve at a time)[50] and in the form of individual publications under the heading, 'new edition,' to reflect the rapidly changing instrumentation of the mid-nineteenth century military band.[51] In the end, a collection of more than five hundred works evolved, organized as follows:

[46] Letter from Wieprecht to King Friedrich Wilhelm IV, dated April 4, 1853, Berlin Secret State Archives, Acta generalia, Cap. 14, Tit 7, Sect. 1, Nr. 4.

[47] Reschke, *Studie zur Geschichte ... Herresmusik*, 55.

[48] The King was fond of Russian military music, both that of the bands and the soldier's chorus. Therefore as this collection developed, it included some thirty-five Russian works, in addition to those compositions by German bandmasters, such as Dörffeld, who served with Russian military bands. See Reschke, *Studie zur Geschichte ... Herresmusik*, 49.

[49] Allerhöcheste Kabinetts-Order, February 10, 1817.

> Um den Regimentern in der Wahl guter Militärmärsche zuhilfezukommen, babe ich eine Auswahl bewahrter Musikstücke veranstalten lassen und jedem Regiment eine Sammlung davon bestimmt. Da die Truppe auf diese Weise in Besitz guter Musikalien gelangen wird, so ist es mein Wille, dass bei allen Paraden und Revuen und besonders, wenn ich denselben beiwohne, keine anderen Märsche gespielt werden.

[50] First editions, Berlin: Schlesinger [scores] and Paris: Ebend [individual compositions], of major portions of this collection can be found in Berlin, Staatsbibliothek, and Vienna, Osterreichische Nationalbibliothek.

[51] Degele, *Die Militärmusik*, 193.

1. Slow (MM.80) Marches for the Infantry (107 marches, including a number of historical ones, such as *Der Torgauer*, *Der Dessauer*, and *Der Koburger*)
2. Fast (MM.114) Marches for the Infantry (243 marches, some 40 of which were based on operatic or ballet melodies)
3. Parade Marches for the Mounted Troops (144 works, including galops, polkas, and various dance movements, together with works based on opera and ballet)
4. Historical Drum and Fife Marches

Aside from the older traditional marches, such as those mentioned, the collection contains many interesting marches of specific aristocratic regiments (not to mention some by Friederick the Great), several states (Hanover, Bavaria, Austria, Russia, etc.) and some dating back to the Thirty Years War.

The Nineteenth-Century Zapfenstreich

One of the traditional German marches, the *Zapfenstreich*,[52] which had begun as a signal to call the troops back from the taverns to their tents, developed during the nineteenth century into an elaborate ceremony which was in part military, religious, and patriotic. The new format had its origin in an order by Friedrich Wilhelm III in 1813,[53] issued after he had been deeply impressed in observing a Russian ceremony, after the Battle of Grossbeeren, which had included the unison singing by the Chorale, 'Ich bete an die Macht der Liebe.'[54] From time to time during the nineteenth century other hymns were tried,[55] but none replaced this one in popularity.[56]

During the course of the nineteenth century, the ceremony developed into one in which all available military units (the Hoboisten, the trumpet corps, the fife and drums, etc.) could participate together. The unison singing was considered as a moment of prayer, during which helmets were removed, and was both preceded and followed by fife and drum signals. The ceremony could include the honoring of an individual, usually included patriotic music, and often included a brief 'serenade' or 'concert' selection.[57]

The form of the Zapfenstreich was such that it could be expanded to suit the ceremonial needs of the moment. How interesting it would have been to have heard the Zapfenstreich

[52] I have outlined the history of this march in volume three of this series. I do not use the usual English translation, 'Tattoo,' as it has no real meaning for American readers today. A literal translation, from the seventeenth century, would be something like 'strike the tap.'

[53] Allerhöcheste Kabinetts-Order, August 10, 1813.

[54] 'I Worship the Power of Love.' According to Stephan, 'German Military Music,' 20, the text for this chorale was written by the German mystic, Gerhard Tersteegen (1697–1769), and set to music by Dimitri Stepanovich Bortniansky (1751–1825).

[55] In volume nine of this series, under 'Germany,' the reader will find sources for extant works for male voices and military band which may be related to this tradition.

[56] The Bavarians used a hymn by Johann Kaspar Aiblinger (1779–1867).

[57] Gottfried Veit, *Die Blasmusik* (Innsbruck, 1972), 57; and Stephan, 'German Military Music,' 21.

given in Berlin during 1872, upon the occasion of 'The Meeting of the Three Kaisers,' when Heinrich Saro conducted a massed band of 1,200 musicians of the Guard!

Infantry Bands, 1820–1838

In 1820 Georg Abraham Schneider (1770–1839) was appointed to the supervisory position of Inspector of Army Bands (Herresmusikinspizienten) in Berlin. Schneider was not an innovator to the extent of his successor Wieprecht, but as he was a distinguished musician[58] I believe perhaps greater credit is due him for helping to establish an artistic climate in which contemporary and later men such as Weller,[59] Neithardt,[60] Piefke,[61] Saro,[62] Schick,[63] and others, would produce Prussian military bands with artistic concert standards which were rarely surpassed by any symphony orchestra of the nineteenth century.

His own extant wind ensemble compositions[64] are all Harmoniemusik and probably date from before his army service.[65] Given this background in Harmoniemusik, both as a player and composer, he would have been very comfortable with the instrumentation of the official Berlin line infantry band in 1820,[66] the year he assumed his new army post, for it might be described—and certainly accurately so with respect to its basic sound—as only an extended Harmoniemusik.

[2] flutes
[2] oboes
[2] clarinets in F
[6] clarinets in C
[4] bassoons
[1] contrabassoon
[2] trumpets
[2] horns
[3] trombones
[1] bass horn
[5] percussion (small and large drum, cymbals, triangle, Schellenbaum)

Such a band is of course larger than any previous ensemble associated with the name Harmoniemusik. The 'extra' players here—in particular the flutes, extra clarinets (in the multiple doublings of the French taste), trombones, and the extra

[58] Schneider began his career as a court hornist and oboist in Darmstadt, Schwerin, and Berlin. He composed masses, cantatas, symphonies, concerti, and his opera *Die Verschworenen* was produced in Berlin while he was Inspector of Army Bands—a rather unusual accomplishment among active military band directors.

[59] Friedrich Weller, Director of the Band of the 2nd Guard Foot Regiment, 1840–1844, a very distinguished musician and the first Prussian bandmaster to skillfully arrange large-scale orchestral works for military band. These included the symphonies of Mozart and Haydn, as well as multi-movement transcriptions drawn from opera. According to Gottfried Veit, in *Die Blasmusik* (Innsbruck: Ed. Helbling, 1972), 54, the reviews in Berlin of the first performance indicated that his arrangement of movements of *Oberon* was particularly successful.

[60] August Heinrich Neithardt (1794–1861), director of the Band of the Kaiser-Franz-Guard Grenadier Regiment Nr. 2, in 1820–1840. In 1838 he became the conductor of the Berlin Cathedral choir.

[61] Gottfried Piefke, Director of the Band of the Life Grenadier Regiment Nr. 8. He was a very distinguished conductor (see the review below by von Bülow, under 'Civic Wind Bands') specializing in the performance of transcriptions of the music of Beethoven and Wagner. He was also a distinguished composer of marches and scored for an instrumentation somewhat unique among the Prussian bands, as he preferred the mellow Austrian Flügelhorns and euphoniums.

[62] Heinrich Saro (1827–1891), distinguished march composer, conductor (participated in the famous international competition in Paris in 1867) and founder of a school of music. In 1872 he made a very successful concert tour to Boston.

percussion—reflect the custom that a regimental band could be enlarged, providing the additional cost was borne by the officers of the regiment and not by the government. As this was one means of competition between regiments, there seems to have been little resistance on the part of those officers who were asked to contribute. The Berlin Guard Infantry and Grenadier Regiment bands, on the other hand, were special, privileged bands and had thirty regular (government supported) players already by 1821.[67]

By 1830 a few new instruments began to appear and the infantry bands became slightly larger, but one can still recognize the enlarged *Harmoniemusik* principle. In an important study of military instrumentation published in 1828, the only new instruments given are the piccolo, basset horn, and signal horn.[68] Degele suggests a typical number of players for the same year as thirty-seven,[69] but one must assume that most of these players were still extra players, supported privately by the officers. Indeed, a document from 1830[70] acknowledges only ten Hoboists as regular members of the line infantry bands, with twenty as 'extra' (*überzählige Hoboisten*) who, in the event of war, had to revert to the role of foot soldiers.

Kalkbrenner,[71] based on the extant scores of Neithardt, Weller and Schick, suggests a typical infantry band for the 1830s, that is just before the period of Wieprecht, as,

large and small flutes
clarinets in F and E♭
clarinets in C, B♭, and A
Bassethorns
oboes
bassoons
contrabassoon
English-basshorn
serpent
4 chromatic horns
4 chromatic trumpets
chromatic altohorn
tenor and bass trombones
Harmoniebass
large and small drum
triangle
cymbals

[63] Friedrich Schick (1822–1847), director of the Kaiser-Alexander Guard Grenadier Regiment and arranger.

[64] All in Berlin, Staatsbibliothek, except for single examples in Vienna, Gesellschaft der Musikfreunde in Wien, and Harburg, Fürstlich Öttingen-Wallerstein'sche Bibliothek, Schloß Harburg.

[65] His *Pièces d'Harmonie*, op. 8 for pairs of clarinets, horns, and bassoons was reviewed in the *Allgemene Musikalische Zeitung* already in 1801 as,

> Pleasant, smooth singing melodic movements. Other outstanding characteristics are successful imitation and good taste.

[66] Allerhöchste Kabinett-Order, October 16, 1820.

[67] Allerhöchste Kabinett-Order, January 1, 1821.

[68] A. Sundelin, *Die Instrumentierung für Sämtliche Musikchöre* (Berlin, 1828). Also, the *Drey Märsche für Militaire Musik*, op. 58, by Neithardt, which appeared in 1826, are scored for a very similar instrumentation. The parts (not the numbers of players) call for: 2 piccolo in D, 2 oboes, 2 clarinets in F, 2 clarinets in C, 2 basset horns, 2 bassoons, contrabassoon, bass horn, 2 trumpets in A, 4 horns (D, F), 3 trombones, and percussion.

[69] Degele, *Die Militärmusik*, 115.

[70] Allerhöchste Kabinett-Order, March 15, 1830.

[71] Kalkbrenner, *Wilhelm Wieprecht*, 34–35.

Cavalry Bands, 1820–1829

An order issued in 1825 seems to reflect a concern that competition for trumpets among the ordinary cavalry regiments might consume too much money. Therefore a limit of three (government supported) trumpets for each squadron was established.[72] Again, however, an exception was made for the Berlin Guard Regiment, which could maintain twenty-one members in its trumpet corps. The document which announces this exception is quite valuable in its detail.[73] First, it specifies that only thirteen of these trumpeters were state supported, the rest had to be paid for privately. In the instrumentation of the full complement we see the final chapter of the ancient trumpet corps tradition;[74] hereafter, under Wieprecht, it would evolve into a true brass band. One sees here for the first time, by the way, the valve trumpet in the cavalry.

> 2 first trumpets
> 1 second trumpet
> 2 first Principal-trumpets
> 2 second Principal-trumpets
> 2 Kenthorns
> 1 chromatic trumpet
> 1 trumpet in (high) E♭
> 1 trumpet in F
> 1 trumpet in G
> 4 trombones (ATBB)

[One first trumpet, one first and second Principal trumpet and the F trumpet were not used if only the basic thirteen players were required.]

[72] Allerhöcheste Kabinett-Order, January 17, 1825.

[73] Allerhöcheste Kabinett-Order, March 21, 1725.

[74] The reader must remember that the presence of the trombones here in what I call a 'trumpet corps' only reminds us that the trombone itself began as a slide-trumpet; it is definitely a 'family member.'

Jäger Bands, 1817–1850

The great figure in the story of the nineteenth-century Prussian Jäger band was Johann Gottfried Rode (1797–1857). When he arrived at the Berlin Guard Jäger Battalion in 1817, he would have found at most a nine-member ensemble of trumpet-types, horns and trombones. By 1828 Rode had a twelve-member ensemble of the same instruments, but now with valved horns and trumpets, together with the new valved alto horn.[75] In 1829 an instrument below the bass trombone was added, the 'Harmoniebass,' which according to Kalkbrenner was a keyed bass horn with nine keys.[76]

[75] This discussion is taken from Reschke, *Studie zur Geschichte ... Herresmusik*, 44; and Degele, *Die Militärmusik*, 136. In 1828 the instrumentation was 2 Kenthorns, 3 horns, signal horn, alto horn, 3 trumpets, and 2 trombones (T, B).

[76] A. Kalkbrenner, *Wilhelm Wieprecht*, 33.

By 1831 the ensemble was much larger, with nineteen members, and the range had been extended on both ends, with the new bombardon and the high F trumpet.[77] In 1832 Rode added the valved bass trombone (Vienna valves), finally arriving at a fairly stable instrumentation for the period 1837–1850:

3 Kenthorns in C (after 1847, cornets)
3 chromatic trumpets
9–10 chromatic horns
1 alto horn (after 1847, alto cornet)
1 chromatic tenor horn
1 valve bass trombone
1 Harmoniebass (later, tuba)
1 bombardon (later, tuba)

One can see that an ensemble with this unique instrumentation would have developed its own repertoire quite apart from that of the infantry and cavalry bands. Indeed, when an Inspector of Russian Jäger Bands visited Potsdam in 1833, he requested Rode to give him thirty compositions to take back to St. Petersburg.[78]

The Wilhelm Wieprecht Era

'Wieprecht is the *l'etat c'est moi* of Prussian military music,' said Hans von Bülow, one of the most important music critics of the nineteenth century.[79] This association with Louis XIV is not altogether inappropriate, for it is difficult to think of any military musician who was more influential. In addition to his military contribution, discussed below, I might add that he corresponded with such musicians as Meyerbeer, Spontini, and Vieuxtemps.[80] He was a close friend of Liszt, who requested him to arrange music from his *Tasso* and *Mazeppa* for band; Mendelssohn also requested Wieprecht to arrange some of his music for band.[81]

Wieprecht came from a very musical family, his grandfather, father, and four uncles all being professional musicians. His father, it was said, could play in the third octave of the E♭ clarinet so softly that one could not distinguish it from a flute.[82]

Wieprecht was born in 1802 and a rigorous musical education administered by his father soon began. He began his studies on clarinet and violin, performing a concerto on the latter

[77] In 1831 the instrumentation was 2 Kenthorns, 8 horns, signal horn, alto horn, 3 trumpets, 2 trombones, Harmoniebass, and bombardon.

[78] Theodore Rode, 'Zur Geschichte der Kgl. Preuss. Inf.- und Jäger-Musik,' in *Neu Zeitschrift für Militärmusik*, XLIX, 149, 161, and 173ff.

[79] Hans von Bülow, 'Zur preussischen Militärmusik,' in *Neue Zeitschrift für Musik* (1858), XLIX, Nr. 1.

[80] Kalkbrenner, *Wilhelm Wieprecht*, 55, quotes several such examples of correspondence, but says the correspondence with Vieuxtemps and Ole Bull are of too private a nature to quote!

[81] Ibid., 52–53, 110.

[82] These notes on Wieprecht's early life are taken from ibid., 6–20.

in public at age ten. On his own, he studied trombone and arrived at such a degree of proficiency that by age twenty he could rival the most famous trombonist in Leipzig.

At age fourteen he took his examination as an apprentice in the civic music of his hometown, Aschersleben, in Thuringen, which consisted of performing a concerto on violin,[83] a set of variations on clarinet, and a composition on trombone. After some years as an apprentice he received his Journeyman's Certificate from the guild in 1820 and also participated in the ceremony marking his manhood smoking his first bowl of pipe tobacco in front of a witnesses!

Although his father expected Wieprecht to take his place in the city wind band, the young man wanted to travel and 'see the world.' This opportunity presented itself when the famous clarinetist, Hermstedt, came to Aschersleben for a concert and gave Wieprecht a letter of introduction to the leader of the civic band, Barth, in Leipzig. In 1821 Wieprecht left for Leipzig; Barth could offer no position at the moment, but gave Wieprecht a letter of introduction to take to the court Kapellmeister, Zillmann, in Dresden.[84] Here Wieprecht was given a position, where he remained for nearly nine months. This was followed by a return to Leipzig, where he worked for nearly two years, and finally to Berlin, where beginning in 1824 he was a chamber musician in the court.

It was in Berlin when the turning point in Wieprecht's life occurred. This metamorphosis began with his chance hearing of a Prussian military band performing the Overture to *Figaro* by Mozart. Wieprecht remembered this moment, as follows:

> When I heard in Berlin for the first time an infantry band in its full instrumentation, I was seized by an emotion I have never been able to explain to myself. Was it the rhythm, the melody, the harmony, or other elements which affected me so deeply? As I then followed this band on their march to the watch parade, and there heard them play the Overture to Mozart's *Figaro* in a closed circle, there came into my heart the firm decision that I would dedicate myself from now on to military music.[85]

The reader may find confusing this confession that a professional orchestral musician, with experience in the royal operas of Dresden and Leipzig, could be so taken by the performance (outdoors) of a military band. But the reader must remember

[83] Wieprecht continued to study violin and tells of walking three hours to nearby Bernburg to study with a student of Spohr, having a three-hour lesson, and making the return walk home only to have to play his lesson again for his father!

[84] Wieprecht also had a letter of introduction to Weber, but was too shy to present it. His introduction to this famous master occurred during an opera rehearsal which Weber was conducting. Wieprecht was playing an off-stage trombone part and mistakenly played a major third in a chord, rather than a minor third. Weber, according to Wieprecht, yelled, 'Who plays alto?' He ran back stage, pinched Wieprecht on the ear and said, 'You probably have not been a musician long.' This led to better times, when Wieprecht was often a guest in Weber's home.

[85] Quoted in Kalkbrenner, *Wilhelm Wieprecht*, 18.

> Als ich hier (in Berlin) zumersten Male eine vollständig besetzte Infantriemusik hörte, wurde ich von einem Gefhül ergriffen, von dem ich mir nie habe Rechenschaft begen können. War es die Rhythmik, die Melodik, die harmonie, oder die Verscbmelzung dieser verschiedenen Elemente, die mich so gewaltsam erschütterte? Als ich nin diese Militarkapelle auf ihrem hinmarsche zur Wachtparade verfolgte und dort dieselbe im geschlossenen Kreise die Overture zu Mozart's Figaro spielen hörte, da wurde es in meinem Herzen zum festen Entschluss mich von nun an dem Fache der Militarmusik ausschliesslich zu widmen.

we speak of a time when most orchestras were opera orchestras; the great repertoire orchestras we know today had not yet emerged. The better military bands sometimes were more disciplined (due to the military) and performed at a higher technical level than these small opera orchestras. As Wolfgang Suppan, one of Europe's most distinguished musicologists and critics, has written,

> Many people today look with contempt at the nineteenth century arrangements and transcriptions. This is completely unjust. A great army band had a higher standard of performance than many opera orchestras.[86]

[86] Quoted in Veit, *Die Blasmusik*, 53.
   Eine grosse Heeresmusik hatte damals höheres Niveau als manches Opernorchester.

Berlioz's memoirs of his tour of Germany in 1842–1843 seem to confirm this in his descriptions of the various orchestras and bands he heard.

Wieprecht could not have chosen a more interesting musical career at this moment. Military bands were receiving the funds to increase their size, yet there seemed to be no unified plan for instrumentation. Nearly all the principal discoveries, developments and refinements which separate the modern woodwind and brass instruments from those of the late eighteenth century were occurring at that very moment.

As a person from outside the military establishment, Wieprecht seems to have understood that his most opportune entrée into military music was through the one kind of band most musicians at that time were less interested in—the trumpet corps of the cavalry. Perhaps he also intuitively understood that it was the brass instruments, not the old court oriented *Harmoniemusik* which lay at the heart of the larger infantry bands, which were more perfectly suited, psychologically, to express the exuberance and pride felt everywhere by the citizens now in the process of rebuilding Prussia.

Through an acquaintance with a Major von Barner, of the Guard Dragoon Regiment, Wieprecht began his career by composing for this regiment six marches, which were very highly regarded. The great harmonic limitations imposed by the instrumentation (natural trumpets in G, F, and C, and trombones) led him to persuade the major to buy instruments with valves, which at this time were not used in Berlin cavalry units. The band in question had thirteen regular members, for whom Wieprecht chose the following instruments.

1 high B♭ valve trumpet
2 keyed trumpets
1 alto trumpet in E♭ with valves
2 tenor horns in B♭
1 tenor-bass horn in B♭
4 trumpets in E♭ with valves
2 bass trombones

The band was allowed an additional seven 'hired' players. Wieprecht writes,[87] 'for these I used four more trumpets, one high B♭ trumpet, one alto trumpet, and another bass trombone. Now I had a full *Blechinstrumental-harmonie* with which I could modulate in all directions.'

The success of this new instrumentation gained immediate attention among cavalry circles. Wieprecht was invited to Breslau in 1829 to reinstrument the First Curassier-regiment and soon after King Friedrich Wilhelm III personally issued an order for Wieprecht to reinstrument his Guard Regiment in Potsdam.

> When this new music corps was presented to his Majesty, who was the leader of this regiment, I was engaged to also instruct the trumpets of this regiment and so I had to go four days each month to Potsdam, where the entire music corps of Berlin and Charlottenburg were brought together for this purpose. For the lessons and travel I received a suitable salary
> ……
> In 1833 I removed the high trumpets, because of their hard tone color, and substituted the soprano cornets. Soon I replaced the keyed trumpets also with cornets, and had an alto cornet made to replace the alto trumpet. The rest I left unchanged, except the bass trombones which I replaced in 1835 with the new tuba, which I invented together with the court instrument maker J. G. Moritz.
> ……
> For this success I made many persons envious, but also many friends, especially His Royal Highness, Prince Albrecht of Prussia, who became my protector and helped advance me. In 1835 the Prince took over command of the Second Guard Cavalry Brigade and gave me the leadership of the music. Soon my military orchestra grew to eighty men, with whom I gave great concerts and increased my reputation.[88]

During this period, Wieprecht also seems to have been thinking of the problems of reorganizing the infantry band, although at this time he could apparently only put his ideas into practice with bands far from Berlin.[89]

[87] Quoted in Kalkbrenner, *Wilhelm Wieprecht*, 22.

[88] Quoted in ibid., 23–24.

[89] It seems to me nearly impossible to determine precisely the chronological development of Wieprecht's ideas on the instrumentation of the infantry band, for the reason that nearly all of his autograph scores have been lost. Were they extant, one could trace this development through them. Two copies in Frankfurt am Main, Universitätsbibliothek Johann Christian Senckenberg, which claim to be based on dated autographs, are scored for an unusually large band for this date. These scores, *March for the Royal Jäger Regiment in Sardinia* ('Turin, 1834') and his scoring of a march by Prochaska for an Austrian infantry band ('Prag, 1835'), also suggest Wieprecht was traveling a great deal by this time. These works are scored for:

piccolo in D♭
oboes
soprano cornets in B♭
alto cornets in E♭
horns in E♭
tenorhorns in B♭
baritone-tuba
small clarinet in A♭
'Mittel-Clarinetten' in E♭
4 'Grosse Clarinetten' in B♭
bassoons
contrabassoon
bass tuba
4 trumpets in E♭
trombones
small and large drums

While serving under Prince Albrecht, Wieprecht was invited by Abraham Schneider, the over-all director of the Guard music in Berlin, to organize, in his place, the music for a royal wedding in 1837. This again brought Wieprecht to the attention of the King.

> The King finally noticed me. I was playing some marches in the garden of Prince Albrecht and included one from the time of Frederick the Great, which I had found among my father's music. The King called to me saying, 'I know that old march and I can sing it to you, so exact is my memory of it.' Thereafter the march became known as the 'King's Fanfare, and soon after, on February 2, 1838, I became Director of all the music of the Berlin Guard.[90]

As Wieprecht says, upon the retirement of Schneider in 1838 he gained this first important military position.[91] Until Wieprecht, this position had only been a part-time one through which little influence had been wielded. It was the goal of Wieprecht to make the position a regular commissioned rank, with uniform. The latter he was to achieve indirectly only a few months after his appointment, in connection with the music he organized for the visit of Kaiser Nicholaus of Russia.

The King wanted a great Festmusik for this occasion and asked Wieprecht how many bands he trusted to participate in this. 'Every band quartered in Berlin,' answered Wieprecht and thus occurred the first of the 'Monster Concerts' which would make Wieprecht one of Berlin's best known persons. The concert was held in an open square before the Berliner Schloss by a combined band consisting of sixteen infantry band and sixteen cavalry bands totaling more than a thousand musicians and two hundred percussionists. Wieprecht conducted the following program:

> Overture to *Rienzi* by Wagner, played by the full ensemble.
> 'Chorus' and 'March' from *Conradin* by Hiller, performed by the bands of the foot troops.
> 'Halleluja' from the *Messiah* by Handel, performed by the infantry bands.
> *March* by Möllendorf, performed by the cavalry bands.
> 'Coronation March' from *The Prophet* by Meyerbeer, performed by the full ensemble.
> The *Dessauer*, *Hohenfriedberger*, and *Coburger* marches, performed by the full ensemble.[92]

[90] Quoted in F. Bücker, 'Beim Generalkapellmeister Wieprecht,' in *Der Bär* (1897), Jahrgang 23, Nr. 2.

[91] This position was held by Quantz, during the period of Friedrick the Great; by Gurlich, under Friedrich Wilhelm II; and by Tausch and Schneider, under Friedrich Wilhelm III.

[92] Degele, *Die Militärmusik*, 148; Reschke, *Studie zur Geschichte ... Herresmusik*, 51; and Kalkbrenner, *Wilhelm Wieprecht*, 26–27.

'Afterwards,' wrote Wieprecht, 'I was brought before the two Majesties, where I had to assure the Kaiser Nicholaus that this performance was created in only two rehearsals over a two-day period.'[93] It was apparently at this meeting that the Kaiser observed that it looked a bit odd to see Wieprecht conducting in civilian clothes before so many hundred soldiers! Thus the King immediately ordered a uniform made for Wieprecht, a blue coat with red-lined collar and red-lined tails, three-cornered hat, dagger, etc., which he wore for the first time four days later when he conducted a combined performance of the Guard bands in the opera house. This performance, of the *Olympia* Overture by Spontini and the *Jubel* Overture by Weber, was apparently intended to demonstrate that the military bands could also play 'art' music.

In 1843 Wieprecht was given temporary leadership of the Tenth German National Army in order to organize a Monster Concert in Lüneburg. Here more than thirteen hundred non-Prussian musicians, representing all the military bands quartered in Hanover, Holstein, Lauenburg, Oldenburg, Mecklenburg-Schwerin, Braunschweig, Hamburg, Lübeck and Bremen, gathered to rehearse and perform. Here Wieprecht once again became acutely aware of the need for a standardized instrumentation, for in order to hold rehearsals he had to write out seventeen different versions of the infantry parts and nine different versions of the cavalry parts! For this performance he was awarded the Golden Service Medal by the King of Hanover, but as he was not an officer he had to receive the official permission of the Prussan aristocracy to wear it.[94]

At home, Wieprecht was no doubt beginning to achieve at least some administrative control, if not yet a standardized instrumentation, as we can see in a report by Berlioz during this same year.

> As for the military bands, one would have designedly to avoid them not to hear at least some, since at all hours of the day, either on foot or on horseback, they are passing through the streets of Berlin. These little isolated bands do not, however, give any idea of the majesty of the grand whole which the head bandmaster of the military bands at Berlin and Potsdam [Wieprecht] can collect whenever he chooses. Imagine, he has a body of upwards of six hundred musicians under his command, all good readers, all well up in the mechanism of their instruments, playing in tune, and favored by nature with indefatigable lungs

[93] Ibid.

[94] The document allowing this is reproduced in Kalkbrenner, *Wilhelm Wieprecht*, 43–44.

and lips of leather. Hence the extreme facility with which the trumpets, horns, and cornets give those high notes unattainable by our artists [in France]. They are regiments of musicians, rather than musicians of regiments. The Crown Prince of Prussia, anticipating my desire to hear his musical troops and study them at my leisure, kindly invited me to a matinee organized at his palace expressly for me, and gave Wieprecht orders accordingly … I was [at first] astonished at not seeing the wind orchestra; no sound betrayed its presence, when a slow phrase in F minor … made me turn my head towards an immense curtain. His Royal Highness had had the courtesy to order the concert to open with the *Franc-Juges* overture, which I had never heard arranged thus for wind instruments. There were 320 players, directed by Wieprecht, and difficult as the music was they performed it with marvelous exactness, and that furious fire with which you of the Conservatoire perform it on your great days of enthusiasm and ardour.

The solo for the brass in the introduction was especially startling, performed by fifteen bass trombones, eighteen or twenty tenor and alto trombones, twelve bass tubas, and a host of trumpets … The middle and high tones of the tuba are very noble, not at all dull like those of the ophicleide, but vibrant, and very sympathetic to the tones of the trombones and trumpets, of which it forms the true double-bass, and with which it blends perfectly …

The clarinets seemed to me equal to the brass: they performed great feats in a grand battle symphony for two wind orchestras by the English ambassador, the Earl of Westmoreland.

Afterwards came a brilliant and chivalric piece for brass only, written by Meyerbeer for the Court festivals under the title of *Torchlight Dance*, in which there is a long trill on the D, kept up through sixteen bars by eighteen cylinder trumpets doing it as rapidly as the clarinets could have done. The concert ended with a very fine and well-written funeral march, composed by Wieprecht, and played with only one rehearsal![95]

This evidently high level of musicianship reported by Berlioz is confirmed in an anecdote by Kastner. Apparently, during a joint appearance of the First Regiment of Prussian Guards with a Russian band at a festival at Kalish, the Prussians, whose clarinets were in F and C, noticed the Russian clarinets were in G and B♭. In order not to embarrass the Russians, all the Prussian clarinetists transposed the concert at sight.[96]

In 1845, Wieprecht turned to the press in his attempt to generate support for the standardization of Prussian military bands. In one of these articles, published on 28 June, in a Berlin newspaper, Wieprecht proposed an extraordinary new concept for military band instrumentation. It called for a band

[95] Berlioz, 'Letter to Monsieur Desmarest,' in *Memoirs*, 325ff.

[96] Kastner, *Manuel Général de Musique Militarie*, 198.

of twenty-one different parts, with players doubling according to the dictates of his desired texture. The instruments were grouped into three registers, which were further balanced, resulting in what Wieprecht called an 'acoustic pyramid.' Given are the numbers of players for each part in both the Guard Infantry and regular Line Infantry bands.

	Guard Inf.	Line-Inf.
Piercing Register, to be played lightly		
flutes, large and small	2	1
clarinets in A♭ or G	2	2
clarinets in E♭ or D	2	2
clarinets in B♭ or A	8	6
oboes in E♭ or D	2	2
bassoons	2	2
batyphons	2	2
Middle Register, to be played stronger		
cornets in B♭ or A	2	1
cornets in E♭ or D	2	1
tenor horns in B♭ or A	2	1
bass horns (Baryton) in B♭ or A	1	1
bass horns in F or E♭	2	1
Low Register, to be played very strong		
trumpets in E♭ or D	4	4
trombones in B♭ or A	2	2
bass trombones in F or E♭	2	2
bass tuba in F or E♭	2	2
triangle	1	1
cymbals	1	1
small drum	2	1
bass drum	1	1
Schellenbaum	1	1
Conductor	1	1

Following the publication of his famous 'Travel Letters over Military and Folk-music in the South German States,' in 1846 in the army newspaper, *Soldatenfreund*, Wieprecht began to see movement toward acceptance of his ideas. Letters of invitation began to arrive requesting his personal appearance when one or another regiment adopted his new instrumentation. In 1847 he was asked by Turkey to reorganize their military music and for this purpose he sent two young instructors and forty-eight instruments. A music school was also founded there after Wieprecht's plans. In 1852 the government of Guatemala hired Wieprecht to organize the small military bands, which would also be used in church, due to a lack of organs. Again, he sent instructors and instruments. Almost eight years later, Wieprecht received a newspaper article from the Consul in Jamaica describing a concert 'à la Wieprecht,' played by forty-eight Moors.

Thus, while a large concert band, such as the one given above, would have been unthinkable only twenty years before, large concert bands were no longer uncommon in Prussia by mid-century. Indeed, according to Kastner,[97] although a band of twenty-four men was in 1848 *de rigueur*, one in fact ordinarily found a band of fifty or sixty musicians. In addition each regiment now also had a soldier's chorus of sixty voices for performing national hymns with the band.

According to a letter by Spontini,[98] the ordinary regiment of Prussian infantry had by 1848 a band constituted as follows:

[97] Kastner, ibid., 197.

[98] Quoted in Kastner, ibid., 196–197.

8 or 10 clarinets given the melody, with two small clarinets
8 or 10 clarinets serving as accompaniment
2 first oboes
2 second oboes
2 basset horns (first and second)
2 flutes or piccolo
2 first bassoons
2 second bassoons
4 horns
4 trumpets, 2 'ordinaires,' two with valves
4 trombones (ATBB)
serpent
contrabassoon (often two)
tuba, bombardon, or bass horn
1 or 2 small drums
cymbals
triangle

Kastner, gives the ordinary instrumentation for the cavalry band in 1848 as,

2 Kenthorns (keyed-trumpets)
2 solo trumpets, nearly always in E♭
2 ordinary trumpets
4 to 6 chromatic trumpets

1 trumpet in A♭
1 trumpet in F
1 trumpet in B♭ alto
1 trumpet in C alto (but rare)
1 chromatic tenorhorn
3 trombones (ATB)
1 or 2 tubas
timpani

The following year, Wieprecht had another massed band performance in Berlin, in the Tivoli park, but it was apparently the last of the 'Monster Concerts' in which he was involved. A contemporary review provides the instrumentation, as well as some hints of other projects Wieprecht was interested in.

> Mr. Wieprecht has apparently been very busy this summer, for on August 22 in the Tivoli he conducted 452 musicians and 300 singers in a concert. The instrumentation included 11 flutes; 14 oboes; 11 basset horns; 19 small clarinets; 63 large clarinets; 24 cornets; 19 tenorhorns; 6 'Tenorbasse,' including both 'Tenortubas,' 28 bass tubas; 15 contrabassoons; serpents, and other bass instruments; 6 alto trombones; 8 tenor trombones; 20 bass trombones; 10 small drums; 7 pair of 41 cymbals; 7 triangles; 2 bass drums; 60 regimental drummers; 11 conductors and the conductor in charge [Wieprecht]. It should be pointed out that no cannons accompanied the music. The whole thing of course made a splendid noise which vibrated the Kreuzberg to its foundations. And to think Mr. Wieprecht still has received no Prussian medals! This has further significance when one remembers that so many of his other hopes have gone unfulfilled. Thus his plans for the general reorganization of all military music rests in peace; his plans for a [military] conservatory rests—not in the peace of God, but in the peace of the bureaucracy; and other needs such as the Choral Society and the Orchestral Union do not really want to bloom.[99]

[99] *Neuen Zeitschrift für Musik* (1849), XXXI.

Prussian Military Bands during the 'Golden Age'

Wieprecht's Unified System

In 1857 Wieprecht reorganized the Prussian brass bands, those of the cavalry and Jäger regiments, finally getting rid of the old key-bugles, or Kenthorns, and replacing them with cornets. These bands were now constituted[100] of the following parts (not numbers of players):

[100] According to Degele, *Die Militärmusik*, 144, 136.

Cavalry
2 cornets in B♭
2 alto cornets in E♭
2 tenorhorns in B♭
trumpets (E♭ and low B♭)
baritone
2 bass tubas

Jäger
soprano cornet in E♭
2 cornets in B♭
1 alto cornet
6 horns (F, E♭)
2 tenor horns
baritone
3 trumpets
2 trombones (TB)
2 bass tubas

In 1860 the War Ministry created thirty-four new infantry and ten new cavalry regiments and gave to Wieprecht the responsibility for creating their bands. These he managed to recruit and supply with instruments in only three months.

This offered him the opportunity to publish yet another reorganization of Prussian bands. This was an ingenious system by which, through the addition of instruments, one could arrive at the instrumentation of the cavalry, Jäger, artillery, or infantry bands. His idea was that if publishers would make compositions available which were scored in accordance with this plan (including the resultant unconventional score order), then the same piece of music could be purchased and used by any of the three basic types of bands.

Wieprecht's Unified Instrumentation System of 1860

	Cavalry	Artillery	Jäger	Infantry
Cornettino	1	3	1	
Soprano cornet	4	6	4	2
Alto cornet	2	3	2	2
Tenorhorn	2	6	2	4
Baritone-tuba	1	3	2	1
Bass tuba	3	6	3	4
Trumpet	8	12	3	4
Horn			4	4
Flute				2
Oboe				2
Clarinet in A♭				1
Clarinet in E♭				2
Clarinet in B♭				8
Bassoon				2
Contrabassoon				2
Trombone				4
Cymbals				1
Small drum				2
Large drum				1
Halbmondträger				1
Total	21	39	21	47

Wieprecht's greatest personal achievement, of course, was his gaining the first prize at the 1867 World Competition in Paris, which will be discussed in detail below. His excitement after winning this event can be seen in his letter to his friend, the Berlin music professor, Ferdinand Sieber.

> Dear friend,
> Everything, everything, everything on which the most wild fantasy can imagine has succeeded for me. We have won! Won and showed that the North German musical arts earned the laurel wreath, given us only with clenched teeth. The first prize was given to me.
> ......

I, the only one of the musical directors, was twice requested to the Imperial table. At the second banquet Kaiser Napoleon gave me the medal of the Legion of Honor and requested me to write a theoretical treatise on the purpose and organization of military bands in general.

At the table I had my place very close to the Empress—between her and myself a court lady was placed who could translate in German, so the Empress could speak to me, which she did especially about Berlin. The Emperor took me into a side room after the banquet where he praised me. The Empress introduced me personally to her nieces and nephew.[101]

[101] Quoted in Kalkbrenner, *Wilhelm Wieprecht*, 64.

Aside from his contributions to the reorganization of Prussian military music, we must not forget his tremendous contribution as a composer and arranger. Although most of his output is now apparently lost, Kalkbrenner[102] supplies the following repertoire known to him to have been contributed by Wieprecht for military bands. We have made a few additions.

[102] Ibid., 68ff.

Original Compositions
1. *Six Marches*, op. 1, for cavalry band, (Berlin: Wagenführ)
2. *Mein erster Defilier-Marsch* (Breslau: Leuckart)
3. *Concerto for Clarinet* (Berlin: Logier)
4. *Einholungsmarsch* (for Friedrich Wilhelm IV in Berlin, September, 21, 1840), for cavalry band (Berlin: Fröhlich)
5. *Armee-Marsch Nr. 133*, for military band (Berlin: Trautwein)
6. *Marsch* (Nr. 30), for cavalry band (Berlin: Schlesinger)
7. *Marsch* (Nr. 21), for cavalry band (Berlin: Schlesinger)
8. Three *Märsche* ('zur Einholung des Prinzen und der Prinzessin Friedric,h Wilhelm von Preussen, am 2. Februar 1858 in Berlin aufgeführt') (Berlin: Schlesinger, 1858)
9. *Wilhelms-Marsch*, for harmoniemusik (Berlin: Schlesinger, 1860)
10. *Musikalische Erinnerungenan die Kriegsjahre 1813. 1814. und 1815*, for military band.

In Manuscript
1. Ouverture militaire
2. Militairsche Trauerparade
3. Huldigungs-Marsch, 'Wir schwören'!
4. (40) Parademärsche, for cavalry band
5. (31) Defiliermärsche for infantry band
6. Festmarsch on Themes of Beethoven's 5th Piano Concerto
7. Trauermarsch
8. Notturno (virually a four-movement symphony)
9. Tone Poem on the Battle of Leipzig for three bands

Instrumental Fantaisies
1. über russische Lieder
2. über hollländische Lieder
3. über altdeutsche Lieder
4. über den Dessauer Marsch
5. über Themata a. d. Zauberflöte
6. über Themata a. Robert der Teufel
7. über Themata a. Der Prophet
8. über Themata a. Euryanthe

Arrangements for Military Band

Beethoven:
1. Overture to Egmont
2. Overture to Coriolan
3. Overture to Prometheus
4. Symphony Nr. 2, for Infantry band
5. Symphony Nr. 3, for combined Infantry and Cavalry bands
6. Symphony Nr. 5, for Infantry band
7. Symphony Nr. 7, for Infantry band
8. Symphony Nr. 9, for combined Infantry and Cavalry bands
9. Symphony, Die Schlacht bei Vittoria
10. Trios for piano', violin, and cello, for Harmonie musik, Nrs. 1, 2, and 3
11. Sonate pathétique, for Orchester Harmonie
12. Trauermarsch, aus Ab Sonate

Gluck:
13. Overture to Armide
14. Finale from Armide

Handel:
15. Chorus from Messiah
16. Marsch from Messiah

Méhul:
17. Overture from Joseph in Egypten
18. Overture from La chasse Henri IV

Mendelssohn:
19. Overture from Antigone
20. Overture from Die Schone Melusine
21. Overture from Hebriden
22. Marsch from Sommernachtstraum
23. Overture militaire

Meyerbeer: .
24. Overture from Feldlager in Schlesien
25. Overture from Die hugenottenn
26. Overture from Dinorah
27. Fackeltänze Nr. 1, 2, 3, and 4
28. Overture from Struensee
29. Krönungsmarsch from Prophet
30. Krönungsmarsch for two bands (and various works from Meyerbeer's operas)

Mozart:	31. Overture from Don Juan
	32. Overture from Die Zauberflöte
	33. Overture from Figaros hochzeit
	34. Overture from Titus
	35. First Finale from Don Juan
	36. Great C minor Fantaisie
	37. C Major Symphony with Fugue
Righini:	38. Music from the Ballet, Die Wiederbelebung der Statuen des Daedalus
Rossini:	39. Overture from William Tell
	40. Overture from Die dibische Elster
	41. Overture from Othello
	42. Overture from Trancred
	43. Finale from Semiramis
Spontini:	44. Overture from Olympia
	45. Overture from Ferdinand Cortez
	46. Overture from Die Vestalin
	47. Overture from Agnes von hohenstaufen
	48. Ballet works from Olympia
	49. Ballet works from Alcidor
Abt Vogler:	50. The complete music from the opera, Hermann von Unna
Wagner:	51. Overture from Rienzi
	52. Entrance of the Guests in Wartburg from Tannhäuser
	53. Entrance and Bridal Chorus from Lohengrin
Weber:	54. Overture from Der Freischütz
	55. Overture from Oberon
	56. Overture from Euryanthe
	57. Invitation to the Dance in a free arrangement
	58. Jubel-Overture

The various contributions of Wieprecht were in large part responsible for the great popularity of Prussian bands through the end of the century. By World War I, no fewer than 541 separate bands were authorized for the various branches of the Prussian military (including naval bands)[103] and on a summer evening in Berlin one could hear any of twenty to thirty different military band concerts![104]

[103] Stephan, 'German Military Music,' 14. Degele, *Die Militärmusik*, gives a large number of instrumentation charts for the various types of bands between 1860 and World War I; they are distinctions in numbers of players, not of new instrumentations.

[104] Veit, *Die Blasmusik*, 57.

The impact of these military bands, especially through their public concerts, helped bring about a tremendous expansion in civic bands throughout Germany—in Berlin especially, where a reported 100,000 players were involved as will be discussed below.

Military Bands of the other German States

The remaining principal states of what is today the modern Germany varied both in quality and in the degree to which they followed the lead of the Prussians. Berlioz, during his tour of Germany in 1842–1843, commented on military bands in Stuttgart,

> They still use a very imperfect instrument with two pistons, which, for tone and sonority, is behind the cylinder trumpet, now in general use elsewhere.[105]

and Dresden,

> The military band is very good—even the drummers are musicians; but the reeds did not strike me as irreproachable. Their intonation left much to be desired, and the bandmasters of these regiments would do well to order their clarinets from our incomparable Sax. Ophicleides there are none; the deep parts are sustained by Russian bassoons [the 'bass horn'], serpents, and tubas.[106]

who were distinctly 'behind the times' with respect to the instruments they employed. Suppan adds that the state of Baden was also slow to follow the lead of the Prussians,[107] the Life Grenadier Guards in Karlsruhe still having by 1830–1832 only an eighteenth-century sized eight 'Bayreuther Hautboisten,' with conductor. In 1833, however, the grand duke's Minister of State established for the Grenadier Battalion a ducal infantry regiment with 12 Hoboisten First Class and with 28 Hoboisten Second Class and at the same time 40 musicians for the First, Second, Third and Fourth Infantry Regiments, each with 10 Hoboisten First Class and 18 Hoboisten of the Second Class and for the regular infantry regiments bands of twenty-eight Hoboisten.[108] Toward the end of the century this band became one of the more famous in Germany. Under

[105] Berlioz, *Memoirs*, 260.

[106] Ibid., 292–293.

[107] Wolfgang Suppan, *Blasmusik in Baden* (Freiburg: Musikverlag F. Schulz, 1983), 83.

[108] Suppan, Ibid., also suggests that in the State Archives in Karlsruhe there are valuable files which have yet to be examined by musicologists, including files on the sending of a Baden band to the famous 1867 competition in Paris, on the military concerts of 1868, on the education of military music directors (as for example one, Loewe, who attended the Potsdam School in 1878), and on the introduction of 'Parisian tuning' [A-435] in Baden military bands.

the fine bandmaster, M. Boettge, the band began accepting only new members who could play a string instrument as well, thus the ensemble could appear either as a band or orchestra according to the desire of the conductor.

Wieprecht reported on military bands he heard in Stuttgart, during his travels through the State of Württemberg in 1845.[109] He found there little support or interest in military bands, the infantry band he heard—combined of two regiments, yet only twenty-one players—he says had 'instruments in the most pitiful shape, their intonation I found lacking, and the ensemble played without any energy.' He also observed that the 'Türkish' instruments ('bass drum, cymbals, or triangle') found almost everywhere else were still unknown there. Their percussion consisted of the constant playing by fifteen old-style tambours.

Wieprecht found much more satisfaction with the cavalry band he heard in Stuttgart, although again he observed their instruments were very poor. Their fine playing, especially their intonation, he attributed to an unusually hardworking chief trumpeter. He was especially astonished, as everyone must have been, that when this band performed mounted—playing pieces which Wieprecht says were 'not easy,' they did so without saddles, riding only on blankets!

One military band which Berlioz was pleased with during his 1842–1843 tour was that in Darmstadt.

> At Darmstadt there is a military band of about thirty musicians, for which I envied the Grand Duke. They play in good tune, with style, and with such a feeling for rhythm that even the drum parts are interesting.[110]

Bavaria seems to have followed the lead of Prussia, indeed, according to Kastner by 1848 one would have found the same organization and the same number of players as in Prussia.

> There is no difference between the Bavarian infantry of the guard and a regiment of the line in Prussia. Each Bavarian regiment has a choir of 60 voices, which are equal to the Prussians. The Bavarian bands have no problems with precision or ensemble, but their brass instruments leave much to be desired; they are poorly made. Lately they have gained a certain renown for their good style of playing before the citizens of Alsace and Lorraine on the borders of our country [France].[111]

[109] 'Second Travel Letter,' dated Stuttgart, August 25, 1845, quoted in Kalkbrenner, *Wilhelm Wieprecht*, 101–102.

[110] Berlioz, *Memoirs*, 343.

[111] Kastner, *Manuel Général de Musique Militarie*, 205.

According to a number of instrumentation charts provided by Degele, this imitation of the Prussian models in Bavaria seems to have held true for the cavalry and Jäger bands as well until World War I.[112]

Wieprecht found nothing to admire among Bavarian military bands during his travels there in 1845. He especially pointed out the lack of suitable instruments in the lower range, the tuba, in particular, being completely unknown there. 'This demonstrates,' says Wieprecht, 'how little care is given to military music in Bavaria.'[113]

Finally, one must mention Joseph Küffner, who, when his native Würzburg fell to Bavaria in 1802, became a military bandmaster and by his death in 1856 had contributed an enormous number of arrangements and original scores for military band.

[112] Degele, *Die Militärmusik*, gives the instruments and numbers of players for the following Bavarian units (in parenthesis Degele's page numbers are given): Infantry of 1860 (125); the 2nd Bavarian Infantry Regiment just before World War 1 (134); the Jäger band of 1913 (138); the cavalry of 1857 (144); the cavalry just before World War 1 (145); the 4th Bavarian field artillery regiment of 1891 (151); the 1st Bavarian foot artillery regiment of the late nineteenth century (153); and an Engineer band just before World War 1 (155).

[113] 'Third Travel Letter,' dated Munich, August 30, 1845, quoted in Kalkbrenner, *Wilhelm Wieprecht*, 103.

2   Military Bands in Austria

Austrian Infantry Bands before Mid-Century

At the end of the eighteenth century a typical Austrian infantry band would have consisted of the traditional *Harmoniemusik* ensemble of about eight players, although still under the old military title of '*Hautboisten*.'[1] During the first decade of the nineteenth century, Austrian infantry bands, in a characteristic acknowledgement of tradition, maintained this *Hautboisten* nucleus. These players in particular were hired civilian artists, rather than from the ranks of the troops, and commanders were cautioned to hire only serious and hard-working Hautboisten.[2] However, to these Hautboisten were added the so-called 'Bandisten,' or additional players, so that Austrian bands during the first decade were considerably larger than those in Prussia.

A reorganization, which took place in 1806, authorized bands to have eight *Hautboisten* and thirty-six Bandisten, although according to Brixel they were often even larger.[3] The fifes were eliminated in the Austrian bands at this time (1806) but the tambours remained for signal purposes. An order in 1809 cautions the commanders not to hire for tambours the 'weak and cowardly boys' as has been the practice, but rather strong men with soldierly qualities who would follow the troops into battle.[4]

An order by the Emperor given in 1822 cuts back somewhat the total musicians allowed in an infantry band; the official limits were now set at ten *Hautboisten* with twenty-four Bandisten.[5] A striking color lithograph of a 'Regiments Banda' in 1823[6] pictures a band of thirty-six or more in a Viennese military parade. Here one sees in the first row the *Hautboisten*, consisting of a flute-type, six soprano woodwinds, two trumpets, bassoon, and a non-playing conductor. Behind them are trombones, three rows of Bandisten, consisting of trumpet-types, trombones (one with the bell to the rear) and percussion. The uniforms of the *Hautboisten* consist of much more gold braid and more elaborate hat design than those of the Bandis-

[1] Panoff, *Militärmusik*, 171. By the nineteenth century the Germans had changed the spelling to 'Hoboisten,' but the Austrians seem to have retained the original French form.

[2] Brixel, *Das ist Österreichs Militär Musik*, 69, 'nur tuchtige und entschlossene Leute.' Brixel, himself a former Austrian military band leader, was a foremost authority on this subject and these pages are heavily indebted to his outstanding book.

[3] Surely a reflection of such larger Austrian bands is Beethoven's only large-scale band work, the *Siegessinfonie*. Although the work had its origin in a request by Beethoven's friend, Maelzel, for a work to suit a mechanical wind band he intended to construct, this score has nothing in common with those musical curiosities by Mozart and Haydn for music boxes. While the latter were written in piano score, Beethoven's work is a fully instrumented score for piccolo, four flutes, four oboes, five clarinets, three horns, four trumpets, four trombones, timpani and four percussion. While it is true that here and there a note is out of the range of some instrument, nevertheless the use of natural trumpets and horns and the general style and character of the work suggest it was conceived in terms of the sound of a real band and not something for Maelzel to 'orchestrate' for his machine. For further information see David Whitwell, 'Beethoven's *Siegessinfonie* for Band,' *Journal of Band Research* 13, no. 1 (Fall, 1977): 3ff.

[4] Brixel, *Das ist Österreichs Militär Musik*, 69.

'nicht, wie bisher, verzagte schwächliche Knaben'

ten. This lithograph seems almost identical to a list of instruments which Kastner suggests was typical for the Austrian infantry after 1827.

> piccolo in D♭
> clarinets in A♭
> clarinets in E♭ (four parts) [!]
> bassoon
> serpent
> trombones (three parts)
> horns (four parts in E♭ and A♭)
> key-trumpets in E♭
> trumpets in low E♭
> trumpet in F
> trumpet in C
> trumpet in E♭
> tambour[7]

Nothing is more alarming to the modern ear than one of these early nineteenth century military band scores with the multiple small clarinet parts—it is almost as if the melodies are an octave higher than we are used to hearing, making any attempt at a dark, homogeneous sound impossible. Novello, touring in St. Pölten at about this time (1829), heard an Austrian band and made the same objection.

> I also heard on the Grand Place to which I accidentally strolled, the Military Band playing before the Officer's Apartments. It is numerous but the Clarionets were of a small kind and of rather a harsh squealing quality—the only piece worth attending to was the Polacca in the Freischütz. The others were of the usual trashy waltz kind, with which I have been hitherto so much disappointed and annoyed in Germany.[8]

Although there are a few outstanding early concert works from Austria,[9] the emphasis before 1840 seems to have been on the functional, rather than the artistic. Indeed, an interesting order of 1835 reads,

> The choice of instrumentation is left to the regiment, but the commander should observe that there is no unnecessary luxury or constant changes, so that the military music is sonorous but not require any musical virtuosity that goes beyond this purpose.[10]

---

[5] Ibid., 88. I would assume these totals were intended as the maximum official limits and that many line infantry bands were smaller. This same order also gave approval for the induction of boys, beginning at age fifteen years. This seems to carry the implication that boys would be easier to train as musicians than the older men from the ranks.

[6] Heeresgeschichtliches Museum, Vienna.

[7] Kastner, *Manuel Général de Musique Militaire*, 195.

[8] Vincent Novello, *A Mozart Pilgrimage* (London: Novello, 1955), 275–276.

[9] As for example the Maschek *Battle of Leipzig* and an arrangement of a Symphony by Krommer, which is also scored for four separate E♭ clarinet parts, with two smaller A♭ clarinet parts.

[10] Quoted in Brixel, *Das ist Österreichs Militär Musik*, 91.

> Die Eintheilung der Instrumente ist jedem Regimente überlassen, jedoch auch diessfalls von Seite der Brigardiere darauf zu sehen, dass kein unnützer Aufwand durch immerwährende Veränderungen und kein übertriebener Luxus statt finde, indem der Dienst eine sonore und ausgiebige Militärmusik, aber keine diesen Zweck übersteigende musikalishe Virtuosität erfordert.

Another very interesting color lithograph[11] shows a special kind of functional music, an outdoor military field Mass held in 1833. Here one sees approximately sixty musicians, standing in a circle before the altar, together with the priests blessing the officers and thousands of civilians watching. Brixel has suggested[12] that this may represent more than one band, as one sees a total of four Schellenbaums. The uniforms, however, are identical.

The outstanding musicality of the Austrian bands, to which many contemporaries testify, begins to appear as a characteristic after 1840 and may have been due in part to the fact that Austria turned to established civilian musicians for its military band leaders. By drawing on band leaders who were trained in the conservatories, rather than in the field, Austria was able to profit from a particularly distinguished group of conductors, including Joseph Fahrbach,[13] Philipp Fahrbach, Senior,[14] Philipp Fahrbach, Junior,[15] Josef Gungl,[16] Michael Zimmerman,[17] Karl Komzák,[18] Julius Fucik,[19] Alphons Czibulka,[20] and Joseph Franz Wagner.[21]

The broad range of duties expected of these military band directors can be seen in Joseph Fahrbach's military contract (with the IR 45 infantry band, then stationed in Verona) of 1841,[22] which stated he was to do everything in his power to assume responsibility for the organization of the band, the training of its members, and the composition of its music! For this he was to receive a rather good salary of 60 Gulden, plus quarters of at least two rooms on the military base, quantities of firewood, candles, etc., and would receive a uniform 'similar' to an officer's.

One can imagine that such an educated musician hired to assume authority over a military band might have found it unpleasant to discover that he was excluded from the social courtesies enjoyed by the regular officers of the regiment with which he was associated. Thus, when Fahrbach was offered a contract in 1844 to lead the IR 44 infantry band stationed in Padua, he demanded that his new contract include the assurance that, as an educated man and artist, he be treated and spoken to in the manner of an officer. Further, he requested complete authority over all musical questions and that his immediate military superior be limited in his jurisdiction to matters of discipline and organization.[23]

[11] Heeresgeschichtliches Museum, Vienna.

[12] Brixel, *Das ist Österreichs Militär Musik*, 96.

[13] Joseph Fahrbach, eleven years older than his more famous brother, Philipp, was born in 1804. He was a prolific writer on military music and led the Austrian IR 44 and 45 infantry bands.

[14] Philipp Fahrbach, Senior, was one of the best loved of all Austrian military band leaders. He alternated between military service and leading civic dance bands, a specialty he learned while a flutist under his friend, Johann Strauss, Senior. Fahrbach formed his own civilian band in 1835, became the leader of the IR 4 infantry band in 1841, returned to civilian life in 1846—alternating in performing for court balls with Strauss, and in the 1850s returned to military service with the Linz IR 14 infantry band, stationed in Vienna.

[15] Philipp Fahrbach, Junior, was a contemporary, and competed with Johann Strauss, Junior. For ten years he was the conductor of the Austrian IR 38 infantry band in Hungary.

[16] Gungl was born in 1810 and was the Hungarian representative of the German dance music tradition. Liszt made a virtuoso piano arrangement of his *Ungarische Marsch*. He was the conductor of the Austrian IR 23 infantry band in Brünn, but left the service in 1843 to form his own touring band, performing throughout Russia and Germany. In 1851 he was engaged to organize the inaugural music for President John Tyler in Washington.

By the 1840s one also begins to find the instrumental characteristics which one associates with nineteenth-century Austrian music, in particular the prominence of the brass instruments, the E♭ trumpets, and the appearance of the Flügelhorns and euphoniums.[24] Brixel[25] gives a typical infantry band for 1845 as,

1 small flute
1 large flute
2 oboes
1 clarinet in A♭
2 clarinets in E♭
3 clarinets in B♭
2 bassoons
1 contrabassoon
1 trumpet in high B♭
8 trumpets in E♭
2 natural trumpets
2 bass trumpets in B♭
2 Flügelhorns in B♭
1 bassflügelhorn
1 'Obligatflügelhorn'
1 euphonium
3 trombones
4 horns (E♭, A♭)
3 bombardons
1 or 2 small drums
2 pair of cymbals

A large Austrian military band still included a sizable number of 'extra' players, hired by the officers of the regiment. Kastner wrote of this period that, although they were only authorized thirty-five or forty musicians, Austrian infantry bands sometimes had as many as seventy or eighty players![26] Of the musical characteristics of these Austrian military musicians during the 1840s, Kastner provides some very interesting contemporary observations.

> The musicians of Austria are very capable, and especially it is in the execution of marches where they have proved a rare energy and great precision which electrifies the troops. One should not fail to point out the admirable dexterity of the tambours. They play with taste and intelligence that is to say they have style. The tambour part is written only as

[17] Zimmerman, born in 1833, conducted the Austrian IR 73 infantry band in the famous international band competition in Paris in 1867. Although he shared the first prize there, he was not allowed to accept subsequently the French Legion of Honor offered him, as he did not hold officer's rank. Disenchanted, he left the service, but soon returned, serving with the Austrian IR 49, 40, 14, and 17th infantry bands.

[18] Komzák, born in 1850 in Prague, was the most important of the Bohemian military music conductors. He led the Austrian IR 7 infantry band in Innsbruck as a young man and later the Austrian IR 84 infantry band in Vienna. In his mid-forties he left the military to become the band director for the convalescent spas in Baden. He toured to the World's Fair in St. Louis in 1904.

[19] Fucik was born in 1872 in Prague, where he studied with Dvorak. In 1897 he became the conductor of the Austrian IR 86 infantry band in Budapest. He was one of the great march composers of the nineteenth century.

[20] Czibulka was the conductor of the Austrian IR 19 infantry band with whom he won the first prize in an international competition in Brussels in 1880. He was popular for his 'Monster Concerts' in the Prater in Vienna.

[21] Wagner was the conductor of the Austrian IR 47 and 49 infantry bands and was Austria's 'March King.'

[22] Quoted in Brixel, *Das ist Österreichs Militär Musik*, 94ff.

a general guide and the players improvise, pointing up the accents of the melody, etc. The snares of the Austrians are very small and have a very determined sound.

......

The Austrian musicians are blessed with a very good memory; they play by heart their marches and pas redoublés, and one is assured that there are regiments where the musicians have memorized nearly their entire repertoire, that is to say something like 50 or 60 works.[27]

At least one Austrian military band conductor was critical[28] of this practice of memorizing so much repertoire. Josef Sawerthal, writing in the Vienna *Allgemeinen Musik Zeitung* in 1846, wondered what growth might be achieved by the time spent memorizing '20 or 30 opera works' by the process of playing them over and over. Through this repetition, he observed,

> ... the player is dulled, he plays his part mechanically, attention and all love of art vanishes, desire for perfection vanishes as the player is exhausted ... all poetry dies and any illusion goes to its grave through the mechanical playing of the piece.[29]

[23] Quoted in Ibid., 95.

> ... jener eines Offiziers gleich, die er als gebildeter Mensch und Künstler verdienen wird, sohin anzusprechen berechtigt ist ... der stets beigegebene Herr Offizier nur auf die innere Ordnung und Disziplien zu sehen haben soll.

[24] Kastner, *Manuel Général de Musique Militaire*, 204, wrote that he believed the Austrian instrument makers to be particularly inventive, pointing to their experimentation with metal oboes and even a metal contrabassoon, 'which has no particular advantage and maintains all the faults of the usual contrabassoon.'

[25] Brixel, *Das ist Österreichs Militär Musik*, 109.

[26] Kastner, *Manuel Général de Musique Militaire*, 201.

[27] Kastner, ibid., 201, 203ff.

---

[28] In general, during the 1840s, the Austrian military music directors seem to have begun to examine their art and medium with critical attention. An article in the Vienna *Allgemeinen Musik Zeitung* in 1844 by Philipp Fahrbach, wonders what nucleus in the band can be compared with the nucleus represented by the string quartet within the symphony orchestra. He observes that while no wind instrument has the tone quality of the strings, the band has the greater variety of colors and that if the band lacks the shimmering tone of the strings, it makes up for this in its manly power which is more impressive and gripping.

> Man wird hier unwillkürlich in den Ausruf ausbrechen 'und doch fehlt diese Seele dem Militärmusikkörper?' Dieser Meinung kann ich aber entgegensetzen: dass sich eine solche Seele in der Militärmusik wieder in der harmonistischen Constellation und Nativtät kund gibt, und dass es am Ende der Musik doch gleich gilt, ob sie ihre Wirkungen den Saiten- oder andern Klängen verdankt. Die Streichinstrumente werden in der Militärmusik durch gewisse Blasinstrumente, so auch die Heterogenität der erstern mit der Harmonie (Blasinstrumentale) im gewöhnlichen Orchester durch die der Holz- und rumentengattungen repräsentiert.
>
> Das Sanfte der Clarinetten, Fagotts und Hörner lässt sich mit der Natur des Streichquartetts so ziemlich in Einklang bringen, nur muss man dabei bedenken, dass sich das an Tonfarbe und Technik Variante der Violine überhaupt durch kein Blasinstrument wiedergeben lässt ... Weiters aber hat die Militärmusik andere und schöne Mittel aufzuweisen, die Ernte der Instrumentengattungen ist dar in bei Weitem ergiebiger, als im gewöhnlichen Orchester; denn da stösst der Instrumenteur auf so manches nacktes Land; seiner ausgriefenden Phantasie wird Objektsmangel entgegengestellt. Das gewöhnliche Orchester besitzt bei zehn Instrumentengattungen, die Militärmusik aber um die Halfte mehr. Zwar ist das Tonfarbenspiel des Streichorchesters wei schimmernder, dagegen das männlich Kräftige, Volubile, Compacte des Militärmusiktonwesens desto ergreifender und imposanter.

[29] The original text:

> ... er bläst seinen Part mechanisch heruner; es schwindet alle Aufmerksamkeit, alle Liebe für die Kunst, es erstickt die Lust, den Drang zur Vervollkommnung; da der Musiker mit dem Auswendigiernen einer saft- und geistlosen Piece oft Tage lang zubringt und seine geistige Spannkraft dadurch erschlafft wird; alIe Poesie der Auffassung des Vortrages erstirbt und jede illuson geht zu Grabe durch des mechanische Herunterleiern eines Musikstückes.

Wieprecht also reports this practice,[30] but adds the repertoire in question was mostly marches and light Italian opera works. 'One does not expect,' says Wieprecht, 'anything more from the South.'

Wieprecht discussed extensively an Austrian band he heard which was stationed in Mainz.[31] The bandmaster, a Mr. Zulehner, organized a special performance for Wieprecht upon his arrival.

[30] 'Fourth Travel Letter' dated Vienna, September 18,' 1845, quoted in Kalkbrenner, *Wilhelm Wieprecht*, 105.

[31] 'First Travel Letter,' dated Mainz, August 20, 1845, quoted in ibid., 98ff.

> It has 64 players, with the brass far outnumbering the woodwinds … They began with an Overture by Reissiger.
>
> The effect, as one can imagine, was powerful, the ensemble good and worthy of praise. The director was wise not to use percussion in compositions they were not written for … I heard various pieces, among them the Overture to *Titus*, in an arrangement of which I was not in approval. I was more satisfied with the pieces composed in a newer style. The marches were played with much precision, in a characteristic military style. The intonation was, astonishingly enough, clear in fortissimo; but the nearer to piano, unsure; and at pianissimo, unclear. The reason for this lies, in the service relationship of the Hautboisten [and the 'Bandisten']. The band has ten Hautboisten … these serve for ten to twelve year periods of enlistment and are good musicians. The others [the Bandisten] are troops from the ranks, chosen for band service whether they are musical or not, slowly educated, and remaining only dilettantes. If such a man does not have talent he can arrive at a technical ability, but he will not grow into the spirit and character of his instrument—and only in such circumstances does an artist arrive at complete control of his instrument. It is well known that dilettantes get a good tone at a louder level, but at softer levels allow the intonation to fail … Their performance has an almost machine-like quality.
>
> If the director is lucky in the Bandisten he gets, he may, with hard work, educate them during their eight years of service into good technicians, or even virtuosos. Thus, I have heard an Hautboisten [Bandisten?] play variations on the chromatic flügelhorn (which we call the cornetto in B♭, the same instrument Mr. Sax calls the saxhorn in B♭) with astonishing ability; if he had the sophistication in tone that Arban has, he would be an even better player [than Arban].

In Vienna, Wieprecht found military bands of only about thirty-five players, as opposed to those of seventy or eighty players in Austrian military bands stationed in the provinces.[32] Again he comments on the mechanical quality of the Bandisten, 'who practice daily, even hourly, just like a machine, or as a soldier with his rifle.'

[32] 'Fourth Travel Letter,' dated Vienna, September 18, 1845, quoted in ibid., 104ff.

He mentions the lack of over-all supervision of military music in Austria, pointing out that he heard oboes and bassoons in the band he heard in Mainz, but did not find these instruments in the bands in Vienna. Contributing to the lack of unification, was the fact that the conductors were not from the military, but were civilian musicians hired to conduct.

As in the case of Kastner, mentioned above, Wieprecht also comments on the great taste with which the Austrian percussionists played.

> The Austrians are especially blessed with their percussion, which play with astonishing virtuosity and raise the military character of the music ... they play with such insight and taste, using their figures to define the melody, their notated part serving only as a guide-line.

Before continuing, one must acknowledge the strong musical contributions of the Bohemian and Hungarian lands of the Austrian Empire. The Bohemians, of course, had been well known for their expertise in wind music since the eighteenth century and Kastner was particularly impressed with the contribution of this heritage to early nineteenth century military music there.

An Austrian military band, ca. 1830, by Michael Tretsensky.

The Bohemians, from the meanest to the greatest, love and cultivate music. As a result of their universal love of music, the military musicians of that country can not be mediocre in quality or poor in resources. In effect, an infantry regiment ordinarily counts 90, and no less than 80 musicians. Each company of soldiers has various kinds of music, because the soldiers of Bohemia sing popular songs, soldier's songs, and they cultivate not only winds but strings and can even put together in the military, an orchestra capable of playing Beethoven symphonies.[33]

The Hungarians also produced fine musicians (in instrumental music not so successful as the Bohemians, according to Kastner) and I shall return to this subject below relative to the birth of the modern march form. Given the huge geographical responsibilities Austria had taken on, one found Austrian military bands stationed throughout Bohemia, Hungary, and Italy, making it difficult sometimes for travelers to identify which culture was responsible for what.[34]

Austrian Cavalry and Jäger Bands before Mid-Century

A new kind of cavalry unit, the Lancers, appeared at the end of the eighteenth century and represented the first of many colorful new troops (Husars, Light-cavalry, Dragoons, etc.), each with their own distinctive uniforms. In 1807 the Court Secretary of War authorized a new 'Musical Horse-Harmonie' for the cavalry, with the usual provision that the individual officers, and not the government, absorb any new expenses.[35] This is the first time we have seen the term Harmonie associated with the Austrian cavalry and may reflect the fact that the Austrians began to experiment with the addition of *metal* clarinets and flutes.[36] Thus instruments from the traditional *Harmoniemusik* appear, yet, at the same time, the all-brass character which had always been associated with these troops was retained. This seems to have been only a brief experiment, for in the instrumentation given by Swoboda[37] for the Austrian cavalry band of 1827 they are no longer seen.

2 trumpets in D
2 Principal trumpets in D
2 horns in D
signal horn in A♭

[33] Kastner, *Manuel Général de Musique Militaire*, 204–205.

[34] Berlioz, in a letter describing the musical scene in Prague, explains his silence on the subject of military bands:

> I do not know if the regiment in question was a Bohemian one, or from some other part of the Empire of Austria, and it would be too absurd to establish a theory which well-informed people might ridicule by simply saying: 'The Bohemian musicians you are speaking of are Hungarians, or Austrians, or Milanese.' [*Memoirs*, 412–413]

[35] Brixel, *Das ist Österreichs Militär Musik*, 132. .

[36] According to Kastner, *Manuel Général de Musique Militaire*, 205, small flutes and clarinets in both E♭ and small [!] B♭ were made of brass and were very piercing and 'somewhat less satisfactory than if they were made of wood … One generally desires to see these instruments abandoned in Austria.' He also adds that they were tried in the French cavalry briefly, but were found 'painful to play and extremely fatiguing for the artists.'

[37] Quoted in Kastner, *Manuel Général de Musique Militaire*, 195.

2 trumpets in A♭
1 trumpet in F
1 trumpet in E♭
1 trumpet in C
3 trombones
1 bass trumpet in D
1 bass trumpet in G

Brixel reproduces several lithographs of these mounted Austrian brass bands, the earliest of which (Husars in 1815 and Lancers in 1814[38]), picture only six or eight trumpets. A lithograph of 1823[39] shows a larger group of thirteen trumpets playing while in full galop! A color lithograph of mounted Dragoons in 1844[40] finally pictures the full brass band, with trombones, horns, and a bombardon, in addition to the trumpets.

The Austrian Jäger bands also experimented with the metal clarinet, as one can see in a typical instrumentation given by Brixel.

1 high metal clarinet
1–2 cornets
4–5 Flügelhorns
2–3 bass Flügelhorns
1 euphonium
4 horns
7–8 trumpets
3 trombones
2–3 bombardons[41]

One Austrian bandmaster, Joseph Sawerthal (1819–1903), was outspoken against the metal clarinet, noting, 'there are too many clarinets in the Trumpet Music [cavalry band] and too many trumpets in the Infantry Music.'[42] He believed that the Jäger band needed to be all-brass to make up in volume what it lacked in size. The Austrian Jäger band received its first published music regulations in 1840 and here one finds the definition of the ordinary march tempo as MM.108 and the fast march as MM.120.[43]

[38] Brixel, *Das ist Österreichs Militär Musik*, plates 74, 77.

[39] Ibid., plate 113.

[40] Ibid., plate 162.

[41] Brixel. *Das ist Österreichs Militär Musik*, 130, without date, but certainly near mid-century. Brixel also provides, in plate 102, a rare painting of a Jäger band in parade (on foot) in 1833. Although it is impossible to define instruments in this reproduction, the band appears to be more than forty in number and seems to have a variety of brass instruments.

[42] Quoted in ibid.

[43] Ibid., 131.

Austrian Military Bands during the 'Golden Age'

The great figure in nineteenth-century Austrian military music was Andreas Leonhardt, who was appointed to a newly created post of Armeekapellmeister, thus giving Austria for the first time the centralized direction comparable to that found in Prussia and France. Leonhardt was a man of vision who immediately fought for a larger band and for the increased social status of the conductor, by giving him regular army rank and pay (in this he was not successful, however).[44] His official duties included the supervision of instrument purchase ('the best and cheapest'), music, and he was supposed to have been consulted by regiments who hired civilian conductors.

The use of civilian band conductors remained a characteristic of the Austrian infantry regiments at mid-century. A typical advertisement in the army newspaper, *Der Österreichische Soldatenfreund*, in 1854 reads,

> *Conductor's Position to be had*
> The Tuscany 8th Dragoon Regiment, stationed at Oedenburg, seeks someone qualified in every respect. The pay is 60 fl. per month, plus quarters and uniform. For the acquisition of instruments and other musical necessities, and for the recruitment of individual, knowledgeable musicians, money will be put at his disposal in sufficient amounts.
> At first he will be hired on a provisional basis but if in a reasonable period of time he proves himself capable he will be hired permanently and be given a bonus of 100 Gulden.[45]

In a reorganization and standardization of all the army music in 1851, Leonhardt was able to achieve a basic infantry band personnel of forty-eight men, with another twelve who could serve as apprentices during peace time. In practice, individual regiments could still add 'extra' players at the officers' expense, thus in a photograph[46] of the Austrian IR 17 regimental band, taken in 1866, one sees some sixty players. Brixel[47] gives the following instrumentation (expressed in numbers of parts, not numbers of players) as typical for this period.

[44] Ibid., 144ff.

[45] A similar advertisement in the same paper by a conductor seeking such a position reads,
> An experienced military band conductor, who because of family reasons gave up his previous post, wishes to be placed again in this capacity. Of his abilities as a bandmaster and artist, the best recommendations are available.

[46] Ibid., plate 238.

[47] Ibid., 149.

1 piccolo in D♭
1 flute in D♭
1 clarinet in A♭
1 clarinet in E♭
3 clarinets in B♭
2 bassoons
4 horns
1 cornet in E♭
2 soprano Flügelhorns in B♭
1 alto Flügelhorn in E♭
1 bass Flügelhorn in B♭
1 euphonium
1 'Obligattrompete' in E♭
4 trumpets in E♭
1 bass trumpet in B♭
3 trombones
2 'Bässe'
small and large drum
cymbals

When on the march, it was the custom at this time for the bass drum cart to be pulled by a large dog, called the 'Paukenhund,' who carried the mallet crosswise in his mouth![48]

The reorganization of 1851 also set the 'official' personnel of the cavalry and Jäger bands at twenty-four each, although again in practice larger bands were to be found. An 1864 photograph of the K.K. 14th Feldjäger-Bataillons-Musik pictures forty-three brass players, including an impressive number of low brass, without percussion. Finally, this order of 1851 attempted to unify the signals of these troops and called for the re-education of these players.[49]

Leonhardt also seems to have followed the lead of Wieprecht in Prussia in giving so-called 'Monster Concerts.' The first of these massed concerts took place in 1853, when Leonhardt gathered together thirty-seven of his bands—totaling some 1,200 musicians and 300 percussion—in a performance of marches and Strauss waltzes before the Tzar of Russia and the Emperor of Austria, Franz Joseph, in Olmütz. A local paper, the *Olmützer Neue Zeit* was astonished that so many musicians could play together and marveled at the precision and the imposing sound.[50]

[48] Brixel, ibid., in plate 153, reproduces a photograph of a regimental band from the late 1850s where one can see a large white dog, harnessed to the bass drum cart.

[49] The original text:

> … theils Hornisten und Tambours sowie Trompeter, von denen einzelnen Armee-Korps hieher berufen, welche von dem Armeekappellmeister den Unterricht erhalten, den sie wieder fortpflanzen, theils wird der Armeekapellmeister zur Ertheilung des Unterrichts zu einzelnen Armee-Korps beordert.

[50] The original text:

> Die Wirkung dieser Stücke durch ein solches Monsterorchester vorgetragen, war imposant und man musste über die Präzision und Reinheit der Ausführungen und das exakte Zusammenstimmen meherer hundert Musiker erstaunen …

Music Schools

During the nineteenth century there developed strong interest among the military band directors for establishing a national school for the training of military musicians and conductors. The first real leader of this movement was Cölestin Netrefa, trumpet professor at the conservatory of the Gesellschaft der Musikfreunde in Vienna, and himself a former military band director. His advocacy during the 1850s was cut short by his untimely death.

Following the death of Netrefa, Emil Urban, bandmaster of the IR 9th Regiment, stepped forward and declared the necessity of such a school in an article in the *Österreichische Militär-Zeitung*. In this article he pointed out that, as was well-known, regiments recruited primarily from the civilian ranks and that the most sought-after persons were Bohemians, as music was so strong a characteristic of those people. But, he said, the musical talent of the Bohemians was more natural in character and that often after one had recruited such a person it was discovered that basic instruction in music was still necessary in order to make them a functional member of the military band. However, by the time they have received enough training while a member of the regiment, soon their enlistment period was over and then they demanded a great deal of money in order not to transfer to another regiment which might offer advantages—so much money, he observed, that 'one would have been shocked twelve years ago that a military musician could demand so high a salary.'[51] He makes the interesting observation that some military musicians were paid as much as the second conductors of provisional opera theaters.

Urban argued for a national military music school funded by the government, with each regiment sending talented young musicians to train there. Urban's efforts came to nothing, primarily because his plan failed to have the support of Leonhardt—indeed, some suggested that Leonhardt was behind an anonymous article which ridiculed Urban and his plan.

Years later, after 1870, a new move was begun by a man who, interestingly enough, was neither an Austrian nor a military musician, the German composer, Wilhelm Westmeyer. Westmeyer developed a careful plan which won the support of the War Ministry and managed to raise the considerable sum

[51] Quoted in Brixel, *Das ist Österreichs Militär Musik*, 211ff.

of 60,000 Gulden in financial support for the creation of the school. The Salzburg Building Counselor, Herr Schwarz, came forward with the donation of a building in Vienna which, if remodeled, would have been suitable for the school. The Emperor, who had given earlier support, turned hostile to the plan when he realized how much the remodeling costs, together with the annual support needed, amounted to. The Emperor declared, 'This matter must be laid to rest,' and that was the end of that! Westmeyer was, of course, bitterly disappointed and wrote in the *Militär-Zeitung* (July 24, 1872),

> The spiritual and material part of this idea I have fought for and laid at people's feet for, for Austria should have the prestige of having an institution such as no other state in Europe has.
>
> ......
>
> If it is not wanted, good!—or rather, it is unfortunate—since in two years time, according to the judgment of those who know, Austria will have no more military musicians.

This prediction was too dark, but no real national school was ever founded.

Only the conservatories of the major cities continued, as they had in the past, to provide the musical education for potential conductors. Near the end of the century such an institution in Vienna began to specialize in this field, but before this time the best-known school was the so-called 'Eleven-Schule' in Prague. Brixel[52] quotes from the guide-lines for prospective applicants to this school:

[52] Brixel, *Das ist Österreichs Militär Musik*, 214.

> 1. Applicants must be between the ages of 16 and 19. Those accepted would be immediately inducted and would receive room and board during the time of their study. After a period of one or two years study they would join a regimental band with a non-commissioned rank and supplemental monies. Exceptional students would receive these benefits while still students.
>
> 2. Students under the age of 16 accepted only if their parents agreed to their induction after their study and paid for their schooling.

This school closed at the end of the century, but the many fine conductors who studied there continued its influence until the period of World War 1.

The Birth of the Modern March

Shortly after the 1848 civil disorders, the modern march appears in the heart of the Austrian–Hungarian Empire. By the end of the century this new march had become so popular that one finds its essential characteristics in not only marches composed in the Empire, but in Germany, America, and even Russia and China.

The *style* of this new march had its most immediate roots in the *verbunkos* (from the German root *Werbung*, 'to recruit'), a form of dance used to recruit troops in the Hungarian part of the Empire until the Austrian administration imposed conscription after 1849. The music of this dance had, of course, much older roots in Hungarian, Slav, and Balkan popular music. By the beginning of the nineteenth century, the *verbunkos* was a dance with varying tempi requiring good coordination. The recruiters would arrive in a village, assemble the young men of military age, and begin the music of the *verbunkos*. The young man who danced best was designated the leader of the young men recruited from that village, under the assumption that the demonstrated coordination represented more general potential. Had not Socrates said, 'The best dancer is the best warrior'?

The musical characteristics which carried over from the *verbunkos* to the modern march style are the very distinguishing characteristics of the march as we know it. The melodies were cast in widely arched, binary, nearly symmetrical phrases, with complementary cadences. More important, I think, was the *character* of the melodies, a character more vocal than instrumental and, in fact, referred to at the time as 'song without words' (*hallgató-nóta*). There was an introduction and, at the end, a traditional cadence which represented the 'clicking of heels' (*bokázó*, or as we say today, 'stinger' or 'bump-note'). None of these musical characteristics are found in wind band marches of the eighteenth century. The adoption of these musical characteristics into the musical language of nineteenth-century Austria is a direct expression of that people's dawning interest in the Hungarian culture, something which had been subservient and repressed for years. As Szabolcsi[53] observed,

---

[53] Bence Szabolcsi, *A Concise History of Hungarian Music* (London: Barrie and Rockliff, 1964), 54.

The abyss of centuries was suddenly bridged over and the bourgeoisie hurriedly and with enthusiasm took over something from the lower social strata.

The actual *form* of the new march was not so different from the eighteenth-century march. Both consisted of a March in two sections, each repeated, and a Trio in two sections, each again repeated. The eighteenth-century march, however, always included a da capo. It is the absence of this da capo which makes the late nineteenth and early twentieth century march so peculiar at first glance—a form which ends in a different key than that in which it began!

It is in a deeper, psychological sense that one has to look for meaning in this unprecedented formal design. The *verbunkos* found a source of variety in contrasting tempi, something impossible in a functional march. Instead, the new march sought variety in the contrast of melodic styles between the more militant and exciting March and the more lyric and contemplative Trio. While there would be the traditional sense of satisfaction felt in the return to previous material through the da capo, this sense of satisfaction would be far out-weighed by the psychological jolt of the abrupt return to the strong militant style after one had reposed in the peace of the Trio. Sousa[54] once expressed his rationale for this form very nicely in an analogy with dining. When asked why he wrote marches which lacked a da capo, he answered, or so the anecdote goes, 'When you have finished the ice cream, who wants to go back for roast beef?'

For the nineteenth-century Austrians themselves, the most popular march of all the thousands of marches composed in this new style was the *Radetzky-Marsch* of Johann Strauss. But to me, memorable as many of these melodies are, none so characterizes that old Empire or seems so 'in tune' with those yellow-washed buildings of Vienna as the first melody of the Trio in Fucik's *Der Florentiner*.

[54] Non-musicians in America are often under the impression that Sousa 'invented' the march; in fact, he represents the final chapter of this form.

3 Military Bands in France

The Napoleonic Period

The impetus of the extraordinary large concert bands associated with the French Revolution at the end of the eighteenth century resulted in unusually large military bands as well by the beginning of the century. A widely reproduced instrumentation list of the French Imperial infantry bands for 1802 reads,

> 1 piccolo
> 1 clarinet in F
> 16 clarinets in C
> 4 bassoons
> 2 serpents
> 2 trumpets
> 1 bass trumpet
> 4 horns
> 3 trombones
> percussion[1]

[1] Henry George Farmer, *The Rise and Development of Military Music* (London: William Reeves, 1912), 81; and Kastner, *Manuel Général de Musique Militaire*, 171.

A few of the revolutionary composers, such as Méhul, continued to compose large-scale works for chorus and band, but this is misleading for the true Napoleonic military music was quite sparse. While in the palace Napoleon lived in the style of an Emperor, in the field he loved to live as a soldier, sleeping on a common metal cot, for example. He permitted larger military bands only in those cases where it cost his government nothing, that is, where the bands were supported privately by the officers. In fact he eliminated cavalry music entirely for a time when he discovered the cavalry music required enough horses and supplies for four regiments of soldiers!

His own taste for military music was much more basic; for him the essential military music was only the trumpet signals necessary for troop movement. Therefore the *one* musical institution which Napoleon enthusiastically supported was the Trumpet School at Versailles. Here as many as six hundred trumpeters were schooled between 1805–1811, under the leadership of the German composer, David Buhl.

Among the more interesting innovations of Buhl were the first signals in more than two-parts, in this case four to six parts. Several specimens of these are still extant in the Paris Bibliothèque nationale, scored for four trumpets, two horns, and trombone. The inspiration for these more musically complicated signals was not art, but rather a military necessity: the need for a means of transmitting more sophisticated instructions for troop movement. Another Frenchman working on this problem was a man named Sudre, who published a paper[2] in which he claimed the potential for holding real conversations in the field through what he described as 'musical symbols.' This in fact was a system in which an entire 13,000-word French dictionary was represented by no more than five musical pitches. After training two trumpeters in this system he held a public demonstration on the Champ de Mars in Paris during which a general gave commands in complete sentences which were then 'translated' at a distance for another general. The remarkable success led to public demonstrations in several countries. However, the telegraph, which had appeared at the end of the eighteenth century, soon eliminated all need for music as a means of field communication and Sudre and his system were forgotten. The name he coined for his system of musical communication, however, remains in the language of all peoples to this day—'la téléphonie.'

Napoleon, as I said, was also determined that as little government monies as possible were available to the normal infantry bands. Therefore one finds an ordinance in 1807 which sets the official limit for these bands at only nine players![3]

In 1815 Anton Reicha, then living in Paris, produced an extraordinary symphony for wind band, with optional possibilities for expanding the work to include two or more additional bands in concertato fashion. His intent was apparently to have ready music which might be used in one of the famous Parisian festivals which had been so popular with the public during the Revolution and continued on an irregular basis. Thus he named the work *Music to Celebrate the Memory of Great Men and Great Events*. This is truly one of the most remarkable large-scale compositions, and one of the most musical, in the history of the wind band. There is no evidence it was ever performed during the composer's lifetime, however. Indeed the score[4] is so clean and unmarked that it appears never to

[2] *L'Art de parler par le son des instruments, ou Instruction pour donner de loin toute espèce d'avis par les sons des instruments, en temps de paix comme en temps de guerre* ... A similar work appeared in Germany, by B. C. A. Weyrich, under the title, *Die Instrumentalton-Sprechkunst oder Anleitung durch instrumentaltone alle Nachrichten in die Ferne zu geben, sowoll im Frieden als im Kriege, beim Civil und Militair, auf dem Lande und Meere* (Leipzig, 1830).

[3] Kastner, *Manuel Général de Musique Militaire*, 187.

[4] Paris Bibliothèque nationale (MS.8.425).

have left the possession of the composer. In this regard I might add that Reicha, a very intelligent and philosophical person, knew the public was not ready for some of his works[5] and in his *Autobiography* he suggests that he considered such works his best, not the ones immediately understood by the public.

> It is impossible to discuss my complete works here. More than a hundred have been published; about sixty are still in manuscript. Among the latter will be found my finest efforts.

The Symphony begins with a dramatic Adagio, which introduces a very Classical sounding Allegro. The second movement, an Adagio, is a very beautiful and expressive theme and variations. I consider this movement one of the most remarkable in the wind band literature. The third, and perhaps the original final movement, is called 'poco Presto' and is light in character, but very charming, with a very strong ending. Following this in the manuscript is a 'Marche funèbre,' which may have been a separate work in spite of its location in this manuscript. The instrumentation is slightly different, lacking piccolos, but maintaining the same canons of the Presto. Reicha wrote of this movement,

> It was principally for the army that I composed this marche funèbre, which may be performed alone.

Aside from the genuine musical values in this score, there is a most unusual foreword in Reicha's hand which contains a number of interesting ideas.

> This work is composed to commemorate: 1st, the memory of great exploits; 2nd, the death of heroes and great men; 3rd, to celebrate any important future event.
> The performance of this work must be assigned to a good conductor only, one who would be well advised to study the work thoroughly before having it performed.
> The place selected for the performance must be large and open (uncovered) and the orchestra must be a distance of 50 steps from the audience.
> It is imperative to use the exact number of instruments mentioned in the score, otherwise the work would not sound as effectively. These instruments are: 3 piccolos, 6 oboes, 6 clarinets, 6 horns, 6 bassoons, 6 trumpets, 3 double-basses, 6 army drums and 4 small field-guns.

[5] In his *Autobiography* (reprinted in *Notes sur Antoine Reicha* [Brno, 1970]), his remarks on the relationship of the composer and the public clearly mark him as a man of aesthetic vision quite above that of the craftsman-composer of his day.

> I have never been interested in writing for the popular demand. To enlighten the public has been my aim; not to amuse it.
> ......
> I have become indifferent to all praise and criticism, being sufficiently rewarded when I instinctively feel I have achieved something worthwhile. If a good work is a failure, it is not the composer's fault, but the public's. It often happens that today a work is damned, tomorrow it is acclaimed. Was it not so with the works of Mozart? At first they were not understood, they were bitterly criticized, publishers refused them. But all of this has not prevented Mozart from reaching immortality.

The musicians must not be too close to each other,[6] so that the sound gets more widely spread.

The double-basses must not be replaced by other instruments as they are absolutely necessary (no other instrument can go so low), neither must the above mentioned number of instruments be increased, unless one more double bass or double bassoons are added.

The drums must be located at about 100 steps behind the orchestra and there must be only 3 drums beating at a time in order to be able to take turns. The beating of the drums must be a muffled (*piano*) rolling, even when the orchestra is playing *forte*.

The conductor must make sure that the drums are exactly starting and finishing in accordance with the time. It is advisable not to display the field-guns to the sight of the audience, in order to get more of an effect of surprise. The march is repeated 3 times, the first time without drums or field-guns; the second time with drums but not field-guns; the third time with both drums and field-guns. It could also be considered to have one or two infantry regiments maneuvering, if there is enough room, in accordance with the march.

[6] Reicha was a very rare early musician to seriously contemplate the subject of acoustics. He discusses this subject further in his *Traité de haute composition musicale, faisant suite au Cours d'harmonie pratique et au Traité de mélodie* (Paris, 1824). Here he wishes for a means of measuring the exact amount of air actually set in motion by a tone. Among other results, he felt such a device would allow the composer to determine how many musicians are necessary to fill (with sound) a particular hall, and how far from the audience the musicians should be.

This is an extraordinary composition in every respect!

French military band, ca. 1806

Since nearly everyone considered the ordinance of 1807, which limited infantry bands to nine players, an impossible limitation, the officers were forced to bear the expense for hiring additional civilian musicians. The typical line infantry band during the Napoleonic period remained fairly small, however, averaging 20–24 players, of whom half were hired civilians.[7] Further growth was impossible due to the losses which occurred during Napoleon's campaigns. It seems almost impossible to imagine, but it is said that more than 2,000

[7] Kastner, *Manuel Général de Musique Militaire*, 171. Degele, *Die Militärmusik*, 127, gives a typical line infantry band for 1809 as piccolo, small clarinet, 6–8 clarinets in C, pairs of bassoons, horns, and trombones, with one trumpet, one serpent, and percussion.

French military musicians perished during the murderous offensive in Russia alone![8] Under such circumstances rebuilding was slow and even by 1825 the typical infantry band was still relatively small at thirty-six players.

[8] Reschke, *Studie zur Geschichte der brandenburgischpreussischen Heeresmusik*, 46.

2 flutes
2 clarinets in F or E♭
12 clarinets in B♭ or C
4 oboes
6 bassoons
2 contrabassoons
2 trumpets
4 horns
2 trombones[9]

[9] Ibid., 99.

The reader will notice that even more striking than the relatively small size is the ancient extended-Harmoniemusik character of the instrumentation. There is no trace to be seen here of the tremendous advances in both brass and woodwind manufacture which had been made in Germany. Indeed, it was only after a report by Spontini to the Academy of Art that the importation of Germany instruments began (ca. 1825–1831).

French military band, ca. 1820, anonymous

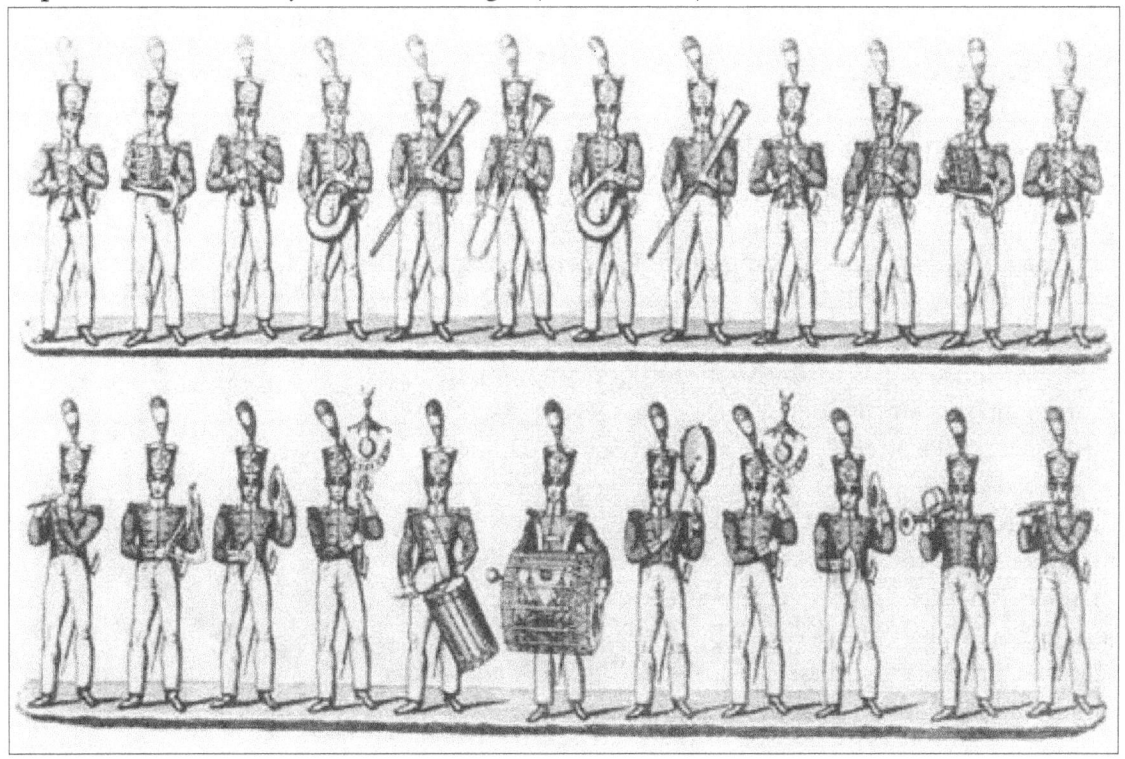

During this period the key-bugle types were imported and there was some experimentation with metal flutes and clarinets. By 1843, however, Berlioz could still complain that the French military as yet did not have valved trumpets or tubas![10]

One institution which tended to preserve the old traditions, no matter how inferior they might have been, was the Gymnase de Musique Militaire. Founded in 1836, under the leadership of musicians such Berr, Klosé, and Carafa[11] the school was open to talented members of all French regiments for the training of both players and conductors until it was closed in 1870. This institution was devoted to preserving the old military instrumentation, based on the traditional Harmoniemusik instruments. In this regard it was closely allied with the Parisian instrument makers, who were geared up to produce only these traditional instruments.

Thus the Gymnase de Musique Militaire and its Director, Michele Carafa,[12] represented all that was comfortable and traditional about French military music and was a formidable establishment against whom a young foreigner named Adolphe Sax had to battle to win his revolution in French military music.

The Period of Sax

Antoine-Joseph (known as Adolphe) Sax (1814–1894) was a talented young instrument maker in Brussels when he came to the attention of the French Général de Rumigny, an aide-de-camp to Louis Philippe.[13] It was probably Général de Rumigny who was largely responsible for sponsoring Sax's move to Paris in 1842, for almost immediately Sax began a correspondence with the Minister of War relative to the poor condition of the instruments of French military music, the social status of the players, etc., all matters of concern to Général de Rumigny.

Sax had arrived in Paris at a time when there was wide public concern relative to military music and his genius in instrument design led to his quickly becoming the focal point for a number of influential persons interested in this subject, including Berlioz, Halévy and Kastner. But to the establishment, chiefly Carafa, the Gymnase de Musique Militaire, and the traditional Parisian instrument makers, this young foreigner was

[10] Berlioz, *Memoirs*, 308.

[11] According to Farmer, *The Rise and Development of Military Music*, 124, fn. 7, Berlioz once applied for the position of Director of the school!

[12] Michele Carafa (1787–1872) was born in Naples but took French citizenship in 1834, thereafter becoming very active in the musical life of Paris. He was an above average composer of ballets and operas, but was over-shadowed by the popularity and genius of Rossini. Rossini, who was a friend from Carafa's Naples days, said of Carafa, 'He made the mistake of having been my contemporary.' (Grove 3:768)

[13] Edward Neukomm, *Histoire de la musique militaire* (Paris: L. Baudoin et ce., 1889), 58.

most unwelcome. Immediately they[204] set about attempting to undermine his ideas and his new business in Paris.[15] Sax was subjected to vicious press campaigns, his best workers were tempted away by higher salaries, a mysterious fire destroyed part of his factory, and he was even attacked physically.[16] Berlioz described all this in his *Memoirs*.

> And yet, will it be believed that this ingenious young artist has all the trouble in the world in making his way and maintaining himself in Paris? Persecutions worthy of the Middle Ages are inflicted on him, corresponding perfectly to those Benvenuto Cellini had to endure from his enemies. His workmen are enticed away, his designs are stolen, he is accused of madness, and driven to litigation. A trifle more, and they would assassinate him. Such is the hatred that inventors always excite amongst those of their rivals who can invent nothing for themselves. Fortunately the gifted inventor has always enjoyed the friendship and protection of Général de Rumigny: but will he be able to count for ever on these aids in the wretched struggle?[17]

It was in this rather inflamed atmosphere, that the Minister of War appointed a commission in 1845 to study the conditions of French military music. The commission members included a group of distinguished composers: Spontini, Auber, Onslow, Adam, Halvéy and Carafa; two French Colonels of regiments which had traditional bands with outstanding reputations: M. le Count Gudin, of the 2nd Lanciers, and M. Riban, of the 74th Line Infantry; two scientists: Baron Seguier and Colonel Savart; Général de Rumigny, as head of the commission, and Georges Kastner, as secretary.

The commission held its first meeting on 25 February 1845, and on that occasion was able to identify its initial areas of study:

1. The question of the hired 'extra' musicians in military bands.
2. The quality of the instruments being used in the bands.
3. The instrumentation of the bands.
4. The question of the size of the bands.
5. The problems of the low military and social status of the military musicians.

[14] Who were these enemies of Sax? According to Kastner, *Manuel Général de Musique Militaire*, 238, they were 'from the region of the obscure; musicians without reputation or talent.'

[15] Sax's flourish of activity can be seen in his French patent records dating from his first ten years in Paris. These include the families of saxhorns (1845), the saxotrombas (1845), the saxophones (1846), as well as numerous patents for improvements in traditional instruments.

[16] Grove 16:530.

[17] Berlioz, *Memoirs*, 308.

Their discussions quickly centered on the impact of the suppression of hired civilian musicians, which had occurred in 1834 with noticeable results. No longer was it possible to acquire fine German and Italian musicians, who not only filled out the instrumentation, but were a positive force in the education of the weaker players. This issue was closely related to the question of size, for clearly the government, alone, would not be able to support bands of the size found in Prussia (fifty to sixty players, according to the commission) or Austria and Bohemia (seventy to eighty players). Spontini told his colleagues on the commission that the absolute minimum must be seventy-four players. This discussion led to a concentration on the question of size and instrumentation and the isolation of three fundamental questions:

1. How many players are strictly necessary for infantry and cavalry bands?
2. Which instruments, either old or new, should be adopted for these bands?
3. How many of each instruments (doubling) are necessary for a desirable sound?

The commission directed the Minister of War to answer the first question and then they set about considering the second. To begin this study they invited all instrument makers in Paris to bring their new instruments before the commission. A variety of French designs of German instruments appeared, such as a French Flügelhorn and a contrabass version of the bombardon, but often were found by the commission to have imperfect mechanisms. Some new instruments appeared, the 'embolyclave,' for example, which was intended as a replacement for the ophicleide. The commission liked the sound of this instrument, but found its mechanism too fragile and complicated for military use.

No doubt frustrated and confused by the individual instruments they had to examine, the commission abandoned this approach and instead decided to consider an 'ideal' instrumentation. To initiate this discussion they invited all interested parties to submit their recommended instrumentation plans.

Carafa, even though a member of the commission, immediately submitted a plan for forty-five players which was dedicated to preserving the traditional instrumentation of the French military band:

1 piccolo
1 E♭ clarinet
2 solo clarinets in B♭
7 first clarinets in B♭
7 second clarinets in B♭
4 oboes
4 bassoons
2 natural horns
2 valved horns
2 valved trombones (Sax system)
2 valved cornets
3 trumpets
4 ophicleides
4 percussion

A plan submitted by Sax was quite different. Here not only were entirely new instruments recommended, but the historic 'extended Harmoniemusik' principle was entirely abandoned:

1 D♭ piccolo
1 E♭ clarient
6 B♭ clarinets
2 saxophones
2 cornets
6 valved trumpets
2 slide trombones
2 valved trombones
2 E♭ soprano saxhorns
4 B♭ saxhorns
4 E♭ tenor saxhorns
2 B♭ baritone saxhorns
4 E♭ contrabass saxhorns
5 percussion

This plan, which recommended entirely new families of Sax's instruments, caused an immediate cry of protest by the other Parisian instrument makers, who saw the possible adoption of such a plan as giving a virtual monopoly to Sax for supplying instruments to the War Ministry. A great 'war' of newspaper articles ensued and one of the participants, as was often the case, was Berlioz.

> A monopoly of bugles, trombones, trumpets and tubas has not been promised to anyone. These instruments will be examined. If those of Sax are better, they must be adopted; but if to the contrary, those of the competitors surpass Sax's, the adoption will be directed to them; nothing is more obvious. Moreover, this question is secondary. This adoption of instruments is not being conducted in the interest of the manufacturer, but for those in the arts and the army. The agitation of the heads of the workshops where wind instruments are made are united, but it will have no more influence on the Commission than would the merchants of brass, who, if the reorganization is put into operation, are assured of a substantial increase. With these parallel considerations, we arrive, following the chain of interests, to the miners who work extracting the ore.[18]

[18] Berlioz, 'Feuilleton,' in *Journal des Débats* (April 1, 1845).

The commission made, at this point, a wise decision. Rather than attempt to resolve the question on an abstract basis, they decided to conduct a live field test. This offered not only the opportunity to test the instrumentation plans in an outdoor environment, as would be typical for a military band, but would offer a wide segment of the interested public the opportunity to make first-hand judgments. The date for this event was set for 22 April 1845, and the place selected was the spacious military parade ground known as the Champ de Mars (where today the famous Eiffel Tower stands).

The commission decided to test primarily the instrumentation plans submitted by Carafa and Sax, as best representing both the older traditional ideas and the entirely new. To this end, both Sax and Carafa were asked to recruit a band and both bands would perform music prepared for the occasion by commission member Adam, in addition to music of their choice. It was decided further to precede this 'battle of the bands' with performances by four actual military bands, so as to give all adjudicators a clear demonstration of the status quo.

At noon on the appointed day a signal was given and the first band began to play. This was the band of the 11th Light Cavalry, a band of thirty-eight players.

1 piccolo
1 small clarinet
12 clarinets (divided 6, 3, 3)
3 horns
2 trumpets
2 cornets
4 trombones
6 ophicleides
7 percussion

This band sounded well, but the observation was made that three of the players (the piccolo, first trombone, and the first cornet) were older hired civilians—the implications of which are not clear today.[19]

Next, the band of the 74th Line Infantry performed, a band somewhat larger, with forty-nine players.

[19] Most of this material is taken from Kastner, *Manuel Général de Musique Militaire*, 261ff.

1 piccolo
1 small clarinet
15 clarinets (divided 8, 3, 2, 2)
4 horns
1 trumpet
1 'néo-cor'
4 cornets
2 Sax bugles
5 trombones
8 ophicleides
7 percussion

This band was judged the very best of the regular military bands, its fast march (pas redouble) performance being thought very remarkable.

Next came a performance by the band of the 1st Line Infantry, a band with the largest number of woodwinds, but not a single trumpet!

1 piccolo
1 small clarinet
20 clarinets (divided 9, 4, 4, 3)
6 horns
2 cornets
1 'clavi-cor'
6 trombones
6 ophicleides
6 percussion

The final regular military band, that of the 62nd Line Infantry was judged by the commission as being weak in all regards.

1 piccolo
1 small clarinet
12 clarinets (divided 5, 3, 2, 2)
2 horns
2 'néo-cors'
3 cornets
3 trombones
6 ophicleides
6 percussion

Now came the main event, the competition between Carafa and Sax. It had been agreed beforehand that each of these bands was to be limited to forty-five players, in order to fairly compare the difference in the instrumentation. Carafa had one important advantage for his players (the professors and best students from the Gymnase de Musique Militaire) were playing on traditional instruments, whereas the players of Sax were playing, in some cases, entirely new instruments they had only seen for the first time the day before!

Carafa, who believed his entire reputation to be at stake, was determined to stop at nothing to win. Accordingly, he not only arrived with four additional players beyond the agreed limit, but had his agents kidnap seven key members of Sax's band. The commission refused to allow Carafa his extra players, so he gave up two bugles and two flutes, performing with the following instrumentation:

1 piccolo
1 small clarinet
16 clarinets (divided 2, 7, 7)
4 oboes
4 bassoons
2 natural horns
2 valve horns
2 valved trombones
2 cornets
3 trumpets
4 ophicleides
4 percussion

Sax, trying without success to locate his missing players,[20] arrived late for the contest, carrying two instruments which he himself alternately played in an attempt to cover the missing parts. The thirty-eight players which he had at his disposal for the contest included,

1 piccolo
1 E♭ clarinet
6 B♭ clarinets
1 bass clarinet
2 cornets
2 E♭ soprano saxhorns
4 B♭ soprano saxhorns
4 E♭ alto saxhorns
4 B♭ bass saxhorns
2 E♭ contrabass saxhorns
2 trombones
2 ophicleides
4 percussion

And so, although they were unevenly matched in size, both bands were positioned and ready to perform. The scene was described by an eyewitness:

> The two bands were separated by approximately one hundred and fifty feet. At the head of the formation was the Commission, presided over by Général de Rumigny, surrounded by several other generals, admirals, superior officers of all the armies, and all of the eminent artists present in the Capital at this moment, and a veritable army of journalists from large and small newspapers. At the other end of the *Champs* were the divers corps of military musicians, armed with their instruments as though for battle, for the presence of the judges and for their public which numbered more than twenty thousand persons.[21]

Anyone with experience in the performance of bands outdoors will not need to be told who 'won' the contest. Carafa, even with his greater number of players, had a band which was sixty percent woodwinds, some of which (oboes and bassoons) were of virtually no use in the open air. Sax's band, on the other hand, was only twenty-four percent woodwinds and furthermore was much stronger in the lower register. As a result we may be sure that Sax's band sounded darker, more homogeneous, and with a bigger sound. It was no contest.

[20] Perhaps some of the 'kidnaped' players were those who might have played the new saxophones. Although these instruments are not mentioned in any account of the actual performance, they we're mentioned in Sax's original proposed instrumentation and when Fessy's *Fantaisie*, composed for this performance, was published it included one saxophone part.

[21] Oscar Comettant, *Histoire d'un inyenteur au dix-neuivièmee siècle* (Paris: Pagnerre, 1960), 102.

Carafa began, performing an 'Andante' composed for the occasion by Adolphe Adam.

> This piece, perfectly played by the principal students of our ancient school of military music and by several professors of the same establishment, was heard with lively attention. The audience applauded, but without enthusiasm.

Then Sax's band, conducted by A. Fessy, music director of the 5th Regiment of the Parisian National Guard, performed the same composition.

> Almost immediately followed the music of Sax, playing the same *Andante*. This good military music was bold, open, sonorous, noble, sustained, less varied in timbre, without a doubt, but more homogeneous, equal throughout, and infinitely more adaptable to soldiers on the march or on the field of battle … The piece played by Sax was followed with cries of enthusiasm and applause.[22]

Next each band played a march by Adam, followed by a joint performance of a fast march, and finally the composition of their choice. For the latter, Carafa performed an arrangement of the Overture to *Muette de Portici* by Auber. Sax's band performed an original *Fantaisie* by Fessy[23] composed for the occasion. This work begins with only the brass instruments, scored at the *piano* dynamic level, with a crescendo leading to a great *forte* chord for the full band. The entire beginning, indeed the entire composition, seems designed to demonstrate the sound of the band at varying dynamic levels.

The summary of the commission acknowledged the greater color possibilities of the Carafa instrumentation, but heard in Sax's band a greater sonority, which carried over a greater distance, and homogeneity with fusion at both piano and forte dynamic levels. On this day the question of the cavalry band instrumentation was also tested. Again, the adjudicators first heard an authentic cavalry band, that of the 74th Regiment of Cavalry, a band of twenty-seven players.

[22] These eyewitness accounts from ibid., 107.

[23] This work was published after the contest by Sax, as Plate Number 1. The title page bears a dedication to Général de Rumigny and mentions it was 'composed for the new instruments invented by Ad. Sax, expressly for the contest on the Champ de Mars in 1845.'

9 cornets
3 bugles in B♭
2 trumpets
1 valved horn
2 'néo-cors'
2 'clavi-cors'
2 trombones
6 ophicleides

This performance was followed, as before, by a band constituted after the ideas of Carafa and one after the plan of Sax. Once again, Sax's band was clearly the more successful.

Carafa	**Sax**
1 small cornet in A♭	2 small saxhorns in E♭
1 small bugle in E♭	4 saxhorns in B♭
2 bugles in B♭	4 alto saxhorns in E♭
2 bugles in A♭	2 cornets
2 alto bugles in E♭	2 valved trombones
4 trumpets	2 trombones 'à coulisses'
2 valved horns	4 bass saxhorns in B♭
2 natural horns	3 contrabass saxhorns in E♭
3 trombones	
4 ophicleides	

Following the performance, the Parisian newspapers had great fun describing the 'battle' as a great military event, Carafa and his friends retreated and formed an association designed to carry on the anti-Sax campaign in the law courts, and the commission continued to talk. These final discussions on instrumentation centered on the recommendation of a larger infantry band, now fifty-five players. In the final recommendations for the infantry and cavalry bands, the victory of Sax was evident:

Infantry	Cavalry
1 piccolo in C	2 'trompettes d'harmonie'
1 clarinet in E♭	4 valved trumpets
14 clarinets in B♭	2 small E♭ saxhorns
2 bass clarinets	7 saxhorns in B♭ (1, 3, 3)
2 saxophones	2 saxhorns in A♭
2 oboes	2 saxhorns in E♭
2 bassoons	2 saxo-trombas
2 cornets	2 cornets
2 valved trumpets	1 valve trombone
4 valved horns	3 trombones 'à coulisses'
1 small saxhorn in E♭	3 baritone saxhorns in B♭
2 saxhorns in B♭	3 bass saxhorns in B♭
2 alto saxhorns in E♭	3 contrabass saxhorns in E♭
3 bass saxhorns in B♭	
4 contrabass saxhorns in E♭	
1 valved trombone	
2 trombones 'à coulisses'	
2 ophicleides	
5 percussion	

The War Department accepted these recommendations with minor changes, and published the ordinance for the reorganization of all military bands in the *Moniteur de l'armée* (September 10, 1845).

This is not quite the end of the story, for the revolution of 1848 brought enemies of Sax into the government and the entire work of the commission was thrown out! But, before following the development of the instrumentation during the second half of the nineteenth century, there were some additional recommendations by the commission which are quite interesting.

First, they recommended to the government that it was essential to re-establish the system of hiring extra civilian players and suggested the government fund such staffing. For the regular army players, the commission recommended additional ranks which might be made available to those players for purposes of morale.

Further recommendations included a proposal for standardization of examinations for conducting candidates and performance levels for players. They recommended the introduction of the metronome, to help bands 'better conform to the intentions of the composer.' The foundation of a military band journal was recommended and, finally, a recommendation that the government buy cases for the woodwind instruments[!] The government accepted most of these recommendations and added a further ordinance relative to the standardization of tuning.

The wide public interest in the discussions of military bands during 1845, not to mention the 'battle of the bands' itself, led to the idea of a 'Monster Concert' the following year, held in a great arena in Paris called the Hippodrome. For this concert forty-one military bands (together with students of the Gymnase de Musique Militaire) were brought together.[24] The repertoire included some works played by all of the bands and some played only by the various types of bands.

> *Marche et fanfare de cavalerie* by Fessy [Cavalry]
> *Clara*, a valse by Mohr [Cavalry]
> *Pas redoublé* by Brepsant [Infantry, played as these bands entered]
> *Overture de Fra Diavolo* by Auber, arranged by Berr [Infantry]
> *Choeur d'Armide* by Gluck, arranged by Fessy [Cavalry]
> *Pas redoublé de la Juive* by Halévy, arranged by Berr [Infantry]
> *Marche de Fernand Cortez* by Spontini, arranged by Klosé [Infantry and Cavalry]
> *La Bénédiction des poignards des Huguenots* by Meyerbeer, arranged by Fessy [Cavalry]
> *La priere de Moïse* by Rossini, arranged by Fessy [Infantry and Cavalry]
> *Fantaisie militaire* by Mohr [Infantry and Cavalry]
> *Chasse* by Rossini, arranged by Fessy [Cavalry]
> *Les Bords du Rhin*, a valse by Hunten, arranged by Klosé [Infantry]
> *Choeur de Judas Machabée* by Handel, arranged by Fessy [Infantry and Cavalry]
> *Marche d'Olympie* by Spontini, arranged by Fessy [Infantry and Cavalry]
> *Le franc Juge*, a pas redoublé by Ennes Berr [Infantry]
> *Bolero* by Fessy [Cavalry]
> 'Apothéose,' the final movement of the Berlioz *Symphony for Band* [Infantry]

Everyone agreed the Berlioz was the most impressive.

[24] Kastner, *Manuel Général de Musique Militaire*, 325ff., identifies these bands and provides the seating chart. Interestingly enough, the bands were broken up into sections of similar instruments, all organized in an inverted [!] pyramid. Kastner, 317ff, also mentions an earlier Monster concert of 1833, somewhat smaller in size, performed by 80 clarinets, 8 small clarinets, 12 flutes, 10 oboes, 20 horns, 20 trumpets, 16 trombones, 18 bassoons, 15 ophicleides, 22 contrabass, 3 timpanists, 2 bass drums and 6 'tambours d'harmonie.' The repertoire included overtures of Rossini (*La Gazza Ladra* and *Guillaume Tell*) and Auber, a '*scène héroïque et prière*' by Berlioz and a battle piece with choir by Schneitzhoeffer. A similar Monster Concert was held during the same year in Brussels, conducted by Fétis. Here 80 clarinets, 4 piccolos, 8 E♭ flutes, 20 bassoons, 36 horns, 16 trumpets, 'various oboes,' keyed horns, a great number of ophicleides (including altos, basses, and Russian serpents), 30 trombones, and percussion performed. Their repertoire included arrangements of Rossini (*Tancrède* and *Guillaume Tell*) by Küffner, an air varié and an arrangement on themes by Donizetti by Bender, the conductor of the famous 'la musique des Guides du roi,' and the *Overture to Oberon* by Weber.

As I mentioned above, the political changes resulting from the Revolution of 1848 caused the entire results of the Commission of 1845 to be thrown out. Sax and all of his instruments were suddenly in disfavor. This in return resulted in another round of public letters and newspaper articles, pro and con. In 1854 the government reversed itself again and issued a new ordinance for the instrumentation of the infantry and cavalry bands. Here one can see not only was Sax back in favor, but now his new family of instruments, the saxophones, appear officially for the first time.

Infantry
2 flutes or piccolos
4 E♭ clarinets
8 clarinets in B♭
2 soprano saxophones
2 alto saxophones
2 tenor saxophones
2 baritone saxophones
2 cornets
4 trumpets
4 trombones
2 soprano saxhorns in E♭
2 soprano saxhorns in B♭
2 alto saxotrombas
2 baritone saxhorns in B♭
4 bass saxhorns in B♭
2 contrabass saxhorns in E♭
2 contrabass saxhorns in B♭
5 percussion

Cavalry
1 sopranino saxhorn in B♭
2 soprano saxhorns in E♭
4 soprano saxhorns in B♭
2 alto saxhorns in A♭
2 alto saxotrombas in E♭
2 baritone saxotrombas in B♭
4 bass saxhorns in B♭
2 contrabass saxhorns in E♭
2 contrabass saxhorns in B♭
2 cornets
6 trumpets
6 trombones (AATTBB)

This essentially was the instrumentation which had so wide an influence on all continental military bands during the second half of the nineteenth century. The saxhorn family contributed one permanent member of today's bands, the baritone or euphonium. The use of the new saxophone family was not immediately adopted in every French regiment,[25] but they too are part of today's band.

Volume nine of this series gives the call-numbers in Paris, Bibliothèque nationale, for thousands of original compositions for military band, which date from the second half of the nineteenth century. This extant repertoire tells the story of the French military band better than any prose account could. One sees evidence of considerable concert activity, with hundreds of major works in the form of symphonies, overtures, fantaisies, great programmatic works, and the astonishing airs varié—theme and variations of often extraordinary difficulty.

There is one very large published collection of works, under the interesting title, *Journal de la Renaissance des Musiques militaries*. Here one finds works primarily composed by the conductors of the various regiments, but also a few works by students and professors of the various military music schools.

The repertoire also includes a great number of solo works accompanied by full military band. These exist for almost every instrument, even such unusual specimens as the *Le Sommeil de Polypheme* by Girard for solo E♭ contrabass saxophone, or a work somewhat difficult to identify with today, Lamotte's *L'Ophicleide sentimental*! There is one *Concerto* by Gustave Wettge, another former director of the Garde Républicaine band, for unison clarinet section accompanied by the full band.

One of the most interesting portions of this repertoire is the vast amount of compositions composed for use in the church service by the full military band. These are often major works and will be discussed in more detail below.

It is my impression that this vast repertoire of original works, and I have not attempted to even mention the thousands of major transcriptions of orchestral music, has been completely overlooked by conductors today. But, if one is looking for serious, major, original band compositions from the nineteenth century, here is a 'gold mine.'

[25] The extant band music in the Paris Bibliothèque nationale varies considerably in the inclusion of the saxophone family, but by the end of the century most scores include them. An overture by Balay, one of the nineteenth-century conductors of the band of the Garde Républicaine, includes not only ten separate saxophone parts, but also Sarrussophone parts as well. There is also some interesting early music for saxophone ensembles in the Bibliothèque nationale, as for example a saxophone octet, for SSAATTBB, by Savari, published in 1861. Another very interesting anonymous octet for saxophones is scored for petit B♭, soprano E♭, B♭, A♭, and E♭ tenor saxophones, with cornet and snare drum!

4   *Military Bands in England*

MILITARY BANDS DURING THE NAPOLEONIC PERIOD

During the earliest years of the nineteenth century, military music in England seems to have been completely supported by the private officers and not from the government. A typical document permits the First Dragoons of Horse Guards in 1802 to enlist 'a person for five years to instruct the band' so long as no cost was passed on to the government.[1] The government issued an order the following year, in 1803, which seems aimed at guaranteeing that the officers, while raising these private bands, would not be tempted to divert men from the ranks of the fighting troops for training in music. Even while permitting two such soldiers to be trained as musicians, the order warns that in time of need they must revert to being soldiers.

[1] Henry George Farmer, *Handel's Kettledrums and other Papers on Military Music* (London: Hinrichsen, 1965), 105.

> It is H. Mys. Pleasure that, in Regiments having Bands of Musick, not more than one Private Soldier of each Troop or Company shall be permitted to act as Musicians, and that one Non Commissioned Officer shall be allowed to act as Master of the Band. These men are to be drilled and instructed in the Exercise [as soldiers], and in case of actual Service [combat], are to fall in with their respective Troops; or Companies, completely armed and accoutered.[2]

[2] Ibid.

From an official governmental point of view, military music was almost non-existent during the Napoleonic period. No record of any bands, for example, is found in either the government or the regimental accounts for the famous Battle of Waterloo.[3] Private accounts, however, reveal that these privately supported bands were indeed present at the front, and even in the midst of the fighting, during these war years. An officer who participated in the battle of Busaco recalled,

[3] Farmer, *The Rise and Development of Military Music*, 90.

> I saw one company waver, but a non-commissioned officer shouted that as long as the music lasted every man should fight, and he would put a bullet into the first person who exhibited signs of cowardice.[4]

[4] Ibid., 89.

The better bands during this period were the ones with foreign conductors, reflecting the more advanced military traditions in Germany and Austria. Fearful of spies, an order of 1805 permits a regiment to enlist in its band 'any Swiss, German, or Italian,' but 'French Men are on no account to be admitted.'[5] One problem with the foreign-born bandmaster was his apparent hesitation to leave England with the troops departing for battle, as he tended to be a civilian hired to train the band but not to die for England.[6] As a result, some English bands on foreign shores may have compared poorly with the disciplined bands from areas such as Germany and Austria. One English officer, reflecting on the Occupation of Paris, in 1814, said he was never so ashamed of England's meanness and neglect of military prestige as when he heard the fine bands of the other members of the Allies as compared to the 'meagre and scanty musical display of the British troops.'[7]

In spite of the lack of official government support, the officers of some regiments were able to support fairly large bands, even early during the century. Documents prove that the Royal Irish Artillery Band in 1802 consisted of a bandmaster with twenty musicians.[8] The English Royal Artillery Band was even larger and an extant document written about 1805, provides the actual instrumentation.

> Sir,
> The General has asked for a description of the Band of Music which appeared at the Palace, so that he might request the Hon. Board [of Ordnance] for sundry new instruments in the place of those which are old and worn out. I have obtained [a list of] these from Mr. Eisenherdt the Master of the Band, who begs that you will have the goodness to approve of his wishes. The Band of Music has 26 musicians, counting the drummers, etc., 3 Tromboners, 2 Trumpetts, 2 French Horns, 2 Bassoons, 1 Serpent & 1 Bass Horn, 6 Grand Clarinetts & 1 Small Clarinett, 1 Small Flute, 3 Hautboys, 1 Long Drum, 1 Small Drum, 1 Tamborin, 1 Cimbals. Mr Eisenherdt would like another Bass Horn instead of the Serpent.[9]

By 1812 this band had grown to thirty-eight musicians, including the percussion.[10] Many bands may have increased in size, due in part to public interest in the Napoleonic Wars, for one reads in a publication for this same year,

---

[5] Farmer, *Handel's Kettledrums*, 105.

[6] Farmer, *The Rise and Development of Military Music*, 96.

[7] Ibid., 90.

[8] Farmer, *Handel's Kettledrums*, 26.

[9] Quoted in ibid., 4.

[10] Farmer, *The Rise and Development of Military Music*, 85.

The *military bands of music* have been much enlarged, and the serpent, trombone and the German flute, as well as the different kinds of smaller flutes, have been introduced in them, which formerly were not generally used. England therefore has at present a great number of excellent performers on the different wind instruments.[11]

[11] Quarterly Musical Register (London, 1812), Nr. 3.

Cavalry bands at the beginning of the nineteenth century remained only trumpets and drums when mounted. Soon, however, they followed the lead of the continental cavalry units in adding horns and trombones. By 1815 both the keyed-bugle and the ophicleide (a bass keyed-bugle) were also available.[12]

[12] Farmer, *The Rise and Development of Military Music*, 85–88.

England, Band of the Marines, ca. 1825

Post-Napoleonic Growth and Experimentation

During the period of 1820–1845, Prussia, Austria, and France experienced a vigorous period of experimentation with new instruments, resulting in a series of official orders dealing with military band instrumentation. England's story is somewhat different, primarily because she lacked during this period a strong personality, like Wieprecht in Prussia, Leonhardt in Austria, or Sax in France, to influence the thinking of the military as a whole. Thus one finds some bands in England during this period which seem to change little, other than in an expansion in numbers of players. Consider, for example, the Royal Artillery Band instrumentation[13] in 1820 and 1839.

1820	1839
2 flutes	1 piccolo, 2 flutes
3 oboes	2 oboes
11 clarinets	11 B♭ clarinets, 3 in E♭
3 bassoons	4 bassoons
2 trumpets	4 trumpets
3 key-bugles	3 cornets
2 horns	2 horns
3 trombones	4 trombones
1 ophicleide	1 ophicleide
2 serpents	2 serpents
2 bass horns	2 bass horns
5 percussion	4 percussion

[13] Ibid., 98, 114. Since the bands were small or large in relation to the private support of the officers, the totals given here do not reflect governmental 'official' limits, which were set at only ten for a regimental band in 1822 and fourteen in 1823. (Ibid., 93–94)

Lacking a centralized policy, the instrumentation of the regimental bands was left to the individual bandmasters during this period. Moreover, the bandmasters were frequently civilians who owed their appointments to well-placed influence by one or other of the various instrument makers. The newly appointed bandmaster would immediately replace all the instruments with those made by his industrial partner. Thus the guiding force was commercial and not an aesthetic one as in Prussia.

Another commercial influence on the developing English military band instrumentation was the proliferation of band 'journals,' beginning just before 1850. Here the influence was indirect, in so far as this was not the immediate purpose of the publisher. However, bands quickly adjusted their instrumentation as necessary to perform the works of the journal to which they subscribed. Therefore, the more popular journals tended to indirectly contribute to the standardization of band instrumentation.

The first of these journals was printed at his own expense by Carl Boosé, bandmaster of the Scots Guards, in 1845. Boosé was another 'imported' German bandmaster, who was born, studied, and served as a professional and military musician in the Darmstadt area before coming to England. The instrumentation he set forth in his journal was, of course, based on the Prussian–German model and was largely influential in pointing England in that direction, rather than after Austrian or French models. I have a portion of his journal for 1856 (by this time published by Boosey and Co.) and it is interesting that in addition to advertising back issues, which contained for the most part marches, polkas, short operatic excerpts, etc., there is advertised a group of works available in manuscript. The latter includes larger Mendelssohn and Wagner overtures and symphonies by Mendelssohn (Nr. 3), Mozart ('Nr. 2 in G minor'), and Beethoven (Nrs. 5 and 6). This issue also advertises an interesting *Preparatory Journal*, edited by J. A. Kappey:

> THIS SERIES, consisting of Nine complete Journals for full Military Bands, is published for the purpose of furnishing *newly-formed* bands with proper materials for their first rehearsals, and assisting them, by a careful selection of easy pieces arranged in a progressive order, to master the different styles of playing in which a Military Band should be efficient.

The following year, in 1847, a new journal appeared, published by Jullian and edited by Charles Godfrey, Senior, bandmaster of the Coldstream Guards.[14] This Journal[15] was scored for [original spellings given]:

1 Flute or Picolo
Clarinet in E♭
Clarinet 1st & 2nd in B♭
Cornet-a-Piston
1st & 2nd Horns
1 Bassoon
Basso
Bass Trombone

[14] Charles Godfrey (1790–1863) was the first member of an entire family of contributors to English wind band music. He was a bassoonist and from 1825 to 1834 a bandmaster. His three sons were:

> Daniel Godfrey (1831–1903), bandmaster of the Grenadier Guards from 1856 to 1896, an organization he toured to Boston with in 1872. He was an arranger, composer, and founder of a musical instrument business.
>
> Adolphus Frederick Godfrey (1837–1882), who succeeded his father as bandmaster of the Coldstream Guards in 1863.
>
> Charles Godfrey, Junior (1839–1919), clarinet student of Lazarus, member of Jullien's orchestra, bandmaster of the Scots Fusiliers Band, and professor of military music at the Guildhall School of Music. He edited the *Army Military Band Journal* and the *Orpheus Band Journal*.

[15] Published by 'Jullien & Co. at the Royal Conservatory of Military Music. 214 Regent Street & 45 King Street.' An example I have also advertises journals for brass bands, orchestra, septet (string quartet with string bass, flute, clarinet, and cornet), and piano, as well as a series of German arrangements by J. Mohr 'for Military Bands of 8, 12 or more Performers.' The Jullien Journal was acquired by Boosey in 1857, after which it appeared as their 'Supplementary Journal.'

[the following were given as ad libitum:]

Oboes
3rd Clarinet
3rd & 4th Horns
1st & 2nd Trombone
2nd Bassoon
2nd Cornet
Trumpets
Euphonion
Drums and Cymbals

Soon other journals appeared in imitation, including the J. G. Jones 'Full Reed-Band' Journal, the Distin's Brass Band Journal,[16] and the Coote's Military Band Journal, although none were so successful as the original two.

Finally, some ancient traditions passed during the first half of the nineteenth century. The small drum was retired as a poor competitor with the ever increasing size and noise of weapons of war. The era of the fife was far removed, but the instrument had been retained as a form of tradition. By about mid-century, however, the final chapter in this long tradition finally came. A former member of the Royal Artillery Band remembered this moment.

[16] Henry Distin (1819–1903), a member of the Distin Family Quintet, became an important manufacturer of brass instruments (he once made an alto horn with seven bells which the player wore in a semicircle around the chest). In 1877 he moved to America where he was associated with the J. W. Pepper Company of Philadelphia.

Not long after [the abolition of the R. A. Drums and Fifes] a man was sentenced to be 'drummed out,' a duty always carried out by the drums and fifes, [the junior drummer or fifer giving the discharge a kick in the posterior at the gate of the barracks]. Mr. Smyth [the bandmaster] was informed that [there being no more drums and fifes] he would have to see it done. The consequence was that half a dozen of us who could play the flute were ordered to look up the *Rogues March* and, accompanied by an equal number of drummers, we fell in one winter morning, and played the said tune behind the scoundrel, who was, I think, the last man in the R. A. to be 'drummed out.'[17]

[17] Farmer, *Handel's Kettledrums*, 75.

THE GOLDEN AGE

In 1851 the first 'Monster Concert' given in England occurred in Chelsea, where some three hundred and fifty musicians joined to perform overtures (by Leutner, Wallace, Meyerbeer, and Weber), operatic selections, and waltzes. The London *Times* made the following observations on this concert.

> The execution of these pieces were so admirable, the ensemble so good, and the energy and decision of the conductors so remarkable, that the unequivocal satisfaction of the auditors was not to be wondered at. We only regretted that with such splendid means so little of real musical importance was effected. The overture to 'Euryanthe' alone among the fourteen pieces presented was worthy of consideration as an artistic performance. Our military bands have reached a very high degree of perfection in regard to the mere talent of execution; but in other respects they have done little or nothing to assist the progress of the art. If the bandmasters who train them so zealously and well would endeavour to instill into them some notion of true music, instead of confining them almost wholly to the most ephemeral productions, their influence would be highly beneficial.[18]

[18] Quoted in Farmer, '*The Rise and Development of Military Music*, 125–126.

The view expressed here was only one facet of a rising tide of concern by many regarding the quality, the organization, and especially the tradition of civilian bandmasters. Farmer[19] summarizes this critical period:

[19] Farmer, *Handel's Kettledrums*, 106.

> The Crimean War opened the eyes of the authorities to the evils of the civilian bandmaster system. When the war broke out, our bands, deserted by their bandmasters [civilians who wanted nothing to do with battle], were soon disorganized. The French, on the other hand, maintained their bands at a high state of efficiency throughout the campaign. The final humiliation came at Scutari in 1854 when, at the grand review of honour of the birthday of Queen Victoria, with some 16,000 men marching past in perfect order, our bands later struck up 'God Save the Queen,' not only from different arrangements, but in *different keys*, and this before the general staff of the allied army.

After the Peace of Paris (1856) more voices were heard arguing for better training of military musicians and conductors and for a general reorganization of military bands. Two important advocates were James Smyth, bandmaster of the Royal Artillery, and Henry Schallehn, of the Seventeenth Lancers. The latter was able to enlist the influential aid of the Duke of Cambridge, who issued a famous circular letter, dated 26 September 1856, to the commanding officers of the regiments. It is widely held that the origin of the famous Kneller Hall dates from this letter.

> His Royal Highness the General Commanding in Chief with a view to relieve regiments from the great expense consequent upon the necessity of employing professional musicians, civilians, as Masters of Bands, has

it in contemplation to recommend the establishment of a large musical class as part of the education of boys sent to the Royal Military Asylum, and for the instruction of persons sent from the Regiments to qualify for Bugle-Majors, Trumpet-Majors, and Bandmasters, and whose training would require especial time and attention.[20]

This famous school finally opened the following year, under the leadership of Schallehn, with a faculty of five and a student body of one hundred.[21] The Duke of Cambridge went on to other important concerns, especially in breaking the close relationships between the conductors and the instrument industry, which had had the effect of keeping the costs of instruments high.

During the second half of the century the English military bands continued to resist the brass orientation of the Austrian bands. The Royal Artillery Band in 1857 consisted of:

2 flutes and piccolo
4 oboes
4 E♭ clarinets
22 B♭ clarinets
2 E♭ saxophones
2 B♭ saxophones
4 bassoons
4 cornets
2 trumpets
2 soprano E♭ cornets
2 Flugelhorns in E♭, 2 in B♭
4 horns
2 baritones
2 euphoniums
4 trombones
4 bombardons
percussion[22]

It was after mid-century that the so-called 'Staff Bands' became so popular. The musical success of these bands lay in the fact that they did not travel with the regiments of troops and thus could attract a higher level of musician and conductor. Perhaps the best known of these bands was that of the Grenadier Guards, led by Dan Godfrey.

---

[20] Quoted in ibid., 107.

[21] Bandmasters were known as 'students,' but bandsmen enrolled there were known as 'pupils.'

[22] Saxophones were slow in gaining a foothold in English bands. I have a copy of a funeral march (1852) by Henry Bishop which has only one saxophone part, and that in bass clef. Farmer, in *The Rise and Development of Military Music*, 127–128, gives a typical line infantry band as:

    3 flutes and 1 piccolo
    1 oboe
    2 E♭ clarinets
    9 B♭ clarinets
    2 bassoons
    4 cornets
    2 trumpets
    1 alto horn
    2 euphoniums
    3 trombones
    3 bombardons
    percussion

5 *Military Bands in Russia*

A CORRESPONDENT WRITING ON RUSSIAN INFANTRY MUSIC in 1813 reports not a band in the tradition of the Western European armies, but only a massed trumpet and drum ensemble. He reports, moreover, that the trumpets did not play actual music, but only 'little works' in the key of D major.[1]

It was the employment of foreign, especially Prussian, bandmasters which brought rapid modernization to Russian military music. The most famous of these persons was Anton Dörffeld, who became Director of the entire Kaiser's Guard Corps. According to Kastner,[2] these bands soon had all the modern instruments of Western Europe and became known for their brilliant execution of marches. Dörffeld took one of these units, some seventy men, to Paris in 1867 to participate in the famous world band competition.

One of the great figures of the nineteenth century, Rimsky-Korsakov, was associated with the music of the Russian military. He was appointed Inspector of Navy Bands in 1873, a post he was to hold for more than ten years. In this position he suddenly acquired rather absolute authority over the instruments, music, and the education of the players and conductors under his supervision.

> In the bands of musicians I was met as superiors are met: stand up front! I made them play their repertory in my presence; caught the wrong notes; detected the slips (and there were very many of them) in the instrumental parts; examined the instruments and made requisitions for new or additional ones ... Occasionally I grew rather peppery and humiliated some bandmasters undeservedly or ridiculed pieces which I did not like, though the performance of these was necessary and unavoidable in military bands.[3]

The transcriptions which Rimsky-Korsakov himself made for these bands are one portion, perhaps only a very small portion, of what may be a vast repertoire of interesting music unknown in the West today. How interesting it would be to see the scores which Rimsky-Korsakov mentions:

[1] 'Feldmusik,' in *Allgemeine Musikalische Zeitung* (1813), Nr. 44, 713.

> Diese bliesen nun nicht eigentlich musikalische kunstmässige Stücke, sondern scbmetterten unter Trommelbegleitung ihre Trompetenstücklein in D-Dur Akkord.

[2] Kastner, *Manuel Général de Musique Militaire*, 174.

[3] Rimsky-Korsakov, *My Musical Life*, 118.

'Coronation March,' from *Le Prophete*
'Finale,' from *A Life for the Tsar*
'Isabelle's aria,' from *Robert le Diable* (solo clarinet)
Marche Marocaine (Berlioz)
'Introduction, first act,' *Lohengrin*
'Scene of the conspiracy,' from *Les Hugenots*
'Nocturne' and 'March,' from *A Midsummer Night's Dream*
Egmont Overture (Beethoven)
Slavska
Marche in B minor (Schubert)

One wonders what musical treasures from the nineteenth century must lie in Russian libraries! The occasional mention of some or another work, such as the original Symphony composed in 1830 by A. Alabieff[4] or the *Fantaisia militaire* on Russian folk-songs, composed in 1835 by Alexis Theodore Lwoff[5] hint of a broad literature waiting for some future scholar of the wind band!

[4] Mentioned by Veit, in *Die Blasmusik*, 60.

[5] Mentioned by Alessandro Vessella, in *La Banda* (Milano: Istituto Editoriale Nazionale, 1935), 153.

6   Military Bands in Italy

As in the case of the rest of Europe, in Italy at the turn of the century one finds small regimental bands consisting of primarily Harmoniemusik with attached fife and percussion players. A pay document, dated ca. 1805, in the Archivio di Stato, Napoli,[1] gives the size and pay for the musicians of a line regiment of that state.

[1] Most of this material is taken from Alessandro Vessella, *La Banda* (Milano: Istituto Editoriale Nazionale, 1935), 166ff.

Bandmaster	1	20 grani
bass drum	1	12 grani
small drum	1	12 grani
cymbals	2	12 grani
musicians	11	15 grani [each]

One must mention, in passing, one famous member of an Italian military company at the turn of the century, the six-year-old Rossini. His name appears in the records of the Cisalpine troops in 1798 as a performer on the 'listaro,' a term no longer clear, but possibly a triangle ('lista,' for 'rod bent in the shape of a triangle'). Later during the same year a newspaper, *Gazzetta di Pesaro*, mentions a trumpet played by 'the excellent patriot Rossini, known by the nickname of Citizen Vivazza.'[2]

[2] Herbert Weinstock, *Rossini* (New York: A. A. Knopf, 1968), 7.

The young Berlioz, writing from Rome in 1831, describes military music he heard which suggests that perhaps some early nineteenth century Italian military bands were not so impressive as those of Northern Europe.

> ... but for this fatal imagination of mine, I should not have been so disgusted by the impious, coarse cacophony of those two groups of quacking clarinets, roaring trombones, crashing drums, and circus trumpets. Had it ushered in old Silenus, riding on his ass, and escorted by a troupe of coarse satyrs and bacchantes, it would have been highly appropriate.[3]

[3] Berlioz, *Memoirs*, 136, 102

One of the most famous of the early Italian bandmasters was Giuseppe Gabetti, born in Torino in 1796 and died in Morra in 1862, who was bandmaster of the First Infantry Regiment Band of Piedmont. In 1834 he won a march composition contest organized by the War Ministry and, while his prize was only 50 Lire [!], his march became an official march of the army for a time.[4]

[4] Vessella, *La Banda*, 170, quotes a poem on the death of Gabetti, published thirty-seven years after his death, which may indicate the local fame of this bandmaster.

88 Military Bands

Musicians from the Italian Grenadiers, 1821

    In 1831–1832 Duke Carlo Alberto, of Piedmont, signed an ordinance which increased the size of the band for each line infantry regiment from eighteen to twenty-four musicians. In 1839 another edict established fifes and drums, but not real bands, for the navy. In general, before mid-century, the Piedmont bands were larger and more improved, and to a greater degree followed the model of the Prussians, than did the military bands of the other states in Italy. Measures were also taken at this time to improve the dignity of the bandmasters.

    In the other states of Italy, political strife retarded the opportunities for the military bands to follow the exciting developments in new instruments which had taken place in Prussia, France, and Austria. The degree to which some of these states were still behind continental developments can be seen in Florence, where a commission on military music was formed in 1848. Presided over by Teodulo Mabellini, the commission set the instrumentation for a regimental band at only eight regular players (piccolo, clarino, two trumpets, ophicleide, trombone, horn, and bass drum), with the possibility of additional 'extra' hired players.[5]

Beginning with the 1840s, one finds some interesting extant examples of the repertoire of these Italian military bands. Among these is the *Luge Qui Legis*, composed in 1842 for military band by Donizetti.[6] The revolutionary turmoil at mid-century produced a number of patriotic compositions for military band and chorus by Florentine composers. These include the *L'Italia risorta* by Leopoldo Compini and the *Giovani ardenti* by Lorenzo Fabbrucci. A score from this period, by the military bandmaster, Professor Egisto Mosell, is scored for:

- piccolo in E♭
- clarinet in F
- clarinet in C
- horns in F
- 3 trumpets in F
- bassoons
- 3 trombones
- ophicleide
- small and large drum

This score apparently carried a recommendation that this instrumentation be considered for the reorganization of military music, but the idea was rejected and bands remained instrumented after the commission of 1848, chaired by Mabellini.

In 1865 another commission on military band instrumentation was appointed, this time chaired by Mercadantes. This commission recommended a standard infantry band instrumentation of,

- small and large flutes
- oboe
- clarinet in A♭
- 2 clarinets in E♭
- solo clarinet in B♭
- 6 clarinets in B♭
- 2 bass clarinets in B♭

---

[5] In Bologna, Civico Museo Bibliografico-Musicale, there is a copy of a *Sinfonia* (Firenze: Paoletti, 1868) by Mabellini, scored for flute, with pairs of oboes, clarinets, horns, and bassoons.

[6] Donizetti's brother, Giuseppe Donizetti (1788–1856) was a military band director of the Reggimento Provinziale di Casale, but was hired by the Sultan Abdul Medjid of Turkey to take charge of that nation's military music. This led to his more famous brother's *Three Marches*, composed for the Sultan in 1835. A notice in the *Pressburger Zeitung* (August 4, 1829) quotes a letter of Giuseppe Donizetti to a friend in which he discusses a musical school he also founded and also comments on the repertoire of the bands there, 'only Rossini and some of my poor works.'

2 cornets
2 Flügelhorns
5 trumpets
3 horns
3 tenorhorns
3 trombones
3 bombardons
contrabassoon
4 'Basses'
percussion

For the cavalry band, the commission recommended thirty players:

2 trumpets
3 cornets
3 Flügelhorns
5 trumpets in E♭
4 horns
3 tenorhorns
3 trombones
3 bombardons
4 'Basses'[7]

Missing in this instrumentation (which had a distinctly Austrian flavor) were the new instruments of Sax. One who campaigned for the adoption of these instruments was the famous Rossini. When he was made a member of the 'Grand Knight of the Order of the Crown of Italy,' by Victor Emanuel II, Rossini composed, in return, his *La Corona d'Italia* for military band. When the score was sent from Paris, Rossini included the following note:

> Instrumenting this little piece of music, to be performed, be it well understood, on foot, I took advantage not only of the old instruments of Italian bands, but also of the excellent new ones we owe to Sax, their celebrated inventor and maker. I cannot imagine that the leaders of Italian bands have not adopted these instruments (as was done everywhere). If by any chance this *only advance of our days* was not embraced by them (a thing that would pain me), I beg Your Excellency to be willing to entrust my score to a good composer of military music (such as often is found among the bandleaders) so that he may adapt it to the standard instruments, preserving with judgment and patience the melodic and harmonic effects of the original.[8]

[7] Veit, *Die Blasmusik*, 61.

[8] Weinstock, *Rossini*, 361.

The first performance of this work occurred in Rome in 1878 by a massed band of three hundred musicians, from the bands of the Rome Fire Department and four regiments.

Another attempt at reforming the instrumentation of Italian military bands occurred in 1884 when a commission was appointed to meet in the Palazzo del Comando, of the Second Army Corps, in Milan. This commission[9] met from February through August 1884, and published comments on repertoire and instrument design, as well as their recommendations on instrumentation.

Their instrumentation plan was based on a concept by which all instruments would serve primarily one of three basic functions: melody, accompaniment, or bass (*Cantabili, accompagnameti e bassi*).[10] To cite some examples, within the 'melody' category the cornet was assigned the soprano and mezzo-soprano roles, with the first E♭ trumpet serving as the contralto (the remaining three E♭ trumpets were 'accompaniment' instruments for the middle range.) Similarly, the first trombone was the 'melody' instrument of the tenor range, with the three remaining trombones filling 'accompaniment' roles. Two flicorni and two bombardini, representing SATB, were also considered as 'melody' instruments.

The commission set the instrumentation of the cavalry band at twenty-nine players and that of the infantry band at thirty-six, as follows:

1 piccolo and flute
1 E♭ clarinet
7 B♭ clarinets
2 B♭ cornets
2 B♭ flicorni
4 E♭ trumpets
3 E♭ horns
3 E♭ clavicorni
4 trombones (with valves)
1 B♭ baritone bombardino
1 B♭ bass bombardino
2 bass bombardoni (F and B♭)
2 pelittoni in B♭
3 percussion

[9] The *La Musica Popolare. Giornale mensile illustrato* (Milan, February, 1884), III, Nr. 2, listed the members as Celestino Terzi (a Major in the 5th Alpini, serving as the president of the commission); Andrea Guarneri, conductor of the Banda Municipale di Milano; Carini Cesare, bandmaster of the 47th infantry regiment; Sparano Giuseppe, bandmaster of the 63rd infantry regiment; Mantelli Lorenzo, bandmaster of the 62nd infantry regiment; and Moranzoni Giovanni, bandmaster of the 10th infantry regiment.

[10] The recommendations of this commission is discussed extensively by Vessella, *La Banda*, 201ff.

The recommendations of this commission had no immediate impact on Italian military bands and many of the problems addressed by the commission again became the topic of wide discussion following a military band contest held in 1898 as part of the l'Esposizione Generale Italiana held in Torino. Some twenty-eight bands participated in this contest and one observer heard all of them as being weak in any concept of 'families' of instruments; in sufficient numbers of bass instruments; and in the weakness of harmony, due to insufficient instrumentation in general.[11] Other observers commented on the lack of artistic training in the conductors and the general absence of any over-all philosophy in instrumentation.

The first important steps which would lead to real reform in Italian military bands were taken in 1901, when yet another commission studied the problem.[12] As was the case with a similar commission in Paris, in 1845, this group included as part of their activities a 'battle of the bands.' In this case they heard a traditional military band instrumentation, the 94th infantry regiment, and one with a more modern instrumentation, the municipal band of Rome, both perform an arrangement of themes from *Mosè* by Rossini. The commission was so taken by the Rome band that they eventually used its number of players (forty-six) as the number it would recommend for the reorganized military bands. This number they subdivided into three categories: fifteen 'effective' players, fifteen 'students,' and sixteen 'aspiring students,' with pay proportioned accordingly. The commission also addressed the need for written norms of ability for the players and questions of appropriate repertoire.

With regard to instrumentation, the commission suggested the addition of saxophones, which they felt offered both power and flexibility. The contrabass saxophone in particular they recommended as a substitute for the string bass, as it was easier to learn and, at the same time, was a better substitute for the B♭ contrabass flicorno. The commission recommended the addition of the soprano A♭ clarinet and two contra-alto clarinets. The latter, in their view, allowed one to use all the soprano clarinets (A♭, E♭, and B♭) in unison and still maintain two-part clarinet sonority. They also recommended the addition of the bass trombone, E♭ sopranino flicorno, and timpani. Two of the four traditional E♭ trumpets, the commission desired changed to B♭ bass instruments.

[11] Vessella, *La Banda*, 205. According to Henri Maréchal and Gabriel Parès, in *Monographie Universelle de L'Orpheon* (Paris: Librairie Ch. Delagrave, 1910), 261, the award of 'Excellence' was shared by the Marine and Carabiniers Bands of Rome, together with those of the First and Second Grenadiers.

[12] This commission met at the Accademia di S. Cecilia and was presided over by the Minister of War, Major General Paolo Spingardi, and included among its members the president of the academy, E. Di S. Martino, the bandmasters of the Legione Allievi (Caioli), the 94th infantry regiment (Ricci), and Vessella, conductor of the Banda Municipale di Rome.

The commission also addressed the artistic and technical training of the military band conductor, observing that traditionally this person had been the best soloist of the band, thus resulting in his over-emphasis of that part.

Among the military repertoire of the second half of the nineteenth century in Italy are several works by the famous Ponchielli. These include several funeral marches, a *Fantasia militaire*, and the very beautiful *Elegia*, 'Sulla tomba di Garibaldi' (1886).

PART 2
Civic Wind Bands

7 *Military Bands in Public Concerts*

I believe general studies of nineteenth-century European music have failed to give credit to military bands for their contribution to aesthetic music. One can understand why the late nineteenth- and twentieth-century authors closed their ears to the medium, for by the end of the nineteenth century military bands had often elected to perform only an entertainment function for society and in that role performed literature of so little aesthetic value that the wind band is to this very day struggling to free itself of the stigma. But to be perfectly fair and honest about nineteenth-century music, one would have to admit that there was an 'entertainment' facet in even the most highly regarded of society's aesthetic jewels. Let us not forget that the Vienna premiere of Beethoven's *Seventh Symphony* shared a program with a mechanical trumpeter![255] This was probably the same one which appeared a few years earlier in 1809 and received a review in the *Journal des Modes*.

> From a tent, Mr. Maelzel led out a fine manly looking figure, in the uniform of a trumpeter of the Austrian Dragoon Regiment-Albert, his trumpet being in his mouth. After having pressed the figure on the left shoulder, it played not only the Austrian cavalry march, as also all the signals for the maneuvers of that army, but also a march and an allegro by Weigl, which was accompanied by the whole orchestra. After this, the dress of the figure was completely changed into that of a French trumpeter of the Guard; it then began to play the French cavalry march, also all the signals of the French cavalry maneuvers, and lastly a march of Dussek's, and an allegro by Pleyel, accompanied again by the full orchestra. The sound of the trumpet is pure, and more agreeable than even the ablest musician could produce from that instrument, because the breath of a man gives the inside of the trumpet a moisture which is prejudicial to the purity of the tone. Mr. Maelzel publicly wound up his instrument only twice, and this was on the left hip.[1]

Shortly after the death of his friend, Beethoven, Maelzel fled to America to escape lawsuits centering around his mechanical chess player [which had a midget inside]. Among the mechanical objects he brought with him was the mechanical trumpet player which he exhibited in Philadelphia for

[1] Quoted in John S. Sainsbury, *A Dictionary of Musicians from the earliest Times* (London, 1825), 97. In downtown Philadelphia today there is an historical plaque marking the location of 'Mr. Maelzel's Hall, 1826–1831,' where the inventor demonstrated his trumpeter, his machine, 'The Burning of Moscow' [which is said to have produced smoke and snow] and his mechanical chess player. See also, John F. Watson, *Annals of Philadelphia and Pennsylvania*, rev. Willis P. Hazard (Philadelphia: Leary, Stuart Co., 1927), 3:453.

several years. An historical journal devoted to early Philadelphia carries this description of how the mechanical trumpeter was built.

> The machinery of the trumpeter is contained within the trunk of the figure, and is worked by a steel spring which drives a revolving barrel, on which are pegs similar to those in a musical-box; a bellows just below the neck of the figure furnishes the wind, and a valve with a steel tongue, which is lengthened or shortened by means of levers working on the pegs of the barrel, makes the different notes.
>
> There is an important difference between this trumpeter and the ordinary mechanical organs or musical-boxes. These have a separate pipe or trumpet for every note of the scale, while in the automaton the notes are all produced by the one horn, the lengthening or shortening of the steel tongue or reed by means of the levers mentioned producing all the tones of the chromatic scale, on the same principle by which the human trumpeter produces them by tonguing the mouthpiece of his instrument.

We are told that Mr. Maelzel's young assistant, a Signor Blitz, would accompany the machine at the piano, no doubt the part which the orchestra in Vienna played in the 1809 performance. One reason we provide this information is to inspire some reader to attempt to locate this mechanical trumpeter, as the indications are that it was left in Philadelphia.

> The trumpeter was placed in the old Masonic Temple and afterward passed into the possession of the late Mr. E. N. Scherr, a music-dealer on Chestnut Street, to whose estate it now belongs.
> ……
> This wonderful piece of mechanism … was exhibited in 1877 to a part of gentlemen at 926 Chestnut Street by Mr. E. N. Scherr, Jr., who now has possession of it.

Even the keyboard instruments were not exempt from entertainment obligations, as one can see in an organ recital given in September 1807, in Frankfurt, by the highly esteemed teacher of Carl Maria von Weber and Meyerbeer, Abt Vogler.

Part I
1. Chorale: How Brightly Shines the Morning Star
2. Song of the Hottentots, which consists of three measures and two words: Magema, Magema, Huh, Huh, Huh!
3. Flute Concerto: Allegro, Polonaise, Gigue

Part II
1. The Siege of Jericho
   a) Israel's Prayer to Jehovah
   b) Sound of Trumpets
   c) Crash of the Walls
   d) Entrance of the Victors
2. Terrace Chant of the Africans, when they seal their flat roofs with lime, during which one chorus alternately sings and the other one stamps
3. The Pleasure Ride on the Rhine, Interrupted by a Thunder-storm
4. Handel's Hallelujah, treated as a fugue with two subjects and counter-pointed with a third subject[2]

[2] Quoted in Arthur Loesser, *Men, Women & Pianos* (New York: Simon and Schuster, 1954), 165–166.

I only wish to make the point that with wind bands, even as it was so with symphony orchestras and keyboard artists, such concerts were not the *whole* story during the nineteenth century. There were bands and band conductors who had aesthetic goals which were quite as serious as those of any other artist.

It is also important to remember that during the beginning years of the nineteenth century, 1) the concept of 'public concerts' in the modern sense was something still relatively new, and 2) the symphony orchestras as we think of them today did not yet exist (most orchestras were opera orchestras; very few of today's famous orchestras existed as concert organizations before 1850). Yet there *were* at this time large military bands who were performing disciplined and artistic concerts before the public. These performances were sufficiently successful that, as the reader will discover below, composers and publishers began asking the military bands to 'prepare' the public, through their performances, for the original orchestral versions of their music.

Finally, as I have mentioned above, one factor which helped create the success military bands had with the public was their technical excellence. In the years before the impact of the conservatories was widely felt,[3] and before the modern, well-disciplined symphony orchestras appeared, the military band may often have exceeded the local orchestra in many technical performance qualities. The reason for this, of course, was because the military bands enjoyed a residual military discipline as the foundation for their music making. The *aesthetic* significance of this was recognized by the famous nineteenth-century critic, Eduard Hanslick.

[3] Most of the modern conservatories were founded during the second quarter of the nineteenth century.

> In this form, the regimental band emerges out of its purely military role and reaches higher artistic purposes. These are the so-called 'Garden concerts' by which the military bands offer the court a favorite recreation and often give small cities a full artistic musical experience. The many and strenuous rehearsals for this concert [a concert of the music of Berlioz, given in Prague] allow us to see the value of military subordination for artistic reasons; no conductor of any civic orchestra would have been able to manage this performance at that time. It may go against some idealistic theories that art could be encouraged through something so very different from personal freedom as subordination, however it is so. Every art has in its technique one facet which can only be developed through constant work, and this technical side is even more important in the work of many together than by the individual virtuoso. The conductor's baton and the corporal's stick both have the purpose of bringing many heads together under one hat … where the artistic subordination joins with the military subordination, 'a good sound results.' In the Garden concerts or other non-military performances the military bands are in a better position than other mediums to pursue purely artistic goals. The position of the conductor appears here more independent, the selection of the repertoire more free, and the means more complete. In any case, from these favorable conditions springs a stronger obligation to art.[4]

The initial references during the nineteenth century suggest that military bands were closely connected to the aristocracy through the associations of the medium itself and its literature. Indeed, during the early years of the nineteenth century a military band 'concert' may have still been primarily an imitation of the court *Harmoniemusik* and its repertoire of partitas. This seems implied in the advertisement in the *Allgemeine Musikalische Zeitung* for March 1801, which has been quoted above.

---

[4] Quoted in Brixel, *Das ist Österreichs Militär Musik*, 107.

> In dieser Gestalt tritt die Regimentalmusik eigentlich aus ihrer rein militärischen Specialität heraus und erreicht höhere künstlerische Wirkungen. Es sind namentlich die 'Gartenproductionen' der Militärkapellen, welche den Residenzbewohnern eine beliebte Erholung, kleinen Städten oft den einzigen musikalischen kunstgenuss verschaffen. Die zahlreichen anstrengenden Proben zu dieser Production liessen erkennen, was militärische Subordination selbst für rein künstlerische Zwecke werth sein könne; kein Chef irgend eines Civil-orchesters würde dies Auffhührung damals zustandgebracht haben. Es mag sehr gegen idealistische Theorien verstossen, dass die Kunst durch etwas von der persönlichen Freiheit so ungemein Verschiedenes, wie die Subordination ist, gefbördert zu werden vermöge, dennoch ist dem so. Jede Kunst besitzt in ihrer Technik eine Seite, welche nur durch anhaltenden Fleiss ausgebildet werden kann, unddiese technische Seite ist bei dem Zusammenwirken Vieler noch ungleich wichtiger, als beim einzelnen Virtuosen. Der Taktirstab und der Corporalstock haben beide den Zweck, viele Köpfe unter einen Hut zu bringen; wo sich also die künstlerische Subordination mit der militärischen vereiget, 'da gibt es einen guten Klang.'
>
> In den Gartenconcerten oder sonstigen ausserdienslichen Productionen sind die Militärorchester am. meisten in der Lage, rein künstlerische Zwecke zu verfolgen. Die Stellung des Capellmeisters erscheint da viel selbständiger, die Wahl der Stucke freier, die Mittel vollzähliger. Aus diesen günstigen Bedingungen entspringt jedenfalls eine strengere künstlerische Verpflichtung.

> ... as many Oboisten from the military and other musical societies now play partitas ...

Similarly, Gerber's *Encyclopedia* (1812) writes of Georg Druschetzky,

> [He] has for the past ten years composed a great number of excellent Partien for wind instruments, namely 2 oboes, 2 clarinets, 2 horns, 2 bassoons. These are not only for the whole Kaiserly army, but have received merit and invigorated all of Germany.

By the second decade of the nineteenth century, one can begin to distinguish between the concert activity by the larger military band and that by the traditional Harmoniemusik. In a notice from Köln, for example, one reads that during the summer of 1816 the full infantry band gave a series of twelve subscription [!] concerts and during the same summer members of the band appeared in the more informal coffee house environment as a Harmoniemusik ensemble.[5]

Reschke believed that such examples of military bands in concert appearances before 1820 were 'of the greatest rarity,'[6] but I wonder if perhaps it is only the information which is scarce. An advertisement in the *Allgemeine Musikalische Zeitung* for 1804 announced a new collection of military music,[7] edited by Herr von Sydow, which by its very publication seems to suggest a ready market. Moreover, this advertisement contains two very interesting comments: first, that it was the *military* ensembles, and not the civic ensembles, who were the more likely to be able to perform the music, and second, it emphasizes the aesthetic as well as the practical value of the collection.

> This present journal is first of all devoted to the military; then to large and small bands and those civil musicians who raise themselves above the level of the ordinary; (the collection) is just as useful as it is pleasant.

The advertisement of the publication of a similar Journal, in 1810 by Steiner in Vienna, again suggests a broad demand on the part of the military for such literature and recognizes the general quality of the military bands as well.

[5] Hans Engel, *Die Musikpflege der Philipps-Universität zu Marburg seit 1527* (Marburg, 1957), 97.

[6] Reschke, *Studie zur Geschichte der brandenburgischpreussischen Herresmusik*, 37.

[7] The *Journal militärisches Musik* was primarily arrangements in six to eight-parts, with and without 'türkische musik,' of the music of Haydn, Himmel, Méhul, Mozart, Paisiello, Righini, Weber, etc. This information, as well as the following advertisement, is quoted from Hellyer, 'Harmoniemusik,' 52.

These will continue to appear frequently in accordance with the requirements of the honorable k.k. regiments and other respected connoisseurs.

There are two rather extraordinary extant military band works which date from before 1820 which should be mentioned in passing. One, of course, is the Spohr *Notturno* of 1817,[8] a major work in six movements which is technically difficult and, in my opinion, still very worthy of performance. The other is an example of military band literature which could have only been used in a concert environment, programmatic music necessitates the listeners knowing at least the titles of the movements. Such music became very popular in all mediums at the time of the great victory over Napoleon during the 1813 Battle of Leipzig. In an era with no television, radio, or daily newspapers, such a composition gave the citizen at home a vicarious taste of the great events of his time. In the extraordinary band work by Paul Maschek, written during 1813–1814, one finds the entire winter campaign covered during the course of its thirty movements.[9] The titles of the three large cycles are:

[8] *Notturno, 6 Stücke für Harmonie- und Janitscharenmusik*, composed for the military band corps in Sondershausen.

[9] The manuscripts are in Vienna, Österreichische Nationalbibliothek, scored for 'Harmoniemusik und türkische musik.' Most movements are for a full band of 3 flutes, 2 oboes, 3 clarinets, 2 bassoons, trumpet, 2 horns, trombone, serpent, contrabassoon, and percussion, however, a few movements, especially those which in topic deal with the Monarch, are for a smaller, true Harmoniemusik.

The Battle of Leipzig
1. The Imperial Royal Austrian and Imperial Russian Armies, under the command of His Grace, Lord Fieldmarshal Karl, Prince of Schwarzenberg, march out to meet the enemy.
2. The approach of the French troops, marching in double-time, is heard.
3. The Russians approach from all sides!
4. The cannons call to battle.
5. The Battle … the French are defeated … the victory march is heard.
6. The victorious armies receive their praise.
7. The Monarchs give thanks to God.
8. General rejoicing because of the victory.

The Occupation of Paris
1. After the Battle of Champenoise, the victorious army pursues the enemy with resounding noise.
2. The Battle of Paris.
3. The great Allies appear before Paris under the leadership of His Royal Highness, the Crown Prince of Württemberg.
4. Jubilation of the Allied troops at the sight of a city which believed itself invincible.
5. Napoleon's sorrowful retreat to Fontainbleau … more Allied troops are still arriving.

6. Officials of Paris arrive at the headquarters of the Allies to plead for surrender …
7. The entry march of their Majesties, the Czar of Russia, the King of Prussia, the Crown Prince of Wllrttemberg, and Fieldmarshal Prince of Schwarzenberg, with their respective troops, into Paris.
8. The Hunter's Battalion enters Paris.
9. General rejoicing of the French, having been freed from a terrible ruler.
10. The Allied troops spread out during the night and are well taken care of.
11. Everywhere the Allies are received by the inhabitants with respect and cordiality.
12. Solemn thanks of the freed population to the Allied Monarchs.

Austria's Triumph, or the Return
1. The longing of the subjects for their adored Monarch.
2. The travels of his Majesty through the lands of his inheritance to the rejoicing of the people.
3. The military, the Home Guard, ride out to meet His Majesty.
4. The Magistrate welcomes His Majesty.
5. Even the Youth honor him!
6. Procession of His Majesty through the triumphal arch toward St. Stefan's.
7. The Clergy receives His Majesty.
8. Prayer with cannons roaring.
9. General rejoicing.[10]

[10] Another extant program work from very early during the nineteenth century is the Anonymous, *General Bertrand's Abschied* for two clarinets, two horns, and bassoon in Paris, Bibliothèque nationale.

The musical demands of the Spohr and the Maschek works, together with the language of the early Journal advertisements and the comments of Hanslick quoted above, suggest to me that in the German-speaking countries one would have definitely found examples of military bands before 1820 who were outstanding in quality and aesthetically oriented. This also seems implied in an 1816 eyewitness account by the French Novelist, Henri Beyle (Pseud., Stendhal), who heard what was apparently a massed band concert in Milan.

> Yesterday at 1:00 in the Giardini was a very excellent instrumental concert. Every German regiment has a band with 80 musicians. A hundred pretty women were eve-dropping on this distinguished music. Played were the most beautiful works of Mozart and the young Rossini. 150 first-rate wind instruments gave these arias an aura of unique melancholy. French military music compares with this as the coarse shoe of the peasant's wife compares with the white satin shoe of the highest society.[11]

[11] Quoted in Veit, *Die Blasmusik*, 61.

> Die französischen Militärkapeıen sind neben dieser Musik, was das grobe Schuhwerk einer Hökerfrau neben dem weissen Atlasschuh einer Welt dame ist.

Stendhal was notorious for his depreciation of the art of France in general.

From the 1820s there are several examples of new forms of military music which must have been used in public concerts. These include works for solo wind instruments, accompanied by military band, as well as 'concert overtures.'[12] Such works, together with the necessary transcriptions,[13] formed the repertoire for concerts which more and more are mentioned in the diaries and accounts of contemporaries. An Englishman, Edward Holmes, touring Germany in 1827, reports, 'There is a magnificent band of military instruments to be heard on Sundays in Cassel.'[14] Another city where he found regular Sunday concerts was Darmstadt. Here a formal military parade, with the band, soldiers, and horses, was timed to occur as people were leaving the churches. Apparently the parade would stop for intervals of thirty minutes or so in order that the band could play its 'concert' music.'

> The congregation flocked out to help digest their theological repast with some of the prettiest airs in Rossini's Barbiere di Seviglia, played by the military band on parade. When the Sunday is fine, the half hour between the conclusion of church service and the beginning of dinner may be spent very cheerfully at Darmstadt; the air resounds with waltz tunes, the ladies are out dressed [as if] for the opera in the evening, the soldiers stand in columns, while the officers as usual restrain their exuberant chargers.[15]

This same Englishman provides a more poignant description of performance he heard in Munich.

> For the benefit of the strollers and holiday-makers in Munich, bands play twice a week in the open square of the King's palace, which both for look and accommodation may vie with the Palais Royal in Paris. Here, while the cooling luxuries of lemonade and ice are imbibed, there is a regale of excellent instrumental music. An overture in E minor attracted my attention from the brilliancy of execution and expression with which the trombone players accomplished some most unwieldy passages for their instrument. The faces of the performers appeared as if animated by a prophetic fury, and their distended checks would have reminded one of the fat-faced cherubims sometimes seen on a church organ, only that they were older, redder, and accompanied by a 'jutting friz' of mustachio that cast a shade. Their enthusiasm, and the earnestness of their manner, were delightful, as those qualities always lead to excellence.[16]

---

[12] In Berlin, Deutsche Staatsbibliothek, there is a manuscript Tone Poem, *Die Schlacht* ('The Battle'), dated 1824, for large concert band with chorus by M. L. F. Wurst.

[13] Necessary because the military band developed its large instrumentation before it had time to develop its repertoire.

[14] Edward Holmes, *A Ramble Among the Musicians of Germany* [1827] (New York: Da Capo Press, 1969), 279.

[15] Ibid., 49.

[16] Ibid., 61–62.

Let us not forget another expert observer of one of these public, noon concerts—Felix Mendelssohn. He was so impressed with a band he heard in Northern Germany during the Summer of 1824, that he immediately composed the work for eleven-part military band which we know today in the later, larger form as the *Overture*, op. 24.[17] The Mendelssohn work is, of course, a serious overture, fully consistent with the quality of bands described at this time by Holmes.

I believe it was from the 1820s that military band concerts began to become truly popular. In a city such as Berlin, for example, in 1822 one would have heard Neithardt and his band performing every Wednesday, 'under clear skies and shade trees, with the aroma of flowers and coffee,'[18] in a public park called, 'Hofjäger.' Nearby, in the 'Schulgarten,' was Weller and his band, while Schick was conducting in the 'Teichmanns Blumengarten.' In 1827 another public concert site opened, the 'Fausts Wintergarten' and in 1829 the famous 'Tivoli,' on the Kreuzberg, named for a park in Paris. In the latter place Neithardt gave Tuesday concerts which were well attended throughout the year, even in the cold of January (two of Neithardt's compositions are entitled, *The Charms of Berlin's Tivoli in Winter*). Holmes who heard one of these concerts in 1829, left us a valuable first-hand account of what they were like.

> One distinguishing characteristic of the excellence of this country [Prussia] in music is the skill of the wind-instrument bands, and the nicety of tunes with which they play pieces containing the most learned modulation. At a concert in the open air I heard a Fantasia of Mozart in C minor (to be found in his pianoforte works) very effectively arranged by Neithardt; a finale from the Zauberflöte of the same; the overture to the Berg König, by Lindpainter; with some lighter pieces and horn music [Jäger musik]. The complete *accord* with which some very difficult enharmonic changes were accomplished by this numerous and magnificent band, showed great knowledge in the arranger and skill in the performers, a perfection, the value of which, is known only to those who are aware of the unmanageable nature of wind-instruments. I found here many young lads who had attained great eminence as practical musicians, and with it (a rare thing to discover among those who associate in large societies) they joined a simplicity of manners and modest behaviour which were in the highest degree attractive. Two of these youths played some variations for two clarinets by Kastner, and another the corno *principale* in an overture for horns by Neithardt, of

[17] The autograph score of the eleven-wind version has now been discovered in Berlin, Staatsbibliothek (BRD:B). See David Reed, 'The Original Version of the *Overture for Wind Band* of Felix Mendelssohn-Bartholdy,' *Journal of Band Research* 18, no. 1 (Fall, 1982): 3ff. Mendelssohn referred to the band he heard as a 'Harmoniemusik,' and scored his work for flute, pairs of clarinets in C, oboes, bassoons, horns, one trumpet, and one bass horn.

[18] Max Thomas, 'Heinrich August Neithardt' (Dissertation, Freie Universität Berlin, 1959), 27, under the heading, 'Die Militärkonzerte.'

Unter freiem Himmel und schattigen Baüumen, von Blumen- und Caféduft umgossen

which last the effort was perfectly extraordinary. The ingenuity of the German horn music [Jäger musik] is completely unimaginable by those who have never heard any, as it presents some of the most curious discoveries of modern combination, with a tone of the richest quality. Neither is the music simple or so much restrained to one key as might be fancied; the thoughts of the composer are not screwed down by this or that apparent impossibility, but the composition flows on as though it were written for instruments presenting the usual facilities.[19]

[19] Holmes, *A Ramble Among the Musicians of Germany*, 234–235.

Soon, unfortunately, there were conductors who acknowledged the appeal which military bands had on the public by lowering the artistic standards of their literature in hopes, perhaps, of attracting an even larger audience. Thus another English visitor to Germany, Vincent Novello, describes hearing already in 1829 examples of band concerts which were harbingers of the darker side of the history of the wind band. In Mannheim,

> Between 11 and 12 I went to hear the Military Band which played for about half an hour in the public square before the Palace. The Instruments were well in tune (a rare thing in a collection of wind instruments) and the band consists of excellent performers—but they wasted their talents upon trumpery waltzes, commonplace trifles, country Dances—and paltry jigs in six-eight time. There was not a single movement played that at all approached the elevated style of compositions or that was worth a moment's attention from a musician.[20]

[20] Novello, *A Mozart Pilgrimage*, 37.

In Munich he heard what must have been a joint concert by a regimental infantry and cavalry bands.

> July 11 … In the Evening at 6 we went to the Garden belonging to the King's Palace (the Hof Garten) to hear the Military Band. It consisted of two Portions, the Brass Band and the Regular Military Band—which consists of about half a dozen small Clarionets, the same number of common Clarionets, 2 Flutes, an octave Flute, 2 Bassoons, 4 Horns, 4 Trumpets, 2 Trombones, 2 Bass Horns, Long Drum, Side Drum and Cymbals.
>
> The Brass Band relieved the principal one by playing alternately with it but both the Melodies and the harmonies of the airs played were of the poorest common-place description, and the effect was altogether coarse, harsh and disagreeable.

Some of the Pieces selected by the other Band on this occasion were of a better kind than what I had before heard them perform and one movement, the Overture to Preciosa by Weber, was a Musician-like affair of the light airy class—and was performed in a manner very creditable.

There were two Performers who were very superior to the rest, the Person who played the principal Clarionet and the Leader who played 1st small Clarionet and whose name I was informed was Witter—the former was principally distinguished by the beauty of his tone and tasteful expression and Mr. Witter by his spirited and brilliant execution.

With the exception of the above-mentioned Overture, I found nothing to admire, most of the pieces being arrangements of Opera Airs by Rossini and his imitators—mixed with waltzes as usual.

I longed to ask them to play some of Mozart's overtures (especially the Idomeneo which I had heard not long since by the King of England's Band at Windsor) or Haydn's Sinfonias—but was fearful of appearing too presumptuous.

Upon the whole I could perceive nothing in this celebrated Band at all superior to our own military Music which is to be heard every day on the Parade at the Horse Guards and at St. James' Palace and very, very far inferior to the King's Band at Windsor under the direction of my friend Mr. C. Kramer.[21]

[21] Ibid., 274ff.

From the 1830s until the end of the century, one finds an increasingly larger number of extant serious, original works for military band. During the second half of the century, the 'Golden Age' for bands, one finds a very large number of major, serious works, including symphonies, overtures, fantaisies and tone poems.[22]

Indications are that the quality of performance reached a great peak beginning after the revolutionary year of 1848. A touring American, Lowell Mason, was impressed with several band concerts he heard in Germany in 1852, first in Berlin,

[22] Some interesting later German tone poems are the Hallager, *Reminiscenzen aus den letzten Tagen auf St. Helena* and the Ruscheweyh, *Vor Sedan* (a twenty-four movement battle piece).

> An excellent military band plays daily at eleven o'clock. It contains about sixty instruments, and we were truly glad to see that the use of the old fashioned military band instruments is continued. Here were Oboi, Faggotti, Clarinetti, Corni, as well as all the modern brass instruments. The band usually plays all overtures and one or two small pieces daily, at the hour above mentioned; and in its performances, it is sufficient to say, that the characteristics of good orchestral playing are carefully observed.[23]

[23] Lowell Mason, *Musical Letters from Abroad* (Boston, 1853), 99.

then in Munich,

> Military music abounds here, and is very fine. One of the best bands I have heard (but not better than the one in Berlin), consisting of about forty instruments, including oboes, clarionets, bassoons, etc., plays daily at eleven o'clock; say an overture first, and then one or two pieces of lighter music.[24]

and with an informal competition in Frankfurt.

> The military music is very fine. There are many bands, as Prussian, Austrian, Bavarian, and others. One of them plays daily in the square in front of the guard house; and, as each one tries to surpass the others, their performances are often carried to a high degree of perfection.[25]

These military bands, as bands still do, continued throughout the century to perform transcriptions of major orchestral works. These performances seem rarely to have been debated with regard to the principle of transcriptions, but rather seem to have been accepted on the same level as orchestral performances. The key to the latter was found in the high quality of performance, especially by the Prussian bands, as one can see in an 1858 review of a concert conducted by Piefke, by the very distinguished musician and critic, Hans von Bülow.

> We had the satisfaction on numerous occasions to attend the accomplished performance of his band and we were always surprised by the technical perfection, the painstaking nuance of every detail, the majestic power of the mass impression and finally the fresh full vibrating spirit of the noble performances.
>
> The A Major Symphony by Beethoven, Wagner's Overture to Tannhäuser, the transcription of the first Finale, Pilgrim's Chorus, Prayer, and Romance from Act III of Lohengrin which we heard were satisfying, as one would not have thought in this sphere and brought to the conducting and the entire band the highest honor. The choice of the Seventh Symphony of Beethoven appeared to us genuinely successful; this apotheosis permitted a unity of character with that which had been played earlier, for example the transcription of Beethoven's C Minor Symphony by Wieprecht—a work by which he had obtained his great reputation. The Scherzo and Trio, as well as the last movement, were in this transcription of such an overpowering and compelling effect that it was possible for one at the moment to completely forget the original instrumentation.[26]

[24] Ibid., 128.

[25] Ibid., 146.

[26] *Neue Zeitschrift für Musik* (July 1, 1858).

> Wir hatten bei mehrfachen Gelegenheiten das Vergnügen, grösseren Leistungen seines Korps beizuwohnen und wurden aufs neue überrascht durch die technische Vol l kommenheit, die sorgfältige Nuancierung aller Einzelheiten, die imposante Gewalt der Massenwirkungen und endlich den frischen schwungvollen Geist, der in dieser Aufführung herrschte. Die A-Dur Sinfonie von Beethoven, die Ouvertüre zu Wagners Tannhäuser, das erste Finale, der Pilgerchor, das Gebet und die Romanze aus dem dritten Akt sowie die samtlichen übertragungsfähigen Fragmente aus Lohengrin, welche wir hörten, waren Leistungen, wie sie in dieser Sphäre meisterhafter nicht gedacht werden können und gereichten dem Dirigenten wie der ganzen Kapelle zur höchsten Ehre. Die Wahl der 7. Sinfonie von Beethoven schien uns eine recht glückliche; dies Apotheose der Künstlerischen und rein menschlichen Freude gestattet eine solche Transkription bei ihrem einheitlichen Charakter weit eher, als z.B. die e-Mall Sinfonie, deren Arrangement durch W. Wieprecht ein so grosses Renommee erlangt hat. Das Trio des Scherzo sowie der letzte Satz waren in dieser Bearbeitung von so überwältigender und hinreissender Wirkung, dass man die Instrumentierung des Originals wohl auf Augenblicke ganz zu verges sen vermochte.

In Prussia, certainly, the term 'Golden Age' is appropriate if one considers that by the 1860s, as I have mentioned above, one could have heard on a summer evening any of twenty or thirty band concerts[27]—this in a city of only 500,000 residents in 1850.[28] The choice of band concerts in Berlin was such that by the 1830s one could hear them at almost any hour of the day, beginning at 5 o'clock in the morning![29]

The Austrians also emphasized the aesthetic and their military bands gave concerts in places far removed from Austria, due to the vast size of the Empire. We have a testimonial to such an Austrian band stationed in Mainz, by none other than Berlioz, whose first priority upon arriving in town was to seek it out.

> On my arrival in Mainz, I hastened to make inquiries as to the Austrian military band which had been there the year before, and … had performed several of my overtures with great verve and power, and immense effect. The regiment had gone; no more *musique d'harmonie* (this was really a *grande harmonie!*).[30]

Another famous composer who was enthusiastic about the musicality of the Austrian military bands was Wagner, who left an account of hearing his music played in 1858 by Austrian bands quartered in Venice.

> … it was the thoroughly German element of good military music, to which so much attention is paid in the Austrian army, that brought me into touch with public life in Venice. The conductors of the two Austrian regiments quartered there began playing overtures of mine, *Rienzi* and *Tannhäuser* for instance, and invited me to attend their rehearsals in their barracks. There I also met the whole staff of officers, and was treated by them with great respect. These bands played on alternate evenings amid brilliant illuminations in the middle of the Piazza San Marco, whose acoustic properties for this class of production were really excellent … The people were gathered round the band in thousands listening most intently, but no two hands ever forgot themselves so far as to applaud, as the least sign of approbation of Austrian military music would have been looked upon as treason to the Italian Fatherland.[31]

There are further interesting details about Wagner's impressions of one of these Austrian bands in an extant letter of thanks, written by the composer to one of these band conductors whom he heard in Venice.

[27] Veit, *Die Blasmusik*, 57.

[28] Oswald Schrenk, *Berlin und die Musik* (Berlin: E. Bote & G. Bock, 1940), 119.

[29] Thomas, 'Heinrich August Neithardt,' 27.

[30] Hector Berlioz, *Mémoires* (Paris: Garnier-Flammarion, 1969), 2:55ff.

> Arrivé à Mayence, je m'informai de la musique militaire autrichienne qui s'y trouvait l'année précédente, et qui avait … exécuté plusieurs de mes ouvertures avec une verve, une puissance et un effet prodigieux. Le régiment était parti, plus de musique d'harmonie (celle-à était vraiment une grande harmonie!)

[31] Richard Wagner, *My Life* (New York: Dodd, Mead, 1911), 2:695–696. In Vienna, Österreichische Nationalbibliothek, there is an autograph arrangement of the *Overture to Tannhäuser* for an Austrian military band, which is dated 1856. Brixel, *Das ist Österreichs Militär Musik*, 177, reproduces a photograph taken near this time, in 1866, of an Austrian band playing just the kind of concert which Wagner describes in St. Mark's Square. One sees here the familiar, if curious, tradition of the Austrian bands playing their concerts seated in a completely enclosed circle. This tradition continued among Austrian bands through the end of the century, as one can see in several additional photographs reproduced in the same book (including one of a concert in St. Polten, in 1900, p. 232). Brixel also reproduces several examples of the printed programs for mid-century Austrian band concerts; they are elaborate works of art in themselves.

Venice, October 24, 1858

Honorable Conductor,

I could not find you in the Piazza yesterday to thank you for the wonderful performance of the *Rienzi Overture*, so today I do this in this written form. I appreciated it very much that your musicians had noticed everything, had marked everything so well and brought everything out correctly. From the very beginning it was perfect, with the tempo entirely correct. [My only suggestion is that] four bars before the Allegro there should be more drums and very strong; that place is dull. Once again, the best thanks and the assurance that you have made it very enjoyable for me. Auf Wiedersehen! Your faithful,

Richard Wagner[32]

Similarly, from the opposite end of Europe, there are very interesting extant accounts of concerts by Austrian military bands in Hamburg and Bremen. These concerts occurred by virtue of the fact that the bands were accompanying the troops who participated in the German-Danish War of 1864. An account in the Austrian army newspaper, *Der Soldatenfreund*,[33] quotes the contemporary reviews which attest to the quality of these performances.

> The excellence of Austrian military music, which takes the first place among similar European institutions, as has long been recognized, has been recently confirmed through the *Hamburger Nachrichten*, which reports:
>
>> The Austrian military band opened the planned cycle of six concerts in the Great Hall of the Sagebiel'schen Kolosseum the evening before last. The rush of the public was so stormy that already during the first piece the places were full and those arriving late had to turn and leave the filled hall … Fifty well-rehearsed members were received very thankfully. The public especially recognized with applause the piece by the conductor, Herr C. Siede, *Konigsberg-Siegesmarsch*, which opened the concert. In the following opera pieces there was great precision and ensemble and in the solo pieces one recognized the masterful handling of the brass instruments, so characteristic of the Austrians.
>
> [Bremen, November 4]
> While a Prussian regimental band creates excitement in Paris, an Austrian one excited the otherwise cool inhabitants of this *Hansastadt* to a level never seen before at even a Schützenfeste. Not only the justly praised (musical ability) of the Austrians, but also their appearance and

[32] Quoted in Brixel, *Das ist Österreichs Militär Musik*, 178.

Venedig, 24. Oct. 58

Geehrtester Herr Kapellmeister!

Ich konnte Sie gestern nicht mehr auf dem Platze finden, um Ihnen meinen Dank für die schone Aufführung der Rienzi-Overtüre zu sagen, und hole es demnach heute schriftlich nach Es machte mir grosse Freunde, dass Ihre Musiker sich alles so gut gemerkt hatten und richtig herausbrachten. Der Anfang sogleich war ganz vortrefflich. Mit dem Tempo vollkommen einverstanden. Nur (4 Takte vor dem Allegro) mehr Trommeln und sehr stark. Die Stelle war matt.—Nochmals—schönsten Dank, und die Versicherung, dass Sie mir viel Freude gemacht haben! Auf Wiedersehen!

Ihr ergebenster

Richard Wagner

[33] September 26, 1864, regarding the concert by the IR 30 band, and November 9, 1865, regarding the concert by the IR 72 band.

behaviour made the highest possible impression on the people of Bremen. All of the daily newspapers were full of praise and recognition, and we quote only as an example the following from the *Bremer Zeitung*:

> The Austrian military band of IR 72 in their two concerts in the Schützenhof and in the Union went beyond the greatest expectations. The perfection of the instruments and the precision with which the presentation took place allows us to praise the musicians as well as their hardworking and intelligent bandmaster, Scharoch without reservation. Like a cloud-burst everything comes out, even the most difficult passages, and the repertoire is to be remembered by its variety and richness.
>
> An audience which was as select as it was receptive gave stormy applause and desired numerous repetitions. Especially the *Nachtigallen Polka* and the *Bauren-Polka-Mazurka* of Strauss (with singing) and the *Radetzky Marsch* brought a rare storm of applause.
>
> The two *Potpourris* were well constructed and contained lovely quotes from every genre.
>
> As a composer, Herr Scharoch debuted with three melodious works. In the Union a portion was performed with string instruments, with which the Austrians proved skill as great as with the brass instruments.

The *Bremen Kourier* said of the Austrians:

> For the first time since the Thirty Years War the Austrian white coats set foot in our city … The forty-one Austrians who came here by train came on a more friendly mission. They come to achieve victory only in the musical area, which is not very difficult for them, armed with instruments which are at times colossal, especially the bombardon, which the musicians sling around their body. It is no risky statement to say that up to now Bremen has never heard such regimental music. It is safe to say their success will be as great in Hamburg, Schleswig-Holstein and even in the enemy lands of Jütlands, where the Danish could not hear enough of the band of the Austrians

The following day this newspaper brought the following:

> [Regarding a concert in the Schutzenhof] Already by 3 PM there was no place to be had, every seat was taken, 2,420 tickets had gone out. The Austrians are never tired as the twelve numbers on the (printed) program became twenty-two. The *Nachtigallen Polka* is stormily demanded at every concert and our music store have reordered copies of this lovely work by Strauss, which was composed already in 1858, however is new to Bremen.
>
> The tubas and bombardons of the Austrians make the room vibrate in the literal sense of the word. A mob of people were enticed to hear the Austrians at the *Kontrescarpe*, in part because of the wonderful sounds of the band, and in part because it was outdoors in lovely weather … The band appeared in gray Winter coats. The instruments were looked upon with great interest by those for whom

the Union is a closed locality. The masses of humanity stood pressed close together, everyone listened attentively to the magnificent sound of the band of Scharach. The program was:

> Overture to *Martha* by Flotow
> *Waldvögel Walzer* by Lanner
> The Soldier's Chorus from *Faust*, by Gounod
> Overture to *Zauberflöte*, by Mozart
> *Radetsky-Marsch* by Strauss
> *Nachtigallen Polka* by Strauss

Finally, the nineteenth-century novelist, Johannes Ziegler, has left a very interesting eyewitness description of a noon concert, in the Burghof in Vienna, given by an Austrian band near the end of the century. Again, it is above all the quality of the performance which the listener remembered.

> In a large circle the regimental musicians have set themselves up, each behind his mobile music stand, with the bandmaster in his feathered hat standing in the middle. He raises his hands and the music begins to play. I don't believe that the St. Mark's Square (in Venice) has any better acoustics than the Vienna inner court, yes I believe the latter gives out an even better sound. Here the tone of the Waldhorns, the deep roaring of the bombardons is so pure, so full, so powerful as is never heard on the St. Mark's Square. As the glitter of the banonets of the troops earlier had pleased, now it was the glitter of the instruments, even more so as the instruments move with the beat as the musicians play. Let people say what they will, the Austrian military music is the best in the world: their ensemble is perfect, their tone pure and it is a pleasure to listen to sixty exemplary players. Many foreign visitors came to hear these noon concerts, but also strolling natives—professors and bureaucrats, painters with red or black beards, ladies … but the music does not last long, soon it is over and the players dissolve themselves into military rows.[34]

If one can judge by the extant repertoire of the French military bands during the second half of the nineteenth century, they too must have had very active concert schedules. The extant *published* repertoire alone includes many hundreds of *original* symphonies, overtures, fantasies, solo and ensemble works with band accompaniment, not to mention thousands of orchestral transcriptions.[35] To me, one of the most interesting forms in France was the *Air varié*. This is typically a set of variations with each section of the band having its own variation to 'show off.' Many of these are of extraordinary diffi-

[34] Quoted in Brixel, *Das ist Österreichs Militär Musik*, 230.

[35] In volume nine of this series shelf-numbers are given for original works, but only very few transcriptions.

culty, indeed one cannot examine these without coming away astounded at the technical level of these nineteenth-century French bands.

There are also extant a great number of lighter works, indicating that these French bands also engaged in performances of a more popular nature. A number of these lighter works, however, seem set aside from the rest and are carefully labeled, 'Concert Polka,' 'Concert Mazurka,' etc.

In England something seems to have gone wrong, aesthetically. There were serious compositions and performances by wind bands in England through the Baroque, but during the Classical Period one finds a strange absence of the original *Harmoniemusik* which was so prominent on the continent. Oddly enough, for a brief period at the beginning of the nineteenth century there is evidence of some interest in serious concert music far military band. In the military 'divertimenti' and 'concerti,'[36] one is impressed by the aesthetic intent, even if the quality is uneven. But these forms rapidly died out and do not appear again after the Napoleonic Wars. It is just at this period, ca. 1820–1850, that one looks in vain for descriptions of the artistic military band concerts which are so frequently described in Germany and Austria.

What went wrong in England? Certainly there can be no doubt with regard to the band's popularity with the public. Military bands were as popular in England as elsewhere during the nineteenth century and important for this reason, for they reached a broad public, an entire working-class of people, who did not feel welcome in the fashionable concert halls. But, the appearance of some fine orchestral transcriptions in the band 'journals' notwithstanding, the broader evidence seems to suggest that in England the bandmasters did not take advantage of the great popularity of their medium to seek to raise the musical understanding of the public, but rather sought to expand the band's popularity by reaching down to select their repertoire at the level of popular taste. An English historian at the beginning of the present century made the same observation, expressed in characteristic example of British tact.

[36] This term has nothing to do with the modern definition, but rather was the final usage of the Baroque *concerto da camera* term to represent an ensemble work for winds. For further information on the development of this form, see volume three of this series.

> The employment of military bands at places of public entertainment enables them to appeal to larger audiences than can be reached even by the leading metropolitan orchestras. At exhibitions and fetes, as well as

at private gatherings, they have enormous opportunities for influencing public taste, and if in turn public taste has reacted on them, it is only fair to say that the musicians of the army in the past—and still more in the present have taken full advantage of the educational openings put before them.[37]

One must mention one notable exception in England: the Royal Artillery Mounted Band, which gave weekly symphonic concerts of transcribed works by Mozart, Haydn, and Beethoven in their complete form.[38] But, as I said, this band was an exception. The aesthetic aim of most military bands during the second half of the nineteenth century in England is perhaps best defined by an expression one used to hear regarding 'concerts' given in Crystal Palace by the best of the London military bands. According to Farmer,[39] one would commonly hear,

> There is no concert to-day, but the band is going to play!

The 1867 World Band Competition in Paris

At no time during the nineteenth century did military bands so capture the attention of the general public as they did on 21 July 1867 when ten bands, representing nine countries, met in Paris for the purpose of artistic competition. This event, organized by Georges Kastner, was held during a great international exhibition and offered a first prize of a gold medal and 5,000 Fr. The jury consisted of twenty men recommended by the participating countries and included distinguished composers, such as A. Thomas, Felicien David, and Leo Delibes, as well the two leading music critics of Europe, Hans von Bülow and Eduard Hanslick.[40]

At 1:00 pm a signal was given and the ten bands, all in new uniforms, marched into the Industrial Palace, where thirty thousand people waited to hear this great competition.[41] The format called for each band to play a required piece, the Overture to *Oberon* by Weber, and one composition of their choice. The first band to perform was the Grenadier Regiment Band from Baden, conducted by Burg. They performed, in addition to the *Oberon*, the 'Finale' to *Loreley* by Mendelssohn. They

[37] William Johnson Galloway, *Musical England* (London: Christopher, 1910), quoted in Farmer, *The Rise and Development of Military Music*, 141.

[38] Ibid., 132. This band received the only Gold Medal given at the International Exhibition in Edinburgh in 1886.

[39] Ibid., 127.

[40] The remaining members of the jury were Général Mellinet, Georges Kastner, Consul Bamberg, E. Boulanger, J. Cohen, Oscar Comettant, Dachauer, Elwertz de Fuertes, Grisar, de Lajarte, Nicolai Romera Adia, Général Rose, Semet, E. von Villiers, and E. Jonas.

[41] Most of these details are taken from Kalkbrenner, *Wilhelm Wieprecht*, 58ff.

were followed by the First Engineer Corps Band from Spain, conducted by Maimo, who performed a 'very good' *Fantaisie* on Spanish melodies composed by Gevaert.

The third performance was by the Prussians, conducted by Wieprecht. This band was actually a combined band, made up of the Second Guard Regiment of Foot and the Second Guard Regiment of Berlin, a step which Wieprecht felt necessary in order to have a band comparable in size with the other countries. Their selected work was a *Fantaisie* on themes from Meyerbeer's *Propheten*, arranged for the occasion by Wieprecht. A reporter from the *Allgemeine Militair Zeitung* wrote of this performance,

> The beauty of the performance was extraordinary. Especially we were pleased by the woodwinds, who distinguished themselves, especially through their tone, purity of intonation, and their unity with the brasses. The applause of the French (9/10th of the audience) was extensive and often repeated.

The Prussians were followed by another outstanding band, the Austrian's 73rd Infantry Regiment Band, conducted by Zimmermann. They performed the Overture to *William Tell* by Rossini and achieved 'lively applause and a great success.'

Next came another combined band, Belgium's Band of the Guides and the Grenadier Regiment, conducted by Bender, performing a *Fantaisie* on themes from *William Tell* 'very well.' They were followed by the Bavarian First Infantry Regiment Band, conducted by Siebenkas, performing the 'Introduction and Bridal Chorus' from *Lohengrin* 'very exactly and tastefully.'

Individual Band Instrumentation
The 1867 World Band Competition in Paris

(Prussia, Baden, Bavaria, Austria, Spain, Netherlands, Belgium, Russia France, Garde Républicaine and France, Guides, as given in Frederick Blume, ed., *Die Musik in Geschichte und Gegenwart* [Kassel, 1949–1968])

	PR	BD	BV	A	ES	NL	BE	RU	FGR	FG
Piccolo	2	1	1	1	1	1	1	1	1	2
Flute	2	2	2	2	2		1	1	2	2
Oboe	3				2	2	2	2	2	3
English horn	1							1		
Small clarinet in A♭	1			2	1					
Small clarinet in E♭	4	2	4	4	2	2	2	2	4	3
Clarinet in E♭	16	15	10	12	13	10	16	15	8	12
Basset horn								1		
Bass clarinet			1	2				1		
Soprano saxophone						1	1	1	2	1
Alto saxophone						1	1	2	2	2
Tenor saxophone						1	1	2	2	1
Baritone saxophone						1	1	3	2	1
Bass saxophone										1
Bassoon	6	2	1	2	3	2	4	2		
Contrabassoon	4				2			1		
Cornet	4	1	3	2	2	2	2	2	4	4
Trumpet	8	5	8	12	6	4	4	8	3	3
Horn	4	3	5	6	4	4	5	8	2	3
Trombone	8	4	3	6	6	3	4	6	5	5
Small bugle		3			1				1	1
Bugle		3	3	6	2	1	2		2	2
Alto saxhorn	4	1	2	3	2	2	1		3	2
Baritone saxhorn	6	3	1	3	2	2		2	2	2
Bass saxhorn	6	1		8	1	2	4		5	6
Contrabass saxhorn in E♭		2	3		2	1	2	3	2	3
Contrabass saxhorn in B♭		3			2	1	3	3	2	2
String bass						3				
Percussion	6	3	4	5	3	5	2	3	3	1
Total	85	54	51	76	59	51	59	70	60	62

A Dutch combined band, consisting of the Chasseurs and Grenadiers conducted by Dunkler, followed with a *Fantaisie* in themes from Gounod's *Faust*, which received much applause, but was judged by one listener as being too long.

Another fine band followed, the French Garde Républicaine Band of Paris, conducted by Paulus, also playing the 'Bridal Chorus' from *Lohengrin*, a performance deemed 'very excellent.' They were followed by the Russian Band of the Mounted Guards, conducted by Dörffeld, performing the Overture to Glinka's *Life of the Tsar* 'very correctly.'

The band of the French National Guard, London, *Illustrated Times*, 1858.

The final band was called the Guides of the Imperial French Guards, but was actually a group of musicians from the theaters of Paris put together only for this performance.[42] They performed, under the leadership of Cressonois, a *Fantaisie* on the 'Carnival of Venice,' arranged in a virtuoso style, but were generally heard as inferior to the other bands.

[42] According to the Parisian newspaper, *Courier française*.

One of the members of the jury, the distinguished critic Hanslick, left his impressions of this afternoon. In particular, he captures for us the enthusiasm of the public, an enthusiasm that almost reads as the description of a great 'popular' concert today!

> It was a tiring piece of work to listen attentively to twenty military band performances in a hall filled with at least 23,000 people, from 1:00 P.M. until 7:00 P.M. My favorite overture, *Oberon*, was made so repelling [through so many performances] at this event that I had to avoid it for several years. But the hard work [of listening] was [repaid] by the shining success of our Austrians. I have never experienced so strongly in myself the feelings of patriotism, which at home so often are asleep or turn critically to the opposite, as at that instant immediately after the astounding performance by the Prussians when our white coats [the traditional dress of the Austrian military] stood themselves in a half-circle. The Prussians had a harvest of applause which could not be exceeded, but after the Austrians played, the hall howled as if in a hurricane; everyone screamed and waved hats and scarves. There was still one serious virtuoso rival, that of the Paris Band, which possessed very good virtuosos and the new Sax instruments; they played with the precision of a clock. It was not easy to decide among these three, so we decided to give three first prizes in equal value to the Austrians, the Prussians, and the French.[43]

As Hanslick indicated, the jury elected to award three first prizes, but it should be noted that the Prussians clearly were the real winners, having received twenty votes in the original balloting, to eighteen for the French and seventeen for the Austrians. The second prize was shared by Bavaria, Russia, and the French Imperial Guards. The third prize was shared by the Dutch, Baden, and Russia and the fourth prize went to Belgium and Spain.

Wieprecht, conductor of the Prussian band, heard in the Austrians a great musicianship; in the French, virtuosity; and attributed his own victory to the Prussian's 'superior musical education, understanding, and technique.'[44] His description of the balloting indicates his initial victory,

> but then the bourgeoisie intervened and the jury left and returned a second time, having decided not to give one 5,000 Fr. prize, but three at 2,500 Fr. General Mellinet had me step forward, announced the results, and asked me if I was satisfied with it—that the Austrians and French be

[43] Quoted in Brixel, *Das ist Österreichs Militär Musik*, 207ff.

[44] Kalkbrenner, *Wilhelm Wieprecht*, 63.

given a share in the laurels. I said yes, naturally, and everyone was happy about it. Especially to me was given, along with the 2,500 Fr. which I gave to my band, and a large gold medal.[45]

[—]

45 Ibid., 64.

After the competition the members of all ten bands were entertained by the Emperor.

> The Emperor Napoleon [III] was prevented from appearing at the competition, due to a death at court. However, he had already the day before, at 6:30 in the evening, had all the musician introduced to him and the Empress in the Tuileries Gardens. He was very personable, had every band play their national anthem and a march, and had the individual bands march past him. On the 30th all the musicians are invited to Versailles for a great festival banquet.[46]

46 *Allgemeine Militair-Zeitung.*

All in all, this competition also represented a great testimonial to the influence of German military music. One notes, for example, that all the conductors were German, save those from France and Spain. This testimonial was observed as well by the *Allgemeine Militair Zeitung.*

> We close our report with the repeated expression of our pleasure of the renewed recognition which the German art has found in foreign lands. In fact, every German can feel proud in the thought that our good German military musicians have achieved, in the height of their accomplishments, such recognition in foreign lands.

A final measure of the enthusiasm of the public can be seen in a 'farewell' concert given by the visiting Austrian band in the famous Tuileries Gardens. It was estimated that 200,000 Parisians (one in five of the inhabitants at this time!) tried to attend this concert. It was said, 'people climbed onto the backs of chairs, onto the backs of their neighbors, trying to see the band.'[47]

47 Brixel, *Das ist Österreichs Militär Musik*, 209.

Military Bands and Opera

The numerous and successful military band concerts created a wide interest on the part of the public. This was a fact not lost on the super-showman, Rossini, who introduced a military band on stage during a performance of *Ricciardo e Zoraide* in 1818.[48] This, in the view of one present day opera scholar

48 Much of this discussion is based on R. M. Longyear's, 'The "Banda sul Palco": Wind Bands in Nineteenth-Century Opera,' *Journal of Band Research* 13, no. 2 (Spring, 1978): 25–40.

was 'clearly a dark day ... for Italian opera,'[49] because the appearance of military bands on stage rapidly became a popular demand.

Gradually the use of the military band in opera began to evolve from mere stage business to a more involved musical role, as one finds in Meyerbeer's *Il Crociato in Egitto* where a band on the stage alternates with the theater orchestra and in one case two bands on stage play antiphonally. Later, in *Le Prophete* (1849), Meyerbeer scored for a full cavalry band in alternation with the pit orchestra. In this case one sees all of the new Sax instruments which had only recently been adopted by the military.

[49] Julian Budden, *The Operas of Verdi* (New York: Praeger, 1973), 1:20.

2 petite saxhorns in E♭
2 first contra-alto saxhorns in B♭
2 second contra-alto saxhorns in B♭
First and second cornets with cylinders in B♭
First and second trumpets with cylinders in B♭
2 first alto saxhorns in E♭
2 second alto saxhorns in E♭
First and second baritone saxhorns in B♭
4 bass saxhorns with cylinders in B♭
2 contrabass saxhorns in E♭
2 Tambours militaires

A similar, musically independent, cavalry band is found in the pages of *Rienzi* by Wagner, here scored for six valve and six natural trumpets, six trombones, four ophicleides, and eight drums. How important was this kind of stage business to Wagner? In a letter of 1842 to a court official, Wagner writes,

> I am not ready to forfeit a single detail of the musical pomp on the stage; it is absolutely necessary and can easily be managed with the help of the military and other musical bands certainly my requirements are not the usual ones—I demand an extraordinary band, not put together like the ordinary band ... See to it that the trumpeters and trombonists accompanying the warlike cortege of Colonna and Orsini in the first act are chosen from the cavalry and appear on horses ... In operas like mine, it must be all or nothing.[50]

[50] Mary Burrell, *Letters of Richard Wagner* (New York: Macmillan, 1950), 103.

In Paris and elsewhere the popularity of the increasingly larger and larger wind bands on stage by mid-century threatened to drown out the music of the opera itself. An appearance by a band of saxhorns[51] on stage during a performance of Halvéy's *Le Juif Errant* in 1852 was heard by one critic as,

> at once shrill and prodigiously voluminous ... Their impression was formidable and out of proportion with the sonorous mass of the orchestra of the [Paris] opera.[52]

By 1863 one finds in Berlioz's *Les Troyens* no fewer than two bands and a wind ensemble, although all were behind the scenes.[53] Verdi, faced with this kind of escalation of instrumental forces in Parisian productions, suggested that the rather innocent off-stage *Harmoniemusik* of the original might be doubled, tripled, or quadrupled as needed, rather than 'modernizing' the band,

> You must adhere strictly to the instruments composing the small orchestra beneath the stage. This little orchestra of two oboes, six clarinets, two bassoons and a contrabassoon produces a sonority that is strange and mysterious, and at the same time calm and quiet, such as other instruments cannot do.[54]

One can see how out of control this all became in a remarkable passage written by Rimsky-Korsakov. He had been asked by the sister to Glinka to reorchestrate that composer's opera, *Russlan and Ludmila*, as the original score had been lost in a theater fire.

> For my part, I was carried away by enthusiasm and did many impractical things, in orchestrating for a military band the respective parts of *Russlan*. Thus in the Introduction to Act I, the band on stage was to be brass, in Glinka's scheme; I followed his idea accordingly, but took a brass band with the full complement current in our Guards regiments. For Act IV, again in accordance with the composer's intentions, I wrote the orchestration for a mixed band of brass and woodwind, both again with the full complement current in the Guards. Thus a performance of *Russlan* called for two complete heterogeneous regimental bands. Glinka himself hardly wanted this! But that is not all. In Act V, I had the imprudence to unite the two bands in full complement—the brass band and the mixed band. The result of this was sonority so deafening that no theatre orchestra could hold its own against it; and this was manifested

[51] Octave saxhorn in B♭, soprano saxhorn in E♭, four contra-alto saxhorns in B♭, three tenor saxhorns in E♭, two baritone saxhorns in B♭, two bass saxhorns in B♭, one contrabass saxhorn in E♭ and one in B♭.

[52] *Dwight's Journal of Music* (1852), 1:101.

[53] I: three oboes and six to eight harps; II: sopranino saxhorn in B♭, 2 natural trumpets in B♭, 2 cornets in B♭, 3 trombones, ophicleide; III: 2 soprano saxhorns in E♭, 2 contra-alto saxhorns in B♭, 2 tenor saxhorns in E♭, 2 contrabass saxhorns in E♭, and cymbals! The one Sax instrument which Berlioz omits, the saxophone, will have its day later. In the *La Legende de St. Christophe* by d'Indy, it is an off-stage saxophone ensemble which accompanies the heavenly choirs!

[54] Quoted in Dyneley Hussey, *Verdi* (New York: Pellegrini and Cudahy, 1949), 149.

once, when Balakireff gave the whole *Russlan* finale at a concert. The theme and all the figures for the strings were completely drowned out by the military bands which performed their parts in my orchestration.[55]

55 Rimsky-Korsakov, *My Musical Life*, 146.

'Popularizing' Orchestral Music

The great bond between military bands and the public, which the above material typifies, did not go unnoticed by composers and publishers, especially in Germany. Several important composers sought out opportunities to have their works arranged for military bands in the hope that the subsequent performances would help to build an audience for the original versions of their music! This point is stressed by Wilhelm Stephan, who, as Inspector of Music for the German Armed Forces, was later a successor to Wieprecht.

> We must realize, however, that in the period before the radio or recordings, it was largely through military music that the work of the great composers, somewhat transformed to be sure, became known to the public through the many military concerts held throughout the country.[56]

56 Stephan, 'German Military Music: An Outline of its Development,' 17.

Thus Liszt, Meyerbeer, and Spontini all asked Wieprecht to transcribe their music for this purpose.[57] In the case of Liszt, when he was in Weimar, the nearby 'Hoboisten-Corps' in Sondershausen seems to have had a special relationship for this purpose.[58]

57 Veit, *Die Blasmusik*, 53.

58 Wilhelm Ehmann, *Tibilustrium* (Kassel: Bärenreiter, 1950), 72.

Wagner's music was, of course, popular with military bands and, remarkable as it may seem, part of *Lohengrin* was performed by a military band in Berlin before the premiere of the opera itself by Liszt and the Weimar Court Opera in 1850.[59] Wagner, himself, makes it quite clear in a letter to Count Redern in Berlin, that he supported such transcriptions and, in fact, he recommends music known to band directors today as 'Elsa's Procession.'

59 Veit, *Die Blasmusik*, 54.

> While I doubt that there are many pieces in my opera that are suitable for production as military music, I permit myself to draw your attention, however, particularly to one number which has gone exceedingly well on parades here in Dresden; I refer to the first section of the fourth

scene of the second Act; it is a kind of March ... that lends itself well to treatment as an effective piece for military band. If now a pendant to this is required, perhaps the Pilgrim's Chorus ... could be chosen.⁶⁰

One nineteenth-century transcription of 'Brünnhilde's Awakening,' from *Siegfried* is of particular interest. It was done by Anton Seidl, one of Wagner's closest protégées and later a famous conductor, together with Gottfried Sonntag, a senior government auditor in Bayreuth. The extant published score (Hanover, Oertel) is a newly orchestrated one by Oskar Junger, but carries a very interesting note relative to the original arrangement.

This work was arranged for military band during the 1770s by Anton Seidl and Gottfried Sonntag for the 7. Bavaria Infantry Regiment in Bayreuth with the *approval* and *under Richard Wagner's Supervision*.

60 Richard Wagner, letter to Friedrich Wilhelm Graf von Redern, dated Dresden, June 26, 1846, in *Sämtliche Briefe* (Leipzig: VEB Deutscher Verlag für Musik, 1983), 2:515:

Ob sich viele Stücke in meiner Oper zur Ausführung durch Militairmusik gut eigenen, muss ich fast bezweifeln; deshalb erlaube ich mir vorzüglich nur auf ein Stück aufmerksam zu machen, welches auch hier in Dresden auf Paraden sich recht gut ausgenommen hat: dies ist das erste Stück der 4ten Scene des zweiten Aktes (der Einzug der Gaste auf Wartburg),—eine Art Marsch mit Chor—H-dur, welcher sich auf entsprechende Art zu einer effektvollen Militar-Musiknummer verwended lässt. Sollte zu diesem nun noch ein Gegenstuck wünschenswerth erscheinen, so könnte dazu vielleicht der Pilgerchor in der ersten Scene des dritten Aktes gewählt werden, für dessen Uebersetzung in die Sprache der Militairmusik ich II den Arrangeur auf des erste Tempo der Ouvertüre verweise, wo dieser Chor für Instrumentalmusik allein verwendet ist; um ibm aber als einzelnem Stücke einen völiigen Schluss zu geben, bitte ich den Arrangeur, die beigelegte Einzelausgabe dieses Chores einzusehen, wo er einen von mir gemachten Schluss zur Benutzung vorfindet.

8   Civic Wind Bands in the German-Speaking Countries

CIVIC WIND BANDS BEFORE 1848

These volumes have traced in some detail the tradition of European civic wind bands during the Middle Ages, Renaissance, Baroque, and Classical Periods. Toward the end of the eighteenth century these institutions, and the ancient guilds which supported them, fade from notice somewhat. This was due primarily for economic reasons, but the rising popularity of civic orchestras played a role as did the presence of military bands quartered in or near many towns, who offered an alternate, less expensive, source of wind music for many of the functions formerly filled by the city musicians.

The period of 1785–1815 saw the development of a new civic institution, the civic milita, sometimes called Schützenkompagnien in Germany and 'Volunteers' in England. These units of civilian-soldiers reflected a political and social scene which was very much dominated by the military and the natural desire of the public to be involved. These militia bands should be thought of as civic bands, and not as authentic military bands, although some of the characteristics of the military they imitated would remain characteristics of German civic bands to the present day (such as the style of the uniforms).

The instrumentation of these new civic militia bands was based on the most popular wind medium of the immediate past, the so-called *Harmoniemusik*, an ensemble with a nucleus of either pairs of oboes or clarinets, with horns and bassoons, to which were added the new 'türkish' percussion instruments.[1] Elsewhere in this series, I have listed the extensive repertoire of the English militia bands. For the German-speaking countries, there are also extant examples of music written specifically for these civic militia bands, although the surviving repertoire is not so extensive as that of England. German examples are the *Geschwindmarsch der Dresdener Communalgarde* by Lasek, the *Der bayerische Schützenmarsch* by Stuntz, and even a *Marsch für Prager Schützengarde* by Carl Maria von

[1] Degele, *Die Militärmusik*, 114, table 4, note 2.

Weber. Austrian examples include the *Marsch der Wiener Bürger* by Eppinger and the *Marsch* 'für das Bürgerl. Schütz en-Corps, Innsbruck, 1819' by Johann Baptist Gansbacher.

While these early nineteenth-century German civic bands bore a new name, and had new instruments and uniforms, their organization was modeled along the lines of civic bands of ancient tradition. One can see this in a document, dated 1806, from the town of Stühlingen, which is quoted by Wolfgang Suppan in his outstanding book on the wind bands of Baden.[2] Because of the extraordinary interest of this memorandum by the civic official, Schwab, I should like to quote it in entirety.

[2] Suppan, *Blasmusik in Baden*, 140ff.

> The local citizens are deserving of praise for their admirable accomplishments in the acquisition of the [new] türkish instruments. Even higher offices have commended the praiseworthy efforts in the organization of this music and money has been provided for this purpose. My predecessor, Herr Court Councilor and Oberamtmann Baur, has with much difficulty and exertion taken care of the organization and Herr Lieutenant Fredle, through his exemplary patience, has taken care of the education of the band members so that in a short time the türkish music of this town has been brought into such perfection that the members of this praiseworthy institution have earned the applause of the citizens and the neighborhood. The enthusiasm with which the citizen-sons of this town have used their free time for the pleasant entertainment, which has brought them usefulness and to the listeners enjoyment, has been praised by all. I, myself, upon taking my office here, have enjoyed noticing that the improvement of the band has been praised from afar.
>
> Recently, however, the enthusiasm of the band members seems to have cooled, the practicing has been interrupted, and the well-known obstacles of these times of war have hindered the advancement of this institution. I have seen, to my sorrow, that the unity of the band members, which previously we had praised so much, is no longer present.
>
> The main reasons, at least in so far as they are known to me, can be summarized in the following points, which I wish the band members would discuss and come to an agreement. They are the following: A. Organization; B. Suborganization; C. Rehearsals; D. Care of the instruments; and E. the Accounting of income, tips and *Dovceren*, attendance, all of which has as its concern the appropriate distribution of monies to the members. I wish to say in advance, however, that each point is only my opinion. The band members should not see this as a regulation or a command, but simply a rough draft, which in the future I will alter and correct according to their wishes.

A. Organization. Each society must choose, for the maintenance of order, a chairman, who should be concerned with the leadership of the whole. In music, this person is called the Kapellmeister. It is not my place to comment on the duties of the Kapellmeister in so far as they are concerned with musical talent and the art itself, however in so far as he is the leader of a society, I believe it is necessary for him to determine when and where the musical appearances will be held—and who should attend—and the repertoire. The Kapellmeister should be elected through a majority of the votes to a one year term of office.

B. Suborganization. If the Kapellmeister is the leader of a society, then I believe the members should be required to give him not only the necessary attention, but also obedience. Obedience, however, is limited to matters of music, that is:

1. To appear when the bandmaster commands it.
2. Not to assemble without telling the bandmaster the reasons.
3. Through a majority of the votes, the bandmaster should decide who receives the *Dovceren*, which is distributed to the band each six months, taking into consideration penalties assessed against those who missed rehearsals or actual performances during this time.
4. Whoever resigns from the band must return his instrument to the bandmaster.
5. Whoever resigns from the band loses the right to wear the band uniform, or must at least remove the green collar and lapels.
6. Anyone who appears at a performance without his uniform is fined as if he were missing. At rehearsals one may dress as he wishes.
7. The band member who is newest, not the youngest, must make the announcements to the band regarding the schedule.
8. Anyone resigning without cause must pay the society 3 Gulden toward the cost of educating a replacement, unless he has instructed a successor in his instrument.
9. Each member is required to accept an apprentice, if one desires to study his instrument; the teacher receives the *Dovceren* for the first half-year, which would ordinarily go to the apprentice.

C. Rehearsals. The bandmaster is required to hold rehearsals, both with the entire band and in sectionals, on Sundays and holidays, although members should never be required to stay more than one hour. He who can excuse himself before the rehearsal because of a compelling reason will not be counted absent. No excuses will be allowed for missing performances.

D. Care of Instruments. The bandmaster is required to see that the [city] instruments are distributed and not lost or damaged. A list should be maintained and signed by those who are issued instruments, as they are responsible for them. If one damages an instrument without cause, he must pay for it from his own funds. Incidental repairs will be paid from the band funds. Without the previous knowledge of the bandmaster, no changes or repairs should be made to any [city] instrument.

E. Accounting. It is necessary to observe justice in the distribution of monies and to be able to pay for the necessary repairs and the purchase of music. The accountant should therefore have a daily book of the income from *Dovceren* and gifts which come to the society. He also keeps a list of those who receive penalties due to absences. He should keep a list of repairs and purchases, but not purchase anything without a majority vote by the members. In addition to the usual *Dovceren*, it is important to encourage donations from the public. Therefore on St. Cecilia's Day the band will march through the village with complete türkish music. This is in thanks for the support of the band and to encourage further donations. On this day the bandmaster and the accountant should go around to each citizen and make an accounting of past donations, missed donations, and received donations.

In closing, I appeal to those former members of the türkish music, who through perhaps one or another oversight have received an insult, to forget the past and rejoin the band. I promise each and everyone of you, according to my possibilities, support and help with their complaints. I request one and all to meet each other with brotherly accord and love, in order to bring honor to the society and to maintain the reputation of the band.

Stühlingen, Aug. 3, 1806 v. Schwab

The statutes for the militia band of the German village 'of Oppenauer in 1824 were very similar.[3]

[3] Ibid., 113–114.

1. Each member is required to give the bandmaster his most respectful attention.
2. Everyone must take care of his own instrument. If a [city] instrument is damaged during official service, it will be repaired and paid for from the military or church funds. If it is damaged when not in official use, the player must pay for the repairs.
3. Everyone is responsible for his music; if the music is lost, the player must pay 2 kr per page for copying.
4. Everyone must attend rehearsals as required.

5. All conversation is forbidden during the time music is being played.
6. The bandmaster will determine the repertoire.
7. Playing without direction (Nebenblasen) is forbidden unless permission is given.
8. If one appears and his keys are not working, and this also applies to horn and other [brass] players, he will be fined 12 kr.
9. Talking about the society is forbidden.
10. No one is allowed to take offense at the directions of the director.

The bandmaster described in these documents was not a military person, but usually a civilian who, in addition to his civic militia band duties, would often direct the church music of the town and perhaps teach school. In some cases he was perhaps not even paid for his service with the militia band, as one can see in the example of a Mr. Haberer, who directed the civic militia band in Sackingen. This town on the upper Rhine had, in 1836, forty-two citizens listed on the roles of the militia, of which twenty-four were in the band. In a memorandum of 1840 to the city leaders, Haberer notes,

> As is well-known, I am not required to instruct or lead the military band of this town. Until now I have done this as a hobby and I hope it will be understood I have done this with pleasure. I have invested more time and effort in the militia band than the noble town councilor, or even my friends, can measure. My engagement contract says nothing about the maintenance of a town militia band, but only requires me to instruct the youth and lead the church choir. I praise myself that I have taken care of my job and have established in this town a very good church music, which has earned precedence over all neighboring towns. I also maintain the hope that, through tireless instruction of the youth in music and their fast progress, the town council as well as the parents are satisfied [with my work]. I believe I have done all that was possible in this respect for the advancement of the general good.[4]

[4] Quoted in ibid., 142ff.

Because these institutions, town, church, and school, were so closely related, the militia band rehearsals were sometimes held in the school building. Suppan quotes an interesting complaint, by a teacher in Obenwolfach, over the noise made by the meetings of the civic militia band in the nearby school house.

> The band is a so-called türkish music, which, as everyone knows, makes a great deal of noise … I have three children, of which the youngest needs to go to bed early and who is often awakened by this noise and can not go back to sleep … One can see that the above-mentioned musicians are not considerate of the teacher and his family in the example of the night of May 1, when the musicians caroused and roughhoused until 4 A.M.

The letter also referred to the consequent 'nervous headaches' of the mother-in-law, which perhaps influenced the city fathers, who forbade further rehearsals in the school building.[5]

The functions these civic bands filled during the first half of the nineteenth century included, of course, appearances at all important civic celebrations. Again, because of the close relationships between the institutions of the town, these celebrations were often church or school related as well as civic in character. The contribution of music to these celebrations was appreciated by the civic government. A typical document from 1840 in Sackingen, reads,

> We can not fail to recognize that through the civic militia band those church and other festivals have been raised and have received a higher value. Just for the civic militia alone, this band is indispensable. The efforts and accomplishments up to now of the civic militia band have earned, certainly, our entire recognition.[6]

A similar civic document, from Zell am Harmersbach, saw in addition an economic value for the town.

> [The civic band] is proved to be a musical education for the sons of the town, because through them anyone is given the opportunity to learn any instrument without cost. On the other hand, this band, when it is in a state of perfection—which is possible only through frequent rehearsals, very often draws, on the high festival days, many visitors to the community, which has economic importance for every citizen.[7]

Most of the functions of the civic wind bands from the Middle Ages, Renaissance, and Baroque had now disappeared. Only the occasional observance of 'tower music' reminded the listener of the ancient traditions, as was the case reported by an Englishman visiting in Leipzig in 1827.

---

[5] Ibid., 166. I am reminded of a similar contemporary story, but with quite a different solution. A citizen, who lived near a large university in the United States, complained constantly to the university regarding the 'noise' of the large marching band which held rehearsals in a field adjacent to his house. This wealthy university simply bought the protester's house, moved him out and tore the house down. Now the marching band could continue its rehearsals in peace, for the neighbors did not fail to understand what was expected of them!

[6] Quoted in ibid., 142–143.

[7] Quoted in ibid., 166.

From the balcony of the ancient Stadt-Haus in Leipzig the inhabitants are regaled three mornings in a week with an instrumental concert, which is played by the town musicians purely for the amusement of the citizens. Perhaps the magistrates who instituted this regulation were influenced by Shakespeare's idea, that the love of music keeps people honest; at all events it is pleasant to find such a sauce sweetening the dry counting-house negotiations, the agreements, contracts, and acceptances which occupy the time of this mercantile city.

......

The echo of the first blast of instruments from the flag-stone pavement across the wide market-place soon brings together a musical crowd for half an hour's enjoyment. The music, after a full overture or two, always concludes with a simple chorale, which, softly breathed from four trombones produces one of the most delicate combinations I ever heard; though a great part of the audience vanishes at its commencement.[8]

One of the largest portions of the extant repertoire of the civic bands in the German-speaking countries, and certainly the most musically valuable portion of that literature, is the music composed for performance together with civic, amateur choral societies. These singing societies had their origin in small societies called *Liedertafeln* which, toward the end of the eighteenth century, met once a week in a local Gasthaus for beer and singing.[9] In the years following the Napoleonic Wars, these societies spread rapidly and often became very nationalistic. These compositions were written for normal concert appearances as well as for almost every imaginable kind of civic celebration, together with more specialized events centering on Freemasonry, hunting, student life, and gymnastics. This great body of choral repertoire includes numerous works with band accompaniment, a repertoire all the more valuable as it includes contributions by some of the greatest nineteenth-century masters.

Among those examples of works composed for choral society concerts is the beautiful *Begräbnisgesang*, op. 13, by Brahms for chorus and wind band. This work was given its first performance in the Gradener's Academy in Hamburg in 1859 and was described by Clara Schumann as 'most glorious.' We should not forget the lovely *Four Songs*, op. 17, for voices, horns, and harp, which Brahms composed for a ladies chorus of whom he, himself, was the regular conductor. Another important work which Brahms often conducted was his *Ellens Zweiter Gesang* for female voices with six winds. Similarly, Robert Schumann

[8] Holmes, *A Ramble Among the Musicians of Germany*, 254–256. Holmes also heard the famous trombonist, Queisser, to whom Wieprecht was a competitor during his residence in Leipzig.

> Here in one of the suburban gardens, may be occasionally heard the famed trombonist M. Queisser, by his townsmen vaunted the greatest performer of the whole empire. He is himself the proprietor of this rural retreat, having captivated the affections and wedded the form of its female possessor, thus enticing the inhabitants to discuss his viands, and enhancing his fortune, as host, by means of his music. I have heard nothing so soft, round, and deep as the tone of this extraordinary player, who has, at the age of twenty-seven, attained the most surprising mastery. At the late music meeting in Zerbst he performed a concertino on his instrument, which will not be soon forgotten. The palm of excellence for the knack in the management of wind instruments must certainly be given to Germany: in this performer there was no appearance of exertion, and the horrors of apoplexy with which swollen veins and starting eyes fill one in ordinary players, were here wholly dismissed from the mind.

[9] Mary Rasmussen, 'The First Performance of Mendelssohn's *Festgesang, An die Kuenstler*, Op. 68,' *Brass Quarterly* (Summer, 1961), 153.

composed his *Jagdlieder*, op. 137, with horns, for a male chorus he conducted, as well as his beautiful *Beim Abschied zu singen*, op. 84 (1847), for band and mixed chorus, composed for a choral society he founded.

The strong sense of German nationalism which began to be felt during the nineteenth century was also expressed through numerous patriotic works for band and chorus. An early example is, of course, the *Bundeslied*, for voices and winds by Beethoven. The large-scale works of this genre often were composed for civic celebrations in honor of various great men of the German culture. In 1840, for example, cities throughout Germany celebrated the four hundredth anniversary of the printing of the Guttenberg bible. On 24 June 1840, for this celebration in Leipzig Mendelssohn composed his *Festgesang* for male chorus and two brass choirs, the second movement of which is the original version of the music we know today as 'Hark! the herald angels sing' (the original 'Gut–ten–berg, becomes 'glo–ry to' etc.). For an identical celebration on the very same day in Frankfurt, another *Festgesang* was performed, here a work for male chorus with large wind orchestra, composed by Joseph Stuntz (1793–1859).[10]

A great variety of other German writers, artists, and musicians were celebrated in similar ceremonies and are memorialized by the repertoire which is extant today. Some representative examples are: a *Gesang* (1870) by Eduard Grell (1800–1886), for male chorus and brass band, for the unveiling of a monument to Hegel; an *Overture* by Fr. Rosenkranz, on the one hundredth anniversary of the birth of Schiller; the Mendelssohn *Cantata* (1828),[11] for male chorus and wind band, for an Albrecht Dürer commemoration in Berlin; and the Joseph Stuntz *Festgesang*, for male chorus and wind orchestra, for the unveiling of a memorial to Gluck.

Another category of the repertoire is the music composed to help celebrate civic festivals devoted to music and the arts. One example is the Stuntz *Bankett Lied* (1840) for an 'Artist's carnival.' In this connection one also immediately thinks of the *Fanfare Zur Eröffnung der Musikwoche der Stadt Wien* and the *Festmarsch der Stadt Wien* by Strauss, although these are for winds alone. A German–Flemish Choral Festival, held in Köln in 1846, commissioned the *An die Künstler*, op. 68, by Mendels-

[10] In the same year, apparently as part of the same celebrations, the *Messe 'St. Louis Philippi'* by Sigismund Neukomm was performed by a chorus of two thousand and a large military band in the Place de Guttenberg, in Mainz. There is also by this composer a *Grand Choeur*, composed for the unveiling of a monument to Guttenberg in Strasbourg, which was performed in 1837 by more than twelve hundred performers, including singers and both military and civic bands.

[11] Lost during World War II.

sohn. This work, for male chorus and brass, was performed by a chorus of three thousand and immediately repeated on the demand by the audience.[12]

The laying of cornerstones for important new civic buildings was another cause for civic celebration. Thus, for example, we have the *Festkantate* (1842) by Karl Leibl (1784–1870), for the laying of the cornerstone of the Köln Cathedral, and the *Festgesang* by Johann Herbeck (1831–1877), for the laying of the cornerstone of the 'new University in Vienna.'[13]

Occasionally various lay societies would commission such music to enrich their celebrations. Examples which come to mind are Mendelssohns's *Begrüssung* (1828), for male chorus, winds, celli, and bass, composed for a Nature society in Berlin and the *Freimauercantate* by Georg Zulehner (1770–1841), for male chorus and winds.[14] Even for such an occasion as the launching of a new ship on the Starnberger See, called for the composition of *Das Dampfschiff*, for male chorus and brass, by Stuntz in 1851!

Before leaving the discussion of the first half of the nineteenth century, I should add that the diaries of travelers mention hearing wind bands and ensembles which were civilian, yet not the official civic wind bands. These were ensembles hired by the city, and sometimes privately, for the enjoyment of the general public.

The traveling Englishman, Holmes, heard this kind of wind ensemble performing in the public gardens in Vienna in 1827.

> After the theatre, which is soon over, the sound of various bands of music invite the passenger to take his supper in open gardens. No place of refreshment, from the highest to the lowest, is without music; bassoons and clarionets are as 'plenty as blackberries.'[15]

Two years later, another visiting Englishman, Novello, observed the same kind of music in Vienna, but found less pleasure in the musicianship he heard.

> Visited the principal Garden (Volksgarten) as we were told that there was to be an Orchestra of wind. To our great disappointment there were only 2 Clarinets, 2 Horns, 2 Bassoons with a Double Fagotto. As we entered they were playing a poor commonplace Waltz. On requesting they would be so good as to play something of Mozart or Haydn the man said, 'O yes, Mozart or Rossini'—but I said, 'No Rossini—some

---

[12] A reporter from the *Neue Zeitschrift für Musik* (1846), Nr. 25, 6–8, 10–12, reports flower-decked streets, cheering crowds, and general civic harmony on the day of this festival, but another reporter, in the *Allgemeine musikalische Zeitung* (1846), Nr. 48, 473–476, speaks of a climate of bitterness and disappointment due to the failure of the festival to live up to its pretensions and the selfishness and mismanagement of the German organizing committee.

[13] Another composition possibly composed for a university occasion is Mejo's *Variations on Gaudeamus igitur* for piccolo, four clarinets, bassoons, three horns, three trombones, and serpent.

[14] A work composed for a similar purpose is the *Feierlicher Einzug Der Ritter des Johanniter-Ordens* (1909) by Strauss.

[15] Holmes, *A Ramble Among the Musicians of Germany*, 137–138.

air of Mozart.' He accordingly went away for the purpose of telling his companions our wishes—but instead of what we had requested they played the Cavatina in A flat (transposed and thereby spoiled to the key of C) and I really believe that they had not a single piece of Mozart in all their book and probably thought we should not detect the difference. They next played two pieces from Auber's 'Muette de Portici' which seems to be all the rage here as well as in every other place I have yet been at in Germany the performance was in every respect totally unworthy of a musicians's notice.

……

The Caroline Gardens [presently, the Stadtpark] as, for want of a better name, I shall term them, are a kind of Vauxhall upon a very small scale. The walks are lighted with small lamps. There is a little orchestra in the centre, filled by about ten or a dozen performers on clarionets and other wind instruments and there are benches placed round for those who choose to sit and take refreshments. The performers here were a better class than those I had heard before at the Volksgarten but the pieces they played were not a whit better, nothing but waltzes, eternal commonplace waltzes.[16]

[16] Novello, *A Mozart Pilgrimage*, 145, 160–161.

In Munich, Novello heard a small wind ensemble of an even lower order, casual musicians who played for donations from members of the dining public. Interestingly enough, however, he found this little band rather musical.

During Dinner, some itinerant Musicians played at the door of the antechamber. There were two Clarinets and two Horns. The performers were much better than what we had heard on the preceding day or two. The piece which pleased me best was the charming Air in Der Freischütz, 'Through the Forest,' which was played with feeling and appropriate expression especially by the 1st Clarionet; on this occasion it was transposed to F, but I prefer it in its original key of E flat.[17]

[17] Ibid., 59.

Civic Wind Bands after Mid-Century

The civic militia bands could not avoid becoming involved in the civil strife of 1848 and this resulted in their being banned, together with the civil militia itself, after that date. However, a new law of 1851, the Land Club and Assembly Law, allowed the establishment of civic bands, provided they were organized only as civic clubs.

The vigilance with which the regional government oversaw such organizations can be seen in an incident in 1862 which occurred in Zizenhausen, in Baden. An official, named Hatz, saw an advertisement for a concert by a band which had not been officially chartered and issued the following order.[18]

[18] Quoted in Suppan, *Blasmusik in Baden*, 135ff.

> Since the Brass Music Society has up to this time not received the police allowance or permit for their existence, and have not requested the same, the head teacher, Winterhalter, is to be told to immediately submit the statutes of this society for examination and approval. Otherwise we shall be required to take action according to the regulations of the Club and Assembly Law.

The following day the conductor, Valentin Winterhalter answered.

> 1. A society with fixed statutes has up to now not existed under my leadership. The rehearsals thus far were simply music education and a time of testing to determine if it were possible to found a society from which one could possibly expect more than the usual dance music and also to determine if I could find it possible to associate myself with such a society without pay or not. I have convinced myself of the same and according to this the society will actually be founded during this week and the statutes will be submitted to the Grand Duke's regional office for review without delay.
>
> 2. In order to show the parents and friends of the musicians what we have learned in the time of a quarter of a year, I have ordered a performance in the school house on the 6th of the month. Following the request of many musical friends, this concert was however held in the [larger] local Brauhaus ... There has never been any talk of a public performance, since such a thing with people who mostly have never played music and only had lessons for a quarter of a year this is simply impossible. Accordingly no admission was charged. The advertisement which appeared in the *Nellenburge Boten* was unknown to me up to the 6th of the month.

Even though these bands often still called themselves 'civic' bands, their by-laws now in fact read more like the by-laws of a democratic club, rather than those of the past which followed aristocratic models. The 1878 statutes of the civic band in Neuenburg (refounded in 1865) even allowed the members themselves to decide, by ballot, on the acceptance of performances.

> Before public performances, concerts, dance festivals, or funeral music may be played, the club must meet and the event in question can be carried out only if there is a majority in favor … If then such a performance takes place, in no circumstances may a member choose not to participate.[19]

[19] This information is taken from ibid., 174.

These same statutes limited membership to persons of irreproachable character over the age of fourteen. The prospective member submitted an application which the members accepted or rejected by secret ballot. Members were fined 10 pfenning for missing rehearsals without an excuse. A heavier fine of 3 Marks was assessed to those who failed to live up to the standards of deportment, which called for behaving tactfully and the avoidance of drinking, dissension, and fist-fighting!

Another paragraph is very interesting. Since the new civic bands were now more democratic and were free of the functional obligations which were the foundation of the ancient civic bands, it was now possible for a band to consider its *primary* purpose as being performance as an art. This was clearly an important objective for this band in Neuenburg, as one can read in the definition of their purpose.

> The purpose of this club is to awaken the sense of that which is lovely and noble in the people through the performance of selected musical compositions and to entertain and bring pleasure to said people.

The use of the word 'entertain' (unterhalten) here was in the sense of 'delight.' The civic militia bands in Vienna, however, not only continued into the second half of the nineteenth century, but were truly entertainment bands in the modern sense, participating in the famous waltzes and marches which one still associates with that city. Indeed, the famous creators of that new style were also bandmasters of regiments of the civic militia—Johann Strauss, Senior, was bandmaster of the First Vienna Burger Regiment and Josef Lanner was bandmaster of the Second Vienna Burger Regiment. While the orchestral waltzes and marches are the more famous, all the contributors to that literature also composed similar original works for band as well.

The most valuable information on the spread of the popularity of civic wind bands during the second half of the nineteenth century is found in a world survey of civic band organizations, conducted just after the beginning of the present century by the Orphéon Society in Paris.[20] Unfortunately, this survey only reflects the reports which were returned from correspondents and is quite incomplete for Germany as a whole. Few details are given, for example, for Prussia.

[20] Maréchal and Parès, *Monographie Universelle de L'Orphéon*.

The correspondent from the area of Alsace-Lorraine (then part of the German-speaking region) gave the names of nearly forty wind band societies. Most were thirty members or so in size, but several were larger than fifty and one, the Harmonie de Schiltigheim, was a band of seventy.

The participation in music in general can be seen in a reference to Mannheim, which with a population of only 160,000 had fifty-three adult musical societies (choral, orchestral, and band).

For most towns and provinces only the total numbers of civic band societies are given, but these are often impressive:

City of Bremen: Nine civic band societies.
City of Hamburg: Eight civic band societies.
Province of Hanover: 'A great number of civic band societies, the city of Hanover alone with eight. This province also has three schools of music devoted only to wind instruments.'
Province of Prussia: Approximately sixty-three civic band societies.
Province of Saxe-Meiningen: Thirteen civic band societies are cited as examples.
Realme of Württemberg: Seventy-three civic band societies.

For Austria, the only details given are for Vienna, where a correspondent reported ten civic band societies, each with forty to fifty players.

The correspondent from Switzerland cited an astounding total of eight hundred civic wind bands (Harmonie) and civic brass band (Fanfare) societies! By regions, these were described as follows:

French Switzerland: Twenty-one wind band societies, of which the most famous was the *Musique de Landwehr* (militia) of Fribourg and the *Harmonie nautique* and *Musique de Landwehr* in Geneve.

The Fribourg civic band was formed in 1804 as a militia band, which, the correspondent writes, during celebrations accompanied patriotic choral music and performed various 'morceaux de musique.' On April 16, 1804, the band of eighteen players was taken over by the French troops.

In 1813 the band was reorganized under the name, *Musique militaire pour la ville de Fribourg*, and reorganized again in 1848 under the name, *Harmonie*. The first saxophone solo to be heard in Switzerland occurred with this band in 1852.

The band took the title, *Corps de musique volontaire de Landwehr*, in 1879 and by the end of the century had an instrumentation of three flutes, oboe, eight clarinets, three saxophones, five cornets, two trumpets, five B♭ bugles, 2 E♭ bugles, eight alto horns, three baritones, four trombones, three tubas, five contrabasses, and five percussion.

In 1906 the band hosted a national band contest with seventy visiting bands totaling approximately two thousand musicians.

The *Harmonie nautique* of Genève was founded in 1883 with thirty-five players and in the first year gave nine concerts. The following year the band had grown to fifty-two players; by 1886, sixty-four players under the name *Harmonie nautique*; in 1887, sixty-nine players; and in 1889, ninety-two players, who toured to Marseille, Toulon, and Lyon. The repertoire included a broad range of transcriptions, including one by G. Parès of the Berlioz *Symphonie fantastique*.

The *Musique de Landwehr* of Genève took part in the campaigns under Napoleon. By the end of the century it was a band of ninety-five players.

German Switzerland: One hundred civic wind band societies, of which the most famous were in Luzern, Berne, Bale, St. Gall, and Zürich.

Italian Switzerland : The correspondent cites only the outstanding band in Lugano, which, by the way, remains a distinguished band today.

The correspondent from Switzerland also gave very interesting details regarding the national civic band contests sponsored by the *Société fédérale*. The most recent contest, as of his writing, was one in 1909 in which fifty civic brass bands and thirty-five civic wind bands participated. The schedule of activities was as follows:

First day:
7:00 P.M. Reception
8:00 P.M. First Concert

Second day:
5:00 A.M. Call to Awake
6:00 A.M. Assembly of the Delegates
8:00–11:00 A.M. Competitive performances in three different locations
1:00–5:00 P.M. Continuation of competition

5:00 P.M. Procession of the civic officials from the participating cities.
6:00 P.M. Concert of choral units, formed from within the civic bands
7:00 P.M. Banquet
8:00 P.M. Concert by the host city

Third day:
5:00 A.M. Call to Awake
7:00 A.M. to Noon. Continuation of competition Noon Official Banquet
2:00–4:00 P.M. Continuation of competition
6:00 P.M. Announcement of the results and the distribution of prizes
7:00 P.M. Banquet
8:00 P.M. Concert by the host city

The regulations for this contest included the following:

Each band was to tune to A=435

Each band performed a work of their choice, another selected by the National Federation, and had to sight-read a third.

Bands were entered in categories according to the numbers of band members who were professional musicians.

The adjudicators were three bandmasters, either foreign or Swiss, who were not participating in the competition.

The performances were judged on the basis of 'harmony, rhythm, dynamics, artistic conception and total effect'

The resultant scores enabled a band to win descriptive titles ranging from the 'Laural Crown of Gold,' down to the 'Oak Laural.'

The official instrumentation was fixed at:

conductor
D♭ piccolo
flute
E♭ clarinet
clarinet (in three parts)
small E♭ bugle (in two parts)
cornet (in three parts)
E♭ horns (in three parts)
B♭ baritone (in three parts)
B♭ euphonium
trombones (in three parts)
bombardons (in E♭ and D♭)
small and large drum

This same survey gives an insight into the extraordinary brass band popularity during the second half of the nineteenth century.[21] For Germany, a correspondent from Württemberg counted no fewer than one thousand five hundred and sixty civic brass bands! No less surprising is the size of some of these bands, the one in Strasbourg given as ninety players!

The correspondent from Switzerland accounts for five hundred and ninety-seven civic brass bands and includes some interesting details regarding a few individual bands. The most extensive account is for a civic brass band called, *Musique militaire les Armes réunies de Chaud-de-Fonds.* The roots of this brass band, like all brass bands are found in the trumpet choir, but a true brass band society was founded in 1831. Among the articles drawn up at that time, one finds the following:

> Rehearsal dates and place were to be determined by the Society. They began at 8:00 p.m. during the period of March 15 to September 15, during the rest of the year, at 7:00 p.m. Rehearsals lasted two hours. Members who were late to rehearsal, or left early, were fined.
>
> During the rehearsal, there was no individual playing between pieces permitted.
>
> Each year, during the first rehearsal in April, each member was examined individually in the performance of his music. If he failed this examination, he had one month to prepare himself.
>
> One who insulted other members could be expelled by a secret vote by the members.
>
> New members were approved by a vote of the membership. They were to pay a membership fee and had to agree in writing to the articles of the Society.

The instrumentation of this band in 1834 was two trumpets, 2 ophicleides with keys, trombone, small E♭ bugle, two B♭ bugles with keys, E♭ clarinet (made of brass), piccolo (also made of brass), and 'other brass instruments.'

A political incident in 1840 resulted in a ban on the performances of the band, although during this period they continued rehearsals in secret. The activities of the band included 'numerous concerts,' together with appearances at political events and civic celebrations.

[21] Suppan, *Blasmusik in Baden*, reproduces numerous nineteenth-century photographs of civic brass bands, many with from six to twelve members. An engraving in the *Illustrated Leipzig Zeitung* (May 20, 1893) shows a nine-member brass band of civilians on a ship, hired to entertain the passengers.

Several other large civic brass bands were also cited by the Swiss correspondent, among them the *Musique d'élite de Genève*, with ninety members, and the *Musique municipale de Saint-Gall*, with fifty members. The *Musique militaire du Locle* was a civic brass band of sixty members, which included saxophones in its instrumentation.

9　*Civic Wind Bands in France*

THE GREAT IMPETUS OF CIVIC BAND MUSIC begun in Paris in 1790, which resulted in great civic festival compositions for band and chorus, as well as serious and important overtures and symphonies for concert use, unfortunately came to an abrupt end with the arrival of Napoleon just before the nineteenth century. There continued, however, occasional civic fêtes in the spirit of those of the revolutionary days and two of those resulted in band compositions which are quite extraordinary.

The first of these was a ceremony to accompany the removal of the remains of Louis XVI and Marie Antoinette to a more appropriate location. It is one of the interesting ironies of history that the French would celebrate this king, whose head they had so recently removed. Nevertheless, the ceremony occurred on 21 January 1815, and the central musical work was a great Requiem for chorus and band by Charles Nicholas Bochsa.[1]

The Bochsa *Requiem for Louis XVI* is a massive work in fifteen movements for ATB chorus, with pairs of flutes, oboes, clarinets, bassoons, four horns, four trumpets, trombone, serpent, and percussion. After a haunting and beautiful opening 'Marche funèbre,' which shares similar melodic motifs and the solo gong with the Gossec *Marche lugubre*, there follows all the major movements of a full Requiem Mass. The soloistic and highly imaginative treatment of the wind band sets this work apart from all earlier large band repertoire. Not only are there movements with solo English horn ('Christe Eleison' and 'Recordare') and French horn ('Pie Jesu'), but even a movement for *Harmoniemusik* (pairs of clarinets, horns, and bassoons), the 'Liber scriptus.' The hour-long work concludes with a 'Recitative' (basically, saying 'we are sorry we cut off your head Louis!') and an 'Apotheose,' the entrance of Louis XVI into heaven, accompanied by his aristocratic trumpets and simulated cannons!

The second of these extraordinary band works was commissioned for a similar fête, this one involving the removal of the remains of the heros of the Revolution of 1830 to a

[1] Bochsa (1781–1855) was a composer of quite above average talent and for a time was one of the leading composers of France, contributing eight successful operas to the Opéra-Comique. As has sometimes been the case with others, Bochsa has not received his appropriate notice in history texts due to his character flaws. After having been charged and sentenced to twelve years in prison for forgery, Bochsa fled to England where he quickly rose to the top of English musical society as a member of the Royal Academy. Here he was involved in some form of swindle, so he eloped with the wife of his rival conductor, Sir Henry Bishop, and set out for the New World. He gave concerts in New York, crossed America by train to San Francisco, and died in Australia—but not before composing another Requiem for himself. Bochsa was a famous performer on the harp and an English contemporary provides a brief picture of the man and his harp playing:

> Mr. Bochsa in his performance displayed great powers of execution, and his music was scientific and pleasing; but there is something repulsive in a gigantic sort of a personage like Mr. Bochsa playing on so feminine an instrument as the harp, whose strings, in my opinion, should only be made to vibrate by the delicate fingers of the ladies (W. T. Parke, *Musical Memoirs* [New York: Da Capo Press, 1970], 183).

newly constructed monument in the Place de la Bastille. The government minister in charge, M. de Rémusat, commissioned a Symphony for band by Berlioz as the centerpiece of this celebration.

The only insights Berlioz left us regarding the actual composition of this Symphony are his rather patriotic sounding ideas on the relationship of his music with the ceremony itself and a very interesting discussion of his struggle to compose the beginning of the third movement.

> I wished to recall the famous Three Days' conflict with the mournful expressions of a march which contains at once terror and grief, to accompany the procession [to the monument]; following this, a sort of funeral oration, or farewell to the illustrious dead, to be played as the remains were lowered into the monument; and finally a hymn of glory, an apotheosis, to be performed after the sealing of the tomb, when the eyes of the public should be concentrated on the column, on the figure of Liberty with her wings outstretched to heaven like the souls of those who died for her.
>
> ......
>
> When I had finished the march and the funeral oration, and found a theme for the Apotheosis, I was delayed for some time by the fanfare, which I wished to bring up by degrees from the very depths of the [wind] orchestra to the high note where the Apotheosis breaks in. I don't know how many I wrote, but I liked none of them. Either they were too common, or too narrow in form, or not sufficiently solemn, or wanting in sonority, or badly graded. What I imagined was a sound like the trumpets of archangels, simple and noble, ascending radiant and triumphant and grandly resonant, as it announced to earth and heaven the opening of the Empyrean gates. Finally I decided, not without some trepidation, on the one now in the score; and the rest was soon written.[2]

For the day of the ceremony (28 July 1840), Berlioz was able to secure the services of several military bands, numbering, he says, two hundred players. Apparently the first movement, or perhaps some form of it, was played as a procession moved through the streets of Paris.[3] The entire Symphony was undoubtedly performed before the public at the monument, although Berlioz assures us that due to the general noise and confusion, 'not a note of it could be heard.'

[2] Berlioz, *Mémoires*, 2:39–40.

> Je voulus rappeler d' abord les combats des trios journees fameuses, au milieu des accents de deuil d'une marche à la fois terrible et désolée, qu'on exécuterait pendant le trajet du cortege; faire entendre une sorte d'oraison funèbre ou d'adieu adressée aux morts illustres, au moment de la descente des corps dans le tombeau monumental, et enfin chanter un hymne de gloire, l'apothèose, quand, la pierre funèbre scellée, le. People n'aurait plus devant ses yeux que la haute colonne surmontée de la liberté aux ailes étendues et s'élançant vers le ciel, comme l'âme de ceux qui moururent pour elle .
>
> ......
>
> La marche et l'oraison funèbre terminées, le thème de l' apothéose trouvé, je fus arête assez longtemps par la fanfare que je voulais faire s'élever peu à peu des profondeurs de l'orchestre jusqu'a la note aiguë; par laquelle éclate le chant de l'apotheose. J'en écrivis je ne sais combine qui toutes me déplurent; c'était ou vulgaire, ou trop étroit de forme, ou trop peu solennel, ou trop peu sonore, ou mal gradué. Je rêvais une sonnerie archangélique, simple mais noble, empanachée, armée, se levant radieuse, triomphante, retentissante, immense, annonçant à la terre et au ciell l' ouverture des portes de l'Empyrée. Je m'arrêtai enfin, non sans crainte, a celle que l'on connaît; et le reste fut bientôt écrit.

One person who did hear it, however, was Richard Wagner. He confirms that the performance occurred at the monument, that it was by combined military bands, and reveals that Berlioz himself conducted.

> It was, however, the latest work of this wonderful master [Wagner had been speaking of the *Symphonie fantastique* and the *Harold in Italy*], his 'Trauersymphonie für die Opfer der Julirevolution,' most skillfully composed for massed military bands [kombinierte Militärmusik] during the summer of 1840 for the anniversary of the obsequies of the July heroes, and conducted by him under the column of the Place de la Bastille, which had at last thoroughly convinced me of the greatness and enterprise of this incomparable artist.
> ......
> It is a fact that at that time I felt almost like a little school boy by the side of Berlioz.[4]

Berlioz, of course, was too experienced a musician to leave this extraordinary Symphony to the fate of being judged by the musicians and critics of Paris in an outdoor premiere. Accordingly, he planned long before to have an indoor first hearing. His original plan, dating from late March 1840, was to acquire permission to use the famous Panthéon for a festival in which the centerpiece would be the new Symphony for band.[5] This plan did not work out and Berlioz engaged the Salle Vivienne. 'This,' said Berlioz,

> was my real performance. Such was its effect that the man who managed the concerts there engaged me for four evenings; the new Symphony had the place of honor each time, and the receipts were considerable.[6]

At least two such concerts did, in fact, occur in August 1840, as we know from a letter Berlioz wrote to Queen Maria-Amelia.[7] According to Berlioz, the public reception of the Symphony at these concerts was quite enthusiastic.

> At each performance of my new work the public seemed to appreciate it beyond any of its predecessors, and indeed praised it extravagantly One evening, at the Salle Vivienne, after the final movement some young fellows [were so excited that they] took it in their head to smash the chairs against the floor, with shouts of applause.[8]

---

[3] It is evident from comments in his *Mémoires* that Berlioz continued to refine and change this composition over many years, including, among other things, the addition of optional string and choral parts. My personal belief, which is presented in detail in my 'Concerning the Lost Versions of the Berlioz Symphony for Band,' in the *Journal of Band Research* 11, no. 2 (Spring, 1975): 5ff., is that the original first movement may have been considerably different from the version we know today.

[4] Richard Wagner, *Mein Leben* (Munich: List, 1963), 228ff. Wagner was only the first of many distinguished persons who wrote of their admiration of this composition. I devote a number of pages to these testimonials in my book, *Berlioz on Bands*.

[5] Some correspondence to this effect, with Jean Vatout, Curator of Public Buildings, is quoted in Jacques Barzun, *New Letters of Berlioz* (New York: Columbia University Press, 1954), 39.

[6] Berlioz, *Mémoires*.

[7] Barzun, *New Letters of Berlioz*, 41.

[8] Berlioz, *Mémoires*, 41.

While Berlioz wrote that the first outdoor performance was by two hundred players, he did not mention the size of the Salle Vivienne ensemble. There are numbers of players given in brackets on the so-called autograph score, which add up to a band of more than one hundred and thirty players. But this surviving score is a rather late copy and there is no way to identify who wrote these numbers in brackets into it.

Yet another possible clue to Berlioz's thinking on the size of band appropriate for this work may be found in a letter to George Hainl, regarding a possible performance in Lyon in 1845.[9] Here Berlioz gives the list of players he requires for the orchestral part of the program, and then a list of additional wind players needed for a 'morceau a 2 orchestres,' which certainly seems to be a reference to the version of the Symphony with doubling strings. If one takes the available wind players from the orchestral list and adds the requested extra wind players, which would be necessary to cover the parts of the Symphony, then one has the nucleus which Berlioz was apparently prepared to accept himself. Even though, in this case some sixty-three strings were going to be doubling for volume's sake, I think it is fair to consider this list, which Berlioz carefully worked out, as representative of what the composer may have imagined as the minimum number of winds necessary to provide the texture he had in mind.

[9] Barzun, *New Letters of Berlioz*, 63.

1 piccolo in D♭
1 small flute in E♭
2 flutes
4 oboes, one doubling in English horn
4 bassoons
1 E♭ clarinet
10 B♭ clarinets
6 horns
2 cornets
4 trumpets
6 trombones
2 ophicleides in C
1 ophicleide in B♭
Percussion

This is a major composition for band and one of great quality. One has only to point to the judgment of Wagner who wrote, after he had already come to know the *Symphonie fantastique*,

> I am inclined to rank this composition above all Berlioz's other ones; it is noble and great from the first note to the last ... I must say with delight that I am convinced this Symphony will last and exalt the hearts of men as long as there lives a nation called France.[10]

The appearance of cornets in the list Berlioz provides for the performance of this work, reminds me to pause in this account of the civic band music of France to mention the popularity which this instrument enjoyed with the public in Paris at this time. Even Wagner, out of financial necessity, agreed to help meet the demand for music for the new instrument.

> As my contributions to the *Gazette Musicale* proved so unremunerative, Schlesinger one day ordered me to work out a method for the *Cornet à pistons*. When I told him about my embarrassment, in not knowing how to deal with the subject, he replied by sending me five different 'Methods' for the *Cornet à pistons*, at that time the favourite amateur instrument among the younger male population of Paris. I had merely to devise a new sixth method out of these five, as all Schlesinger wanted was to publish an edition of his own. I was racking my brains how to start, when Schlesinger, who had just obtained a new complete method, released me from the onerous task. I was, however, told to write fourteen 'Suites' for the *Cornet à pistons*—that is to say, airs out of operas arranged for this instrument.[11] To furnish me with material for this work, Schlesinger sent me no less than sixty complete operas arranged for the piano. I looked them through for suitable airs for my 'Suites,' marked the pages in the volumes with paper strips, and arranged them into a curious-looking structure round my work-table, so that I might have the greatest possible variety of the melodious material within my reach. When I was in the midst of this work, however, to my great relief and to my poor wife's consternation, Schlesinger told me that M. Schiltz, the first cornet player in Paris, who had looked my 'Etudes' through, preparatory to their being engraved, had declared that I knew absolutely nothing about the instrument, and had generally adopted keys that were too high, which Parisians would never be able to use. The part of the work I had already done was, however, accepted, Schiltz having agreed to correct it, but on condition that I should share the fee with him.[12]

[10] Quoted in Jacques Barzun, *Berlioz and the Romantic Century* (Boston: Little, Brown 1950), 1:350.

[11] In 1974 I acquired in a rare book store in Paris a manuscript volume of just such material. Dated 1844, it contains numerous opera arias transcribed for the cornet, a few with piano accompaniment.

[12] Wagner, *My Life*, 229. According to Richard Goldman, in *The Band's Music* (New York: Pitman, Publishing Corp., 1938), 62, Gounod also wrote a cornet method, in 1845. The spurious Brahms Etudes for trumpet may also be related to this period.

Details of individual French civic bands between 1815 and 1850 are rather rare, although some information is provided relative to the early history of some of the better bands in the Orphéon survey published in the early years of the twentieth century.[13]

The civic band in Armentières had thirty-five members already in 1806 and frequently participated in band contests between 1807 and 1838. Another band which enjoyed success in early contests was the Musique municipale de Valenciennes. This band, which dated from the guild days of the beginning of the eighteenth century, took first prize in the 'Concours de Condé' in 1806.

The Musique municipale de Douai, founded in 1791, was conducted by Pierre Lecomte from that date until 1827. In 1806 Lecomte founded a civic school of music, which offered courses in solfège and wind instruments. His sucessors included Bauduin, 1827–1835, Noury, 1835–1837, and Lefranc, 1837–1871. A similar school was founded by the civic band of Maubeuge, called the Société philharmonique de Maubeuge (founded in 1836).

The Musique des Canonniers de Lille was founded in 1814, with about twenty players under the leadership of Brun-Lavainne. He was followed by J.-J. Printemps in 1817, at which time the band consisted of two flutes, ten clarinets, four 'basses et hautbois,' serpent, buccin, four trombones, three horns, two trumpets, and percussion. A similar instrumentation is given for the Musique municipale du Mans at the beginning of the nineteenth century.[14] This band became a military band briefly and was reorganized as a civic band in 1817. At that time the repertoire included Fantaisies on Italian opera arias, overtures by Rossini, Spontini, Boieldieu, Auber, etc., and '*harmonies* de Krommer, Meyerbeer, Nicolini, etc.,' the latter probably representing original literature. The instrumentation of this band in 1840 is given as piccolo, small clarinet, nine clarinets, bugle, piston-trumpet, ophicleide-quinte, two bass ophicleides, three trombones, bass trumpet, two horns, and percussion.

The civic band in Tourcoing, called the Société philharmonique, was founded in 1805 with twenty-two members and grew to fifty members by 1853. Here again a civic school of music was founded in support of the band.

[13] Maréchal and Parès, *Monographie Universelle de L'Orphéon*, 216ff.

[14] Four flutes, clarinet in F, ten clarinets in C, three bassoons, two trumpets, three horns, two trombones, two serpents, buccin, and percussion.

One important early bandmaster was Prudent-Louis Aubéry du Boulley (1796–1870), who in 1835 founded a society of wind bands in the towns west of Paris. Twice a year these bands came together to form a massed band of several hundred performers.[15]

Civic Bands after Mid-Century

After the political turmoil of 1848 there was a tremendous growth in the development of civic bands in France. This development was helped by the creation of band societies in imitation of the successful civic choral organizations, called Orphéon, who had become nationally organized in 1833.[16] In the following decade a division of Orphéon for bands was formed. In addition to providing a model for the organization of a band society, the national Orphéon society evidently sponsored composition contests for original band literature and published many band compositions.[17] A contemporary description of the social status of these Orphéon band societies was given by the famous critic, Eduard Hanslick.

> Every city and village in France has their Musique d'harmonie, or at least a 'Fanfare' [brass band]. In general, they recruit from the same social levels as the Orphéons [the choral societies], from craftsmen, businessmen, lower government officials, etc., only these wind societies go somewhat lower and higher in age range—one sees there twelve and fifteen year old boys along side old grey-beards. Among the latter are often veterans, an important element, as veterans of military bands for the most part founded the civic bands after they retired to their home towns.
>
> Compared to these bands, the Orphéons see themselves somewhat higher artistically, but the community views them both as 'equally loved children.' Not every community can have a military band, so the Fanfares are supported by civic funds and collections of donations. The government sponsors competitions, organized in higher and lower levels of ability.
>
> As to the artistic meaning of these groups, like the Orphéons, they stand in the second rank with the social clubs. Only the best of the French Harmonie Societies [bands of woodwinds and brass] achieve that which is musically perfect or even special, but even the least of them can take pride in drawing some souls away from drink and card playing. For the working man, even a crude encounter with art has something which frees and ennobles; the desire to belong to a musical group gives a further push upwards.[18]

---

[15] Grove 1:684, where it is also mentioned that Aubéry du Boulley published an account of his band society, under the title, *Des associations musicales en France et de la Société philharmonique de l'Eure, de l'Orne et d'Eure-et-Loir* (Verneuil, 1839).

[16] Grove 13:870; and 6:751.

[17] In going through the nineteenth-century band literature in the Paris Bibliothèque nationale, I noticed a great number of published works with the publisher given only as 'Orphéon.' An example is the *Overture* (Vm.27.8432) by Kelsen which carries a note that it was composed for a contest sponsored by the Orphéon Society and published by them.

[18] Quoted in Eugen Brixel, 'Musikpapst und Blasmusik,' in *Österreichische Blasmusik* (October, 1975), 5.

At the time of his writing, Hanslick indicates there were two thousand such civic band societies in France. The Orphéon survey at the end of the century lists a staggering total of seventeen hundred and eleven 'Harmonie' societies (Paris alone having sixty-eight!), of which sixty-two are classed Division d'Excellence (one of five categories) and between four and five thousand 'Fanfare' societies. The latter alone, according to the survey, represents more than one hundred thousand participants![19]

The Orphéon survey presents detailed information regarding only the best of the French Harmonie societies, those of the Division d'Excellence. Among these are many very large bands, including (numbers of players are given in brackets) the Philharmonique Avignonaise [76], the Lyre Biterroise [105], the Harmonie municipale de Clinchy [103], the Harmonie des Mineurs de Denain [102], the Musique municipale de Douai [127],[20] the Harmonie des mines de Liévin [103], the Harmonie Fanien Sainte-Cécile (Lillers) [102], the Lyre Narbonnaise [85], the Musique municipale de Reims [130],[21] the Musique municipale de Rouen [115], la Harmonie municipale de Saint-Étienne [90], the Musique municipale de Tourcoing [118], and the Musique municipale de Valenciennes [91].[22]

A few of the correspondents have given additional information which provides insights regarding the activities of these large wind orchestras. The Harmonie de la Bénédictine of Fécamp, a band made up of employees of the famous distillery there, had regular rehearsals three times per week. The number of concerts varied from four per week all year by the Musique municipale de Nice to twelve per year by the Musique des sapeurs-pompiers de Nîmes.

The repertoire is often given and usually consists of well-known overtures and fantaisies on famous operas. The correspondent of the Musique municipale de Reims mentions that his band won the 'Prize of Honor' at the Paris Exposition of 1889 with a performance of the *Reformation Symphony* by Mendelssohn.[23] The Harmonie des mines de Lievin included in its repertoire the same work, plus the Third and Sixth Symphonies by Beethoven. La Société philharmonique d'Armentières held a concert in 1890 of transcribed works by Massenet, conducted by the composer.

[19] At this time 'Harmonie' refers to a wind orchestra of woodwinds and brass; 'Fanfare' refers to a brass band.

[20] 11 flutes, 8 oboes, 2 small clarinets, 32 clarinets, 15 saxophones, 6 bassoons, 3 trumpets, 7 cornets, 9 trombones, 5 bugles, 4 horns, 3 alto horns, 2 baritones, 11 'basses,' 2 contrebasses in E♭, 2 contrebasses in B♭, 2 string contrebasses, and 3 percussion.

[21] 5 flutes, 3 oboes, 40 clarinets in B♭, 3 E♭ clarinets, 2 alto clarinets, 2 bass clarinets, 10 saxophones, 2 bassoons, 2 string basses, and 61 brass.

[22] The survey also gives the specific instrumentation for the civic bands of Armentieres, Belfortaise, the Lyre Belfortaise and the Harmonie des Usines de Belfort, the Harmonie les Enfants de la Plaine (Lens), Lille, Lyon, Mons, Nice, Ouveillan, and the Harmonie des ateliers de la Belle Jardiniere and the Harmonie de Montmartre of Paris.

[23] One of the interesting scores I examined in the Paris Bibliothèque nationale was the *Grand Overture* by Georges Rauchenecker, which carries a note that it was composed for the famous Paris Exhibition of 1867, thus indicating there were civic bands performing as well as the famous military band competition discussed in the introduction to this chapter. I might mention that Rossini also composed for this same exhibition a *Hymne to Napoleon III* for military band, orchestra, and chorus. The sense of celebration which accompanied this exhibition can be felt in Rossini's dedication, 'To Napoleon III and his valiant People.—Hymn for Large Orchestra, Military Band, Baritone, a Pontiff; Chorus of High Priests, Chorus of Vivandières, of Soldiers, and of People.—Dances, Bells, Side Drums, and Cannon.'

The availability of chromatic brass instruments, especially those of the saxhorn family, made possible a tremendous development of brass bands in France after mid-century. The Orphéon survey lists more than four thousand brass band societies and noted that no community in France was so small as not to have at least a fanfare ensemble.

Again, some of the brass bands are of extraordinary size, among these are (number of players given in brackets) those of Hautmont [87], Onnaing [85], the La Sirène de Paris [123],[24] Port-Brille [104], Saint-Denis [90], Tilleul [81], Trélonnaise [70], and Trith-le-Poirier [110].

The repertoire of these large brass bands again consisted of major orchestral transcriptions, although the correspondent representing the La Sirène de Paris mentions that after 1886 a great number of original works by Tillard and Hemmerlé were performed. This same writer mentions works such as fantaisies on operas, waltzes, gavottes, and marches belonging to a special literature for 'small concerts.'

The correspondent of the Union musicale de Saint-Denis describes a special music school run by the brass band, which offered courses in solfège and in the various instruments two evenings per week from 8:00 to 11:00 PM. Study in these classes, and success in their exams, was the means for gaining membership in the band. An identical school was associated with the Fanfare des Forges et Aciéries du Nord et de l'Est: Trith-le-Poirier.

Other interesting comments included by the various correspondents include a reference to the conductor of the Fanfare Trélonnaise, M. L. Nicolas, whose predecessors as conductor included his father and grandfather. The representative of the Fanfare Delattre de Roubaix mentions that band's having won first prize in a Paris contest of 1878.

In addition to the development of these large bands, one must also not fail to acknowledge France's contributions to smaller wind ensembles during the nineteenth century. In this regard it is, of course, the Quintets, op. 88, 91, 99, and 100 of Anton Reicha which first come to mind. These remarkable works are typical of this ingenious man, being major works for a medium which hardly existed before. A contemporary,[25]

[24] This band described itself as follows:

> Instruments which replace the strings of the orchestra: small bugle in E♭, 10 solo bugles, 10 first bugles, 7 second bugles 7 third bugles, 9 alto horns, 3 baritones, 6 solo basses, 10 basses, 10 contrebasses (2 in E♭, one of strings);
>
> Orchestral brass instruments: 4 horns, 4 trumpets, 12 trombones;
>
> Instruments necessary for color: solo cornet, 2 first cornets, 3 second cornets, 1 E♭ sopranino saxophone, 2 soprano saxophones, 5 alto saxophones, 3 tenor saxophones, baritone saxophone, bass saxophone, soprano sarrusophone, tenor sarrusophone, bass sarrusophone, contrebass sarrusophone; and 4 percussion.

[25] Sainsbury, *A Dictionary of Musicians*, 2:344. This same contemporary also gives an interesting persona description of Reicha, then living in Paris.

> Reicha is still in the vigour of life, of middle stature, and most urbane manners, his general courtesy greatly endearing him to strangers, to whom he is uniformly obliging. In private life he is cheerful and amiable; his favourite amusement is a game of a tric-trac. His rooms are decorated with a profusion of elegant and curious articles, which have been presented him by numerous individuals in public and private life, as testimonies of friendship, and of the respect and admiration due to his genius and perseverance. In Germany, Reicha is very commonly called the restorer of fugue.

who oddly mentions their being for English horn rather than oboe, captures the excitement which these works have always generated for some listeners.

> [His] practical skill has been shown in a variety of compositions, but especially in some admirable quintets, composed expressly for the flute, clarionet, cor Anglois, French horn, and bassoon; these are performed frequently at L'École des Fils d'Apollon, and, indeed, on all occasions when first-rate performers on the appropriate instruments assemble together. No description, no imagination, can do justice to these compositions. The effect produced by the extraordinary combinations of apparently opposite-toned instruments, added to Reicha's vigorous style of writing and judicious arrangement, have rendered these quintets the admiration of the musical world.

Another distinguished contemporary, Ludwig Spohr,[26] heard these works with mixed enthusiasm.

[26] Quoted in Louis Spohr's *Autobiography* (London, 1865), 2:130–131.

> Two days ago I heard two more quite new quintets of Reicha, which he wrote for the morning-concerts ... They were played at a rehearsal, which appears to me to have been given solely for the purpose of fishing for more subscribers to the morning concerts, among the numerous persons who were invited ... It is sad to see what means artists here are obliged to resort to, in order to procure support for their undertakings. While the Parisians press eagerly forward to every sensual enjoyment, they must be almost dragged to intellectual ones.—I found the composition of these two new quintets, like those I had previously heard at Kreutzer's, rich in interesting sequences of harmony, correct throughout in the management of the voices, and full of effect in the use made of the tone and character of the different wind instruments, but on the other hand, frequently defective in the form. Mr. Reicha is not economical enough of his ideas, and at the very commencement of his pieces he frequently gives from four to five themes, each of which concludes in the tonic. Were he less rich, he would be richer. His periods also are frequently badly connected and sound as though he had written one yesterday and the other today. Yet the minuets and scherzi, as short pieces, are less open to this objection, and some of them are real masterpieces in form and contents. A German soundness of science and capacity are the greatest ornaments of this master.

In my opinion it is clear that Reicha, a man whose background was Bohemia and Vienna, was writing specifically for the current French taste and so these works fail in the profound depth of expression which nearly always follows such an aim. However, one must give Reicha his due: with these works he almost single-handedly was responsible for the later emergence of the repertoire for this medium.

Later during the century another extraordinary chapter in French chamber wind music begins with the creation of the Société de Musique de Chambre pour Instruments à Vent, founded by Paul Taffanel (1844–1908). This series of concerts, begun in 1879, had for fourteen years a tremendous influence throughout Europe.[27] The first concert, given 6 February 1879, in the Salle Pleyel in Paris, included performances of the Beethoven *Octet*, op. 103, an *Aubade* for wind quintet by Barthe, and the Rubinstein *Quintet* for piano and winds. The second concert, 20 February 1879, included the Mozart *Partita*, K.375, a *Prelude* for five winds by Pessard, and the Spohr *Quintet* for piano and winds.

This Society was responsible for commissioning a number of substantial new works for wind ensemble, among them, the Gounod *Petite Symphonie* (1885), the Lazzari *Octuor* (1889), the *Octuor* and *Suite Gauloise* by Gouvy, the two *Suites* by Dubois, and the *Sextuor* by Boisdeffre.[28]

The great value of this activity was to keep alive the potential of the wind ensemble as absolute music, during a time when the military bands had elected to serve primarily as an entertainment medium. In addition, it was students of this ensemble who moved to Boston to become members of the Boston Symphony Orchestra early in the twentieth century who helped found the professional wind ensemble there, the Longy Club.

Finally, I must include here a touching account which mentions an itinerant wind ensemble, in this case apparently an ancient shawm ensemble, so typical of the street music which is still a hallmark of Paris.

[27] Grove 18:521.

[28] After the death of Taffanel the society changed its name to the 'Société Moderne pour Instruments a Vent,' and commissioned the Roussel *Divertissement*, op. 6 (1914) and the Schmitt *Lied et Scherzo*, op. 54 (1910).

> At a café ... at the corners of the Boulevards Saint-Michel and Saint-Germain, we used to notice an elderly gentleman, scrupulously neat and exquisitely clean, though his clothes were very threadbare. He always sat at the same table to the right of the counter. His cup of coffee was eked out by frequent supplements of water, and meanwhile he was always busy copying music—at least, so it seemed to us at first. We soon came to a different conclusion, though, because every now and then he would put down his pen, lean back against the cushioned seat, look up at the ceiling and smile to himself—such a sweet smile; the smile of a poet or

an artist, seeking inspiration from the spirits supposed to be hovering now and then about such. That man was no copyist, but an obscure, unappreciated genius perhaps, biding his chance, hoping against hope, meanwhile living a life of jealously concealed dreams and hardship. For he looked sad enough at the best of times, with a kind of settled melancholy which apparently only one thing could dispel—the advent of a couple or trio of pifferari. Then his face would light up all of a sudden, he would gently push his music away, speak to them in Italian, asking them to play certain pieces, beating time with an air of contentment which was absolutely touching to behold. On the other hand, the young pifferari appeared to treat him with greater deference than they did the other customers; the little girl who accompanied them was particularly eager for his approval.

In a little while we became very friendly with the old gentleman, and, one evening, he said, 'If you will be here next Wednesday, the pifferari will give us something new.'

On the evening in question he looked quite smart; he had evidently 'fait des frais de toilette,' as our neighbours have it; he wore a different coat, and his big white neckcloth was somewhat more starched than usual. He seemed quite excited. The pifferari, on the other hand, seemed anxious and subdued. The café was very full, for all the habitués like the old gentleman, and had made it a point of responding to his quasi-invitation. They were well rewarded, for I have rarely heard sweeter music. It was unlike anything we were accustomed to hear from such musicians; there was an old-world sound about it that went straight to the heart, and when we looked at the old gentleman admist the genuine applause after the termination of the first piece, there were two big tears coursing down his wrinkled cheeks.

......

Then I understood it all. He was the professor of pifferari, an artist for all that, an unappreciated genius, perhaps, who, rather than not be heard at all, introduced a composition of his own into their hackneyed programme, and tasted the sweets of popularity, without the accompanying rewards which, nowadays, popularity invariably brings. This one had known Paisiello and Rossini, had been in the thick of the excitement on the first night of the 'Barbière,' and had dreamt of similar triumphs. Perhaps his genius was as much entitled to them as that of the others, but he had loved not wisely, but too well, and when he awoke from the love-dream, he was too ruined in body and mind to be able to work for the realization of the artistic one. He would accept no aid. Three years later, we carried him to his grave. A simple stone marks the place in the cemetery of Montparnasse.[29]

[29] Albert Vandam, *An Englishman in Paris* (New York: D. Appleton, 1892), 1:259–263.

10 *Civic Wind Bands in Italy*

OUR KNOWLEDGE OF THE ORIGINAL COMPOSITIONS performed by nineteenth-century Italian civic bands is made difficult by the fact that many civic libraries have not yet cataloged their music collection. But it appears that the repertoire is extensive and one scholar summarizes this activity as follows:

> During the first half of the nineteenth century, the town bands of Italy, similar to the one conducted by Giuseppe Verdi in Bussetto, consisted of whatever instruments and players that were available at a given time. Ranging in size from just a few players to a larger band of fifty or more, the instrumentation not only varied greatly from town to town, but from year to year, as players joined or left the band ... Towards the mid-century, the use of the various instruments developed by Adolphe Sax and others in Northern Europe also began to find their way into Italian bands.
>
> Various general terms were, and are today, used to describe the band as an entity. These were *concerto musicale*, *corpo musicale*, *complesso bandistico*, and *filarmonica* among others.[1]

One civic band for which there is some documentation[2] for the period before mid-century is that of Rome. The fortunes of this band varied with both the fortunes of the city and the papacy. In 1818 the civic government suspended the band, called 'concerto di tromboni e cornetti,' due to 'incredible debts.' The ensemble apparently emerged as a new band, called, 'Banda Capitolina,' supported first by both the pope and the city and then by the civic militia, the Guardia Capitolina. In a document of 1820, the band sought new uniforms for a procession to be given a new senator, Don Tommaso Corsini. By about this same period the band seems to have begun to have regular civic support again and, according to Vessella, consisted of a piccolo, six clarinets, bassoon, trumpet, two clarini, three or four horns (*corni da caccia*), trombone and percussion. The conductor, Giuseppe Manfredi, was also a clarinetist; the musicians were called 'Professori.' Vessella dates the addition of the oboe as 1834 and the ophicleide in 1839.

---

[1] James W. Herbert, 'Wind Bands of 19th Century Italy: A Short Sketch' (unpublished manuscript). Herbert points out that Elisabeth Abbott, in her translation of Carlo Gatti's *Verdi: The Man and His Music*, continually refers to the documentation that Verdi was conductor of the 'philharmonic orchestra' of Bussetto. In translating the term 'filarmonica,' she incorrectly assumes, in this case, that the ensemble was an orchestra, when, in fact, it was the town band!

[2] Vessella, *La Banda*, 176ff.

Vessella also mentions that before mid-century the ancient civic trumpet choirs were still active, in particular in Tuscany. In Rome, a document of 1850, relative to the annual civic carnival, mentions the participation of the city's civic trumpets in the official procession.³

³ Ibid., 177.

Before leaving the subject of Rome before mid-century, I should like to quote a passage from the autobiography of Ludwig Spohr in which he describes hearing a small ensemble of itinerant musicians in Rome in 1816.

> During the time of Advent, when all public music is forbidden, the theatres closed, and a real deathlike stillness prevails, whole troops of virtuosi on the bagpipe come from the Neapolitan territory, who play first before the pictures of the Virgin and Saints, and then collect in the houses and in the streets a *viaticum*, or traveling penny. They generally go in pairs, one playing the bagpipe and the other a shepherds-pipe. The music of all, with a few unimportant deviations, is the same, and is said to have its origin in a very ancient sacred melody; but from the way in which these people now play it, it sounds profane enough. Heard at a certain distance it nevertheless does not sound badly; the one who plays the bagpipe produces an effect somewhat as though three clarinets were blown, he of the shepherds-pipe a sound like that of a coarse powerful hautboy. The purity of the notes of the bagpipe and shepherds-pipe is very striking. Wherever one now goes, be the part of the city which it may, one hears the above music.⁴

⁴ Spohr, *Autobiography*, 1:297.

The period of real growth and expansion in Italian civic bands occurred after the period of the unification of Italy, known as the 'risorgimento' (1860–1870). This period also saw an increase in the composition of original works for band, particularly those of a patriotic nature.

During this period, one also finds the civic bands serving as civic militia bands as well. In Milan, for example, the Banda Civica, under the direction of Gustavo Rossari, became after 1859 the Corpo di Musica della Guardia Nazionale, at which time it had sixty-four players. In 1876 the band returned to civilian status, although a smaller band of forty-one musicians. After Rossari's death in 1882, he was succeeded by Andrea Guarneri.⁵ One of the great successes under the new director was a combined concert with the civic band of Torino, conducted by Rossi. The two conductors alternated in conducting works by Wagner, Meyerbeer, Rossini, Gounod, Bizet, and a military fanfare by Ponchielli which imitated cannons.⁶

⁵ Gianfranco Buzzi, *Cenni storici del Corpo di Musica Municipale di Milano* (Milan, 1894).

⁶ Vessella, *La Banda*, 165.

Similarly, the Banda della Guardia Urbana of Bologna became the Banda della Guardia Nazionale in 1860 and a civic band again in 1873, called the Banda musicale di Bologna. In 1857 this band, combined with several military bands, had given the premiere of a new band composition, *Marcia Triofale*, by the Austrian composer Hallmayr, as part of the ceremonies marking a visit by Pope Pius IX. This same composition was repeated in Florence by eight bands when the pope visited that city later in the year. On this occasion the well-known civic band, led by Pietro Mattiozzi, was joined by all the bands of the city in a procession, followed by a concert under the pope's window of 'various symphonies.'[7] The pope made a generous donation to all of the various bands.

In Naples, during 1859–1869, there were no fewer than twelve civic militia bands, each with a distinguished conductor. Three of these men, Paoalo Savoia, Domenico Gatti, and Salvatore Caccavajo, remained on as conductors when these musicians were reconstituted into three separate bands within the 'Banda Comunale.'[8] In Siena, as well, the leading musicians were associated with the Banda del Municipio, among them the conductors Rinaldo Ticci[9] and Pietro Formichi.[10] Formichi also formed, in 1854, one of the rare brass band societies in nineteenth-century Italy, the Società della Fanfara Senese.[11]

During the second half of the nineteenth century many civic bands had come into existence. According to one contemporary, by 1888 there were some six thousand civic bands in Italy![12] Some of the larger of these are cited in the Orphéon survey, including the Musique municipale de Milan, which, according to a correspondent, had a repertoire of some two thousand works;[13] the Musica civia de Novare;[14] and the Musique municipale de Turin, the repertoire of whom also included contemporary works.[15]

The Banda Municipale di Roma had been formed as the La Banda di Roma after the Banda della Guardia Nazionale was disbanded.[16] Unde the conductor, Giuseppe Mililotti, the band was then divided into two sections, each with fewer than forty players, who performed separate services and together for important occasions.

[7] Quoted in Vessella, ibid., 161–162.

…una magnifica riunione di tutte le bande della città, precedute ed accompagnate da moltissimi soldati portanti dei torcetti assesi. Fermatosi questo numerosissimo corpo musicale, sotto le finestre del quartiere del S. Padre, suonò scelte sinfonie …

[8] Ibid., 166.

[9] Rinaldo Ticci (1805–1883) was a leading composer, including works for band, and director of the municipal music school.

[10] Pietro Formichi (b. 1829) was an excellent pianist, chief conductor of the Cappella Senese and the Societa orchestrale, and head of the civic music school.

[11] Rinaldo Morrocchi, *La Musica in Siena* (Siena, 1886). The world survey of bands by Henri Maréchal and Gabriel Parès, *Monographie Universelle de L'Orphéon* (Paris: Libairie Ch. Delagrave), 291, made just after the beginning of the twentieth century, found no normal civic brass band societies in Italy, but rather only small brass ensembles which played marches for the 'sociétés cyclists ou de gymnastique.'

[12] Alceste Murri, *Sulle bande musicali: Pro-memoria* (n.p., 1888).

[13] Maréchal and Parès, *Monographie Universelle de L'Orphéon*, 261ff. The instrumentation (but not numbers of players) is given as piccolo, flute, oboe, small clarinet, clarinets in three parts, bass clarinet, saxophones (SATB), string bass, trumpets, horns, trombones, cornets, small and large bugles, alto horns, baritones, basses, contrebasses, and percussion.

[14] Ibid., giving the instrumentation as piccolo, flute, 2 oboes, 2 E♭ clarinets, 10 B♭ clarinets, 2 bass clarinets, 3 saxophones, 2 string basses, 2 E♭ trumpets, 2 cornets, 4 horns, 4 trombones, 3 bugles, 2 alto horns, 3 baritones, 2 basses, and 4 percussion.

In 1882, under the direction of Maestro Pezzini, the band was reunited as one ensemble of sixty-eight players. In 1885, under Vessella, the band was again reorganized, now as eighty players consisting of sixty players of the 'first class,' followed by twenty 'students' divided into two classes.

Alessandro Vessella (1860–1929), together with Raffaele Caravaglios (1860–1941), conductor of the Concerto Civico di Napoli, was one of two important Italian band conductors who were conservatory trained musicians and who were active in teaching (Vessella in the Santa Cecilia in Rome and Caravaglios in the conservatory San Pietro Maiella in Naples) future band directors.

In 1894, Vessella published a proposal for a standardization of instrumentation, based on the concept of 'families' of instruments, which had an influence on Italian bands lasting well into the twentieth century.[17] Following is Vessella's thoughtful system for the instrumentation for three sizes of bands, large, medium, and small, and is quoted on the following page (the lines indicate Vessella's division of instrumental 'families').

[15] Ibid., giving the instrumentation as piccolo, flute, 2 oboes, 2 bassoons, 2 E♭ clarinets, 8 first and 5 second clarinets, 3 bass clarinets, 4 saxophones, 4 horns, 4 trumpets, 4 trombones, small E♭ bugle, 2 bugles, 2 alto horns, 2 baritones, 3 'solo basses,' 3 basses, 3 contrabasses, and 3 percussion.

[16] The newspaper, *La Capitale* (August 14, 1878), calling the band 'Il concerto municipale,' mentioned hearing forty-five players perform in the Apollo Theater as part of ceremonies in honor of Voltaire.

[17] Ibid., gives Vessella's own band at the turn of the century as piccolo, 2 flutes, 2 oboes, A♭ clarinet, 3 E♭ clarinets, 17 clarinets (solo, 8 first and 8 second), 2 E♭ alto clarinets, 2 B♭ bass clarinets, 6 saxophones (soprano, 2 alto, tenor, baritone, and bass), bass and contrabass sarrusophones, contrabassoon, E♭ cornet, 2 B♭ cornets, 2 E♭ trumpets, 2 B♭ bass trumpets, 4 horns, 4 trombones (2 tenor, Bass in F, and bass in B♭), 2 E♭ bugles, 4 B♭ bugles, 4 E♭ alto horns, 2 tenor flicorni in B♭, 2 B♭ baritones, 2 B♭ basses, ophicleide, contrabass in F, contrabass in E♭, 2 B♭ contrabasses, and 5 percussion.

	BANDA GRANDE	BANDA MEDIANA	BANDA PICCOLA
flute	4	1	1
A♭ soprano clarinet	1		
E♭ soprano clarinet	2	2	2
first B♭ clarinet	9	6	4
second B♭ clarinet	8	6	4
E♭ alto clarinet	2	2	2
B♭ soprano saxophone	1	1	
E♭ alto saxophone	2	1	
B♭ tenor saxophone	2	1	1
E♭ baritone saxophone	1	1	1
B♭ bass saxophone	1		
oboe	4		
B♭ bass sarrusophone	1		
E♭ contrabass sarrusophone	1		
B♭ contrabass sarrusophone	1	1	
string bass	4		
horn	4	2	2
E♭ cornet	1		
B♭ cornet	1	1	1
trumpet	2	2	2
B♭ bass trumpet	2	1	
B♭ tenor trombone	2	2	2
F bass trombone	1	1	1
B♭ contrabass trombone	1		
E♭ soprano flicorno (Flugelhorn)	1	1	
B♭ soprano flicorno (Flugelhorn)	3	2	2
E♭ alto flicorno (Flugelhorn)	2	2	2
B♭ tenor flicorno (tenor horn)	2	2	1
B♭ bass flicorno (euphonium)	4	2	1
F bass flicorno grave (tuba)	1	1	
E♭ bass flicorno grave (tuba)	1		
B♭ contrabass flicorno	2	2	1
timpani	3		
small drum	2	1	1
bass drum	1	1	1
cymbal	2	1	1

11 Civic Wind Bands in England

AFTER THE NAPOLEONIC WARS, the strong tradition of local civic militia bands in England gave way to more regular civic bands, called 'reed bands' by present day English writers to distinguish them from the strong tradition of the brass bands which replaced them. Some of these civic bands were still called 'waits' and this transition can be seen in the example of the York Civic Waits which disbanded in 1835, although two members had begun double-duty in forming a civic brass band in 1833.[1]

Because the civic 'reed' band tradition was rather short-lived during the nineteenth century, information on these bands is difficult to find, although a considerable extant repertoire can still be found in the British Museum. One of these bands, the Stalybridge Band, in Lancashire, which survived until the 1830s, is said to have had an instrumentation of four flutes, four clarinets, two bassoons, trumpet, bugle, two horns, serpent, bass horn, and percussion early during the century.[2] The Bramley Band in 1828 had a similar instrumentation of four clarinets, two trumpets, bugle, two horns, two trombones, serpent and percussion.[3]

Some of the most famous brass bands of the century also began as regular civic bands with woodwinds. The Black Dyke Mills Band, which only became a brass band in 1855,[4] had its origin in 1816 as the Peter Wharton Band. Similarly, the Besses o' th' Barn, which became a brass band in 1853, had begun as Clegg's Reed Band in 1818, with an instrumentation of piccolo, three clarinets, two bass horns, trumpet, keyed bugle, two horns, trombone, and percussion. This band is described in its appearance during the celebration of the coronation of George IV, in 1821, as wearing uniforms of scarlet tunic, white hats and white trousers.[5]

Before leaving this period, I should mention that Grove cites[6] an Italian-born hornist, Giovanni Puzzi (1792–1876), who moved to London in 1817 and established there a professional wind quintet which gave a series of concerts called 'Classical Concerts for Wind Instruments.'

[1] Grove 3:210; and John F. Russell and J. H. Elliot, *The Brass Band Movement* (London: J. M. Dent, 1936), 47.

[2] Russell and Elliot, ibid., 41.

[3] Ibid., 42.

[4] Grove 3:210.

[5] Quoted in Lilla M. Fox, *Instruments of Processional Music* (London: Lutterworth Press, 1967), 33.

[6] Grove 15:481.

The Birth of the Brass Bands

During the nineteenth century the normal civic bands were swept aside in an extraordinary wave of enthusiasm in England for the brass band. For the moment, let me quote, by way of introduction and as an indication of this early enthusiasm, the reaction of one who heard a band mentioned above, the Besses o' th' Barn.

> The effect was marvellous; my hair stood on end; I was in ecstasies; my soul was raptured; all around me seemed a vision of Heaven. Oh, what joy!! What bliss!![7]

[7] Ibid.

A photograph of the Besses o' th' Barn band, ca. 1860.

The origins for a band which could have had such an impact is found in the densely peopled manufacturing districts of Yorkshire, Lancashire, and Derbyshire. There the cottage industries were giving way to new industrial centers with mills, workshops, miles of slums, smoke, and noise. There also the poorly paid worker, often displaced and homesick for the fields of his village, toiled for twelve to fourteen hours a day. It has often been pointed out that while English folk songs can be found from the purely agricultural counties, few are found from the industrial areas.

Civic Wind Bands in England

A man might sing on a lovely summer's morning as he ploughed the fields, though he was poorly paid and badly clad; but in the stifling damp heat of a cotton or woollen mill, the glare, noise, and filth of an iron foundry, the dark, sweaty fetidness of a coal-mine, could a spontaneous song be expected to arise?[8]

Yet music as a domestic and social recreation after work did flourish in these same industrial counties, taking the form of choral societies in the years just before the rise of brass bands.

The first of several factors which made possible the civic brass band development was the arrival of the new instruments fundamental to it, beginning in the 1830s with the cornet, first called the 'cornopean' in England. Here was a melodic instrument capable of considerable musical effect and tonal accuracy which was not too difficult for a working man to learn in his little spare time. The *Musical World* (December 8, 1837) referred to the new instrument as 'beloved of coachguards and cads,' and in the following issue reviewed a new publication of music, *The Cornopean*, but confided, 'We cannot at present boast of sufficient knowledge of the instrument to speak with much confidence.'[9]

Shortly thereafter came the new family of saxhorns, which gained almost immediate popularity due to the extraordinary success of the tours of the Distin family quintet. This ensemble was founded by John Distin (b. 1798), who was a member of the South Devon Militia Band and later the court band of the Prince Regent in London. With his four sons,[10] accompanied by his wife on the piano, they began touring first as an ensemble composed of a slide-trumpet, three horns and a trombone. They began extensive concert tours during the mid-1830s throughout England, Scotland, and Ireland. Already in 1838 one finds accounts of a series of daily concerts in London, in the Argyll Rooms, Willis' Rooms, and at Drury Lane Theatre. Accounts indicate these concerts were very successful, as one can see in a review from a Glasgow paper.[11]

> ... An arranged piece from ... *Norma*, for five brass instruments, struck the audience with astonishment.

[8] Russell and Elliot, *The Brass Band Movement*, 60.

[9] Quoted in ibid., 51.

[10] George (d. 1848), Henry (b. 1819), William (d. 1884), and Theodore (1823–1893).

[11] Quoted in Russell and Elliot, *The Brass Band Movement*, 54.

The significant turning point, both in terms of the fortune of the family quintet and the British brass band movement, came when the quintet discovered the saxhorn while on tour to Paris in 1844. This vital moment was recalled by one of the members of the quintet, Henry Distin, in a letter written in 1895, by which time he was living in Philadelphia.

> When in Paris in 1844, I made special visits to the factories of known brass instruments makers, with the ultimate intention of becoming a manufacturer myself. Our family quintet were playing one night at a concert given by a famous singer. On that occasion I, to my great astonishment, heard a new brass instrument entitled on the programme 'Sax horn' … [and was] struck amazed by the remarkable purity and sweetness of tone produced from the new instrument … I learned that M. Adolphe Sax … had completed but three instruments built on the new model … At the time, however, he had not one of them for sale. Before leaving I arrived at an arrangement for the loan of the three instruments. That very afternoon they were fully and fairly tried by the family at our hotel. The trial raised within us all an indescribable artistic enthusiasm. The delicious evenness, combined sweetness, and general purity of intonation and tone, were recognized and admitted by each member of our family. Adolphe Sax was at once sent for; and, after hearing us play several trios, duets, and solos on them, he eagerly agreed to certain suggested alterations, and gave his word to complete, on the suggested system, without delay, five instruments bearing his name, as needed for the practical musical outfit of our quintet party. We waited in and around Paris, concertizing, until Sax completed the order to our satisfaction; when, having by hard practice attained sufficient facility in their use, they were brought out in public by us as Adolphe Sax's grand new invention, 'Sax horns.'
>
> The first introduction of these instruments was at a grand concert at the Opéra Comique given by M. Berlioz, the famous composer … and in this our novel quintet of Sax horns met with such vehement demonstrations of approval from the delighted audience that the same evening we were awarded the high honour of being engaged to perform upon them at the Conservatoire … From that time the Continental tours of the Sax horn Distin family formed a complete succession of triumphs. The press belauded us, the public everywhere was enthusiastic …[12]

[12] Quoted in ibid., 54ff.

A French writer, Comettant, gives quite a different version of this event. According to him, the Distin quintet had performed in Belgium and had been greeted with laughter and cat-calls and had failed ignominiously when they attempted to acquire an engagement to perform in the rue Vivienne concerts in Paris. Sax, Comettant writes, listened patiently to their

The Distin Family Brass Quintet, ca. 1834.

tale of woe (and to their playing) and began by replacing the Distins' inferior instruments by fine saxhorns of his own making. Then, one by one, he made them play, showed them the nuances, and after a first lesson made them play together.

> Father Distin, surprised and marvelling at the effect of the well-blended combination, and filled with admiration for the homogeneity, fullness and sweetness of the new instruments, could not restrain his joyful emotion. Looking at his four sons, he said, 'we are saved,' and throwing himself on the inventor [Sax], embraced him in a transport of joy.[13]

[13] Quoted in Adam Carse, 'Adolphe Sax and the Distin Family,' *The Music Review* 6 (1945): 196.

Whatever was the circumstances of the Distin's discovery of these instruments, there is no doubt that not only the fortunes of the family immediately increased, but that their following tours had profound influence on the spread of these instruments in England and, in turn, helped make possible the growth of brass bands there.

> Everybody in the remotest degree interested in brass instrument playing endeavoured to hear this famous family.
> ......
> Thanks mainly to the Distins the year 1845 may be taken as the approximate beginning of the extraordinarily marked increase in amateur brass bands, and it was among the new bands that the Sax instruments were largely found.[14]

[14] Russell and Elliot, *The Brass Band Movement*, 55–56.

Another source of encouragement for the development of brass bands came from religious institutions, who were interested in improving the leisure activities of the workers, who otherwise were tempted by drink and gambling. Thus a number of bands were founded by the temperance movement, beginning with the Bramley Band of 1836.[15]

Related to this was the rise of Salvation Army bands which also played a great role in the development of the brass band movement. The first of these was formed in 1878 by the Fry family, a father and three sons, who played cornets, trombone, and euphonium. Soon General Booth encouraged his Army to take up bands (including women) and within six years there were four hundred Salvation Army bands.[16]

Finally, but by no means of less importance, the development of brass bands among the workers in industrial England was due in part to the encouragement of the factory owners and the aristocracy. The factory owners, while perhaps also having some genuine interest in the well-fare of their workers, often admitted that they hoped the bands would keep the men's minds off such 'dangers' as Trade Unionism or Socialism.[17]

Among the aristocracy, the concern was for public order. To some degree their support of the worker's bands must be seen as an attempt to control the lower classes through encouragement of 'safe' afterwork activities. Russell and Elliot[18] provide the background of this attitude.

> If the Georgian period had one salient feature that stood out above all else, it was the arrogance of the aristocracy. The quality moved along, engrossed in the importance of living; a gambling, dissolute, yet polished lot. Veritably the earth was made for them, and birth was the only standard by which to judge a man's integrity! The middle classes, made wealthy by the amazing expansion of trade and industry, were reaching up for power, but even their purchasing and spending capacity did not at first readily admit them into the charmed circle. The lower classes? Well, their place in the scheme of things was to minister to the material welfare of the two upper classes in every degree. The rulers had to some extent been frightened by the excesses of the populace in the French Revolution and determined, by repression, to prevent any possibility of a similar occurrence in England. It was really this psychological reaction which resulted in the drastic criminal laws[19] and the attempt to keep the under-dog in his kennel by denying him such elementary culture as might lie within his power if he were taught to read.

---

[15] The civic pub, however, remained a social center for the bandsmen of nineteenth-century England. In The Netherlands today, many civic bands still have their traditional 'headquarters,' where their flags and trophies are housed, in a local pub.

[16] Grove, 15:481, observes that today more than thirty thousand players are performing with these bands!

[17] Fox, *Instruments of Processional Music*, 32.

[18] Russell and Elliot, *The Brass Band Movement*, 61–62.

[19] It was a time when children could be hung for quite trivial offences and anyone could suffer that fate for any one of nearly three hundred different 'crimes.'

Early Brass Band Contests

Band contests in England date from at least 1818, well before the arrival of the brass band movement with which they are so much associated today. The early contests were local and small, often organized spontaneously on occasions where several bands gathered together in various civic celebrations. With the brass bands of the workers the idea spread quickly, for it made the band the subject of wider civic interest and stimulated civic ambition.

One of the early contests which was organized in advance was the Chichester Brass Band Contest in 1845. The contest was but one event in a day of celebrations which included games, falconry, archery, as well as a fruit and flower show. A judge, a Mr. Richard Hall, organist at Hull, was engaged and advertisements were sent out offering cash awards for both winners and losers. A limitation of twelve members was placed on prospective bands; percussion instruments were not allowed, for fear they might cover some of the finer points!

The citizens did not seem to know for sure in advance which bands would participate and therefore great enthusiasm grew as, one after the other, the bands arrived in decorated wagons. A contemporary describes the arrival of the Wold Band.

> … dashing into the park, comes a four-in-hand coach in full May Day panoply … each horse decorated with rosettes and long streamers of narrow various-coloured ribbons attached to its headgear and neck; the gorgeous portly driver with red beaming face, attired in crimson coat and gold-corded hat, and long whip streaming with ribbons, completed the resemblance. Small flags and rosettes peeped from every projecting portion of the coach, partly concealing the happy musical occupants, whose highly polished brass instruments gleamed as gold among the bedecking ribbons.[20]

There is an extant eyewitness description of the contest itself which is so rich in detail I should like to quote it in full.

> The first brass band to mount a contesting platform in Yorkshire was the Brocklesby Yeomanry Band, formed of four cornopeans, two Sax tenors, three trombones, a Sax bass, and two ophicleides. They chose as their competitive piece a selection from the works of Sir Henry Bishop,

[20] Quoted in Russell and Elliot, *The Brass Band Movement*, 82.

consisting of *Should he upbraid*, *Mynheer van Dunk*, etc. That the performance of this band gave enjoyment to the assemblage was distinctly proved by the applause that greeted them as they re-entered the park from the platform.

Their place was taken by Holmes Tannery Band, with a similar instrument formation; excepting that the leader played a Sax's recent *cornet-à-pistons*, as introduced by the Distin family in their last 1844 tour. This band's musical choice was a wise one, being a selection from Mozart's *Twelfth Mass*. Rapturous cheers, not unmingled with religious party zeal, greeted their really excellent playing of this very grand music.

The Hull Flax and Cotton Mills Brass Band was the third band seeking honours on the platform. The instruments of this band unfortunately were not equal to those of the two preceding them; and, although they played *Hail, Smiling Morn* fairly well, their best efforts fell flat on the assembled crowds, and they left the platform with but few hands in their favour.

The fourth band to ascend the rostrum was entered as the Wold Brass Band, led by Mr. James Walker of York, who played upon a D-flat soprano cornet. This band contained one Sax *cornet-à-pistons*, two cornopeans, two valved French horns, three trombones, one ophicleide, with one solo valved bass, and one valved tuba, both made (as was also the soprano) by the rising musical instrument maker of Yorkshire, Mr. Wigglesworth of Otley. The music selected by this band, from Rossini's *Barber of Seville*, was specially arranged to show the artistic skill of each member of the band. Enthusiastic shouts of pleasure mixed uncannily with the delightfully airy playing of the band: a new school of playing was being introduced, and on the conclusion of the piece tremendous cheers followed their retirement from the platform.

The Patrington Band, as fifth and last competitor, next occupied the attentions of the judge by a small *pot-pourri* of country airs. Unfortunately their instruments were perverse, as well as imperfect, and caused their well-meant efforts to pass totally unregarded by their friends and the populace. After they had quietly retired [it was announced that] the judge wished to hear the second and fourth bands play again: the second band this time to play a secular piece, and the fourth band to play a sacred piece, thus enabling him to determine accurately each band's respective and combined excellences.

After a short interval the second band, amidst loud applause, resumed their place upon the platform. The conductor raised his arm and the band commenced, *pp*, the Prayer from Weber's *Der Freischütz*, followed by a spirited selection from the same opera, full of fire and brilliancy. The spectators seemed assured that this band would easily win first place, and loudly gave free scope to their belief; but the Woldsmen smiled cheerily, not at all discouraged at the hostile demonstration. Without delay the fourth band remounted the platform, and calmed the hubbub with their fine style of playing the well-known introductory strain of the chorus so dear to every Yorkshireman, Handel's sublime *Hallelujah*

Chorus. 'Uncover! Uncover! Hats off!' resounded on all sides; and in bareheaded reverence the assembled rustics listened motionless to the finest performance they had ever heard of their deeply loved chorus. The expression of feeling evinced on the band leaving the stand can only be understood by musical enthusiasts.

After a short pause [the judge] announced his decision of the result of the playing, viz., that the Wolds Brass Band (the fourth) was the winner of the first prize of twelve pounds; and the Holmes Tannery (the second) was the winner of the second prize of eight pounds. Escorted by Lord Beauclerc [sic], the Ladies Chichester [sic] ascended the dais and presented the prizes to the leaders of the two winning bands, with an extra purse of sixteen pounds to be divided, five pounds each to the non-winning bands, and the odd sovereign to be given to the judge.[21]

[21] Quoted in ibid., 84ff.

The First 'National' Contests

Interest in brass bands was beginning to spread during the 1840s and perhaps the great display of brass instruments at the Industrial Exhibition of 1851 (in the newly constructed Crystal Palace) reflected the public interest. It was out of discussions held at the time of this exhibition, between Enderby Jackson, a key figure in British brass band contests for the rest of the century, and others which led to the plans for the first brass band contest on a larger scale, the Belle Vue Brass Band Contest of 1853 in Manchester.

There were several important new features in this contest, one of which was the ingenious idea of involving the railroads in offering special fares to the public attending the event. By 1855 the railroads were actually running special excursions in conjunction with these contests. Regarding the actual contest, now there were three judges, who were screened from the view of the players—a basic element of these contests ever since. Although there had been considerable fear that the public would not support such a contest by amateur musicians (because the Manchester orchestra under the famous Charles Halle had only slowly been able to build an audience), in fact some sixteen thousand people formed the audience.

The brass bands who participated (with numbers of players given in brackets) were those of Dewsbury [11], Bury Borough [10], Saddleworth [12], Newton Bank Print Works, Hyde [16], Nantwich [11], Woodside Halifax [13], Bramley, near Leeds [18] and the Mossley Temperance Saxhorn Band [10]. According to the reports in the *Manchester Guardian*[22] the repertoire for the day included the *Hallelujah Chorus*, Rossini's *Tancredi Overture*, 'The Heavens are telling,' from the *Creation* by Haydn, as well as arias from the works of Bellini and Donizetti.

Other important innovations came with later Belle Vue contests which had become an annual event, in particular the idea, introduced in 1854, of a test piece to be played by each band. By 1854 the public had become quite enthusiastic for these contests and followed their results closely. Local newspapers carefully reviewed and critically compared the competing bands, as one can see in the example of the *Hull Packet* (1854).

[22] Quoted in ibid., 101.

> Of No. 1 [Buslingthorpe] the less that is said the better; the intonation was particularly defective. No. 2 [Leeds Joppa] passed very well through its various performances ... No. 3 [Black Dyke Mill, who was awarded second prize] was superior to No. 2, and its performances were in better style than either of its predecessors. No. 4 [Huddersfield] was moderate. No. 5 [Gawthorp] and No. 6 [Bridlington and Quay] were better than No. 4 in the tone of the introduction, but were indifferent in time. No. 6 was the only East Riding band that had the courage to stand on the same ground as the men of the West, and, if the object was to show the marked difference between the music of the hills and that which bears a similar name in the plains, the demonstration was perfect. No. 7 [Smith's Leeds Band] was a very fine band; indeed we have rarely, if ever, heard a finer private band ... They played in perfect time; their tone was of a rich quality; they observed the points of expression, and there was much sweetness about the subdued tones of the *piano* passages ... the whole of their performance exhibited great tact in training.

Truly national contests began with the Crystal Palace Contest of 1860, the first great contest to be held in the South of England. As a measure of the growing interest in brass band contests, one might note that seventy-two bands made application for participation in the first of the two-day contest—although only forty-four actually appeared when the event occurred. The audience, too, was growing, for twenty thousand persons heard the bands on the second day!

One unusual feature of this contest was the combining of all the bands into a massed band of nearly fourteen hundred. Under the baton of Enderby Jackson, the principal organizer of the contest, this huge band[23] performed Mendelssohn's *Wed-*

[23] There were 144 soprano cornets, 184 first and 210 second cornets, 83 E♭ alto horns, 71 first and 51 second D♭ alto horns, 100 baritones, 74 tenor and 75 bass trombones, 80 euphoniums, 133 ophicleides, 155 E♭ tubas, 2 B♭ tubas, 26 small drums and a specially constructed monster gong requiring two players.

ding March, Handel's *Hallelujah Chorus*, Haydn's *The Heavens are Telling*, together with patriotic music. The *Daily Telegraph* reported that one could 'not hear the music for the sound.'

The size of the Crystal Palace made possible a contest with so many bands, for it was possible to have six stages, each with three judges, operating simultaneously.

The London newspapers were more than impressed by the musical results, the *London Era* commenting,

> The excellence of these bands has proved what rapid strides music has been making in our manufacturing districts. No military band in Her Majesty's service could at all compete with some of the bands that played. Among such a number it was a difficult matter for the judges to define the excellence of each, more especially where so many were equal.

The *Times* made the interesting observation that the Darlington Saxhorn Band was 'generally known as the Catholic band, and ... plays sacred music exclusively.' The *Daily Telegraph* summarized the state of the art at that time.

> It is interesting to observe that these workmen are daunted by no difficulties ... The Saltaire band is composed entirely of men in the employment of Mr. Titus Salt, at the establishment (or should we say the town?) near Bradford, which is called after his name. It is rumoured that Mr. Salt promised a considerable sum of money to his band in the event of their winning the first prize. This band affords an example of the rivalry which has resulted in these gigantic performances. The natural rivalry between factory and factory gradually extends to towns and cities, until, at length, entire districts are roused to emulation. All these bands have some distinctive features ... Indeed, though it is a *sine qua non* that every executant shall be a practical weaver, cotton spinner, miner, or working man of some description or other, some of these bands may be almost said to be nurseries for professional players.[24]

The Crystal Palace contests continued for three additional years.[25] The contest in 1861 featured a solo competition for players of bass instruments, the prize being an 'E♭ contrabass sonorophone.' This event was won by a member of the Keighley Band, performing on a contrabass trombone of his own invention. The final contest in this series, held in 1863, drew only twenty-one bands, perhaps due to a restriction which stated, 'No band will be allowed to compete unless it is tuned to the pitch of the Crystal Palace organ!'

[24] Quoted in ibid., 117. The final statement remains true today.

[25] The contests resumed during the twentieth century.

Brass Bands after 1860

After 1860 the brass band movement developed into immense proportions, with many new bands being formed during the 1860s and 1870s. Some of these were inspired by the Volunteer movement of 1859,[26] in particular this was the cause for the spread of the brass band movement into Scotland, where by 1862 brass band contests were being organized in Glasgow.[27] Other bands came into being through the enthusiasm generated by the contests, one of the latter was the Irwell Springs Band, begun by six residents returning home from the 1864 Belle Vue contest. An organizational meeting was announced which drew fifteen persons and soon the first rehearsal occurred in a private home, with a bedstead used as a conductor's podium. By the following year the band had nineteen members and appeals were made to the citizens for donations for instruments.

[26] Ibid., 133.

[27] Ibid., 157ff. In Wales, brass bands began at mid-century, but spread rapidly during the 1880s.

> Respected Neighbours and Friends,
>
> We, the members of the Irwell Springs Band, beg to appeal to you on behalf of ourselves to help us a little in subscribing towards the purchasing of two drums which we are yet in want of, as the instruments we have got has been all at our own expense, we can assure you it has been very hard for us being (as you know) all working men, but we were determined our little village should have something to enliven it. We think if we only wait upon you, you will do a little towards helping us in getting the same, which will cost upwards of 5 Pounds.
>
> Hoping you will excuse
>
> Yours truly,
> The Band[28]

[28] Quoted in ibid., 130.

An extraordinary band was founded in 1869 when a John Dennison was approached by a group of pit workers from the St. Hilda Colliery with the idea of forming a band. Although none of these persons had any musical knowledge whatever, and some were completely illiterate, within five years they were winning prizes in competition![29]

During the final twenty years of the nineteenth century the contest tradition grew to extensive proportions. The 1888 Belle Vue contest drew some eight thousand people, on fifty excursion trains, to view thirty-five bands performing selections from Wagner's *Flying Dutchman* as the required

[29] Ibid., 123.

composition. By the following year the *Daily News* observed that between Easter and August 'some hundreds of brass band contests take place.'[30] By 1895 there were two hundred and twenty-two contests in Great Britain and by 1896 two hundred and forty![31] One of several journals devoted to brass bands which came into existence during the final twenty years of the nineteenth century, the *Cornet*,[32] remarked on the positive influence of the contest system.

> Without a doubt the main factor in this all-round advancement is the contesting movement. Contesting has literally revolutionized the whole world of brass music, and its beneficial influence has more or less affected every brass band in the country. Bands everywhere are awaking and striving to improve their position; the introduction of contests has imbued them with a commendable desire to press to the front; and as a result we have better instruments, better music, better teachers, better officials, and better bandsmen.[33]

All this notwithstanding, as everyone knows competition can also unleash less commendable characteristics in man. In any contest, of course, most entries are 'losers,' as there can only be one 'winner.' By the end of the nineteenth century there began to occur in England some rather ugly instances of behavior on the part of the unsuccessful band members. An adjudicator of a contest in 1888 wrote to the *British Bandsman*, 'As soon as one band had found that they were unsuccessful, the members thereof launched out with a torrent of epithets which I doubt if the lowest riff-raff of Billingsgate could supersede or equal.'[34] Even at the famous Belle Vue Championship contest of 1888 the judges were hissed and hooted and even subjected to physical abuse. The *British Bandsman*, in commenting on this, noted,

> We have never ceased to condemn those meetings which, under the disguise of music, were little more than sporting assemblies, and when the result was a foregone conclusion among 'those in the know.' Matters have at last become so bad, that if an adjudicator is honest, and stands by his own opinion, he is almost sure to be insulted if nothing worse happens to him, and one by one the self-respecting judges keep dropping out of the field.[35]

[30] Ibid., 154.

[31] Ibid., 137, 170.

[32] Others were the *Brass Band Annual*, *Brass Band News*, and the *British Bandsman and Orchestral Times*. The *Brass Band Annual* carried a notice in an issue in 1895 which read:

> CONCERT MANAGERS AND COMMITTEES
> Don't be carried away with Challenges made by Certain Bands; it is only Empty Bounce and Bluster, and is only intended as cheap glory.

[33] Quoted in ibid., 137.

[34] This discussion is taken from ibid., 138ff.

[35] This association with 'sporting assemblies,' used by the British Bandsman in 1888, I find very interesting. I once attended the final stage of one of the modern versions of these national contests, in Albert Hall in London. I, too, had the impression I was observing some sort of physical, rather than musical, contest. If the printed dynamic were *piano*, the challenge seemed to be who could play at the most inaudible level, without regard to the musical logic of the work; the same, of course, held true for *forte*. Tempi also seemed a physical contest—I heard a Glinka overture which must have been performed at least twice as fast as any orchestral performance ever given! As a frequent participant of American contests, which are of course much younger chronologically, I could not help but be alarmed that I was seeing into the future of our own 'festivals.'

In addition, some smaller contests were actually corrupt; with the results altered by bribery or threats, the tampering of the instruments of contestants, etc.

The repertoire of these bands consisted of a great deal of trivial music, but also major transcriptions of important orchestral music. Although all this activity did not attract original composition by major composers during the nineteenth century, there is nevertheless something impressive in the fact that the brass band movement introduced thousands of working men (by the end of the century there were an estimated twenty thousand of these bands[36]) to the music of Mozart, Mendelssohn, Verdi, and Wagner.

[36] Grove, ibid., 210. Even today, according to this source there are some three thousand of these bands and the distinguished Guildhall School of Music offers a diploma in brass band conducting.

Court Wind Bands

12 Court Wind Bands in Austria

THE FINANCIAL COSTS of the Austrian-Bohemian participation in the Napoleonic Wars brought an end to many luxuries in the smaller courts, among them the aristocratic Harmoniemusik wind bands[1] which had so flourished during the Classical Period. If this activity was no longer so wide-spread, nevertheless the two most famous of the Viennese *Harmoniemusik* ensembles continued to be active during the first third of the nineteenth century. For the remainder of the century, the taste of aristocratic Vienna would turn to the dance music played by the civic orchestras and bands of Lanner, Fahrbach, and Strauss.

THE LIECHTENSTEIN *HARMONIEMUSIK*

In volume four of this series I have discussed the early history of this Harmoniemusik, especially with regard to the activity of Joseph Triebensee, who became 'fürstlichen Kammer- und Theater Kapellmeister' in 1794.[2] Although many of the Liechtenstein court records between 1792 and 1814 are lost,[3] it is nevertheless clear that Triebensee remained in this capacity until some point between 1809 and 1812, when he was succeeded by Wenzel Sedlak.[4]

The extant manuscripts of Triebensee for the Liechtenstein Harmoniemusik are extensive and include trivial marches and dance music, transcriptions of operas and other forms, together with serious original partitas. The music itself tells us that the *Harmoniemusik* performed both as functional music and for concert occasions. As an example of the latter, a court document of 1807[5] speaks of the *Harmoniemusik* giving concerts during the early Summer in the Gartenpalais every Sunday, Tuesday, and Thursday evening at 6:00 P.M.

As Triebensee neared the end of his tenure with this Harmoniemusik, he obviously began to think of trying to secure additional profits from the tremendous amount of effort he had invested in arranging and composing for this medium, for he began to attempt to sell copies of these works to other

[1] The term Harmoniemusik during the Classical Period meant usually an ensemble of pairs of oboes or clarinets (or both), horns, and bassoons. During the nineteenth century this term gradually becomes synonymous, usually in the shorter form of Harmonie, with the larger concert band, after the last of the true Harmoniemusik ensembles die out just before mid-century.

[2] Des regierenden Fürsten von Liechtenstein in Wien, Fasz. H-2, 159, 160 ex 1794, May 1. Triebensee (1772–1846), an active oboe player in Vienna beginning about 1791, studied composition with Albrechtsberger and oboe with his father Georg Triebensee.

[3] Hannes Stekl, 'Harmoniemusik und "türkische Banda," des Fürstenhauses Liechtenstein,' *Das Haydn Jahrbuch*, vol. 10 (1978), 173, fn. 20.

[4] The Harmoniemusik of Prince Liechtenstein in Vienna disbanded apparently in about 1809. But it appears to have been reformed with Sedlak as the leader in about 1812. Sedlak is associated with this ensemble in his arrangements in Vienna, Österreichische Nationalbibliothek, and is clearly identified as the Kapellmeister of the Liechtenstein court on the title page of Artaria's publication in 1814 of Sedlak's arrangement of *Fidelio* for Harmoniemusik.

[5] Liechtenstein Hausarchiv, Fasz. H-2, Nr. 27 (May 25, 1807).

courts. Indeed, a few copies of his works are found in other court libraries, but it would appear he sold very few, due to the decline in the numbers of these ensembles as mentioned above.

His first attempt was one of trying to enlist in advance a group of aristocratic subscribers. For this purpose he placed in the German journal, the *Allgemeinen Musikalischen Zeitung* (January 1804), an advertisement offering to the potential subscribers each year six opera transcriptions and six original partitas. He promised each opera transcription would be at least twelve movements in length and invited the subscribers to request specific operas they would like to have included in the series. The number of movements in a Partita, he says, 'is well-known.'[6]

The advertisement also reflects both the fact that such music was still popular in aristocratic circles in 1804 and Triebensee's own awareness of the skill he had gained through his countless hours of service for Prince Liechtenstein.

> Because for some time several masterworks of the most famous composers have been transcribed for Harmonie, in which often the spirit of the composer has been totally deformed, often totally unrecognizable, without consideration for the instruments, their range and their usefulness, and through this the enjoyment of the artist in the performance must be diminished, all of which the natural result is that the expected enjoyment of the listener, where it is not totally destroyed, is at least extremely reduced. Because of all of this, Joseph Triebensee, without wanting to praise himself, has enjoyed for quite sometime the fact that he has been rewarded by undivided applause by the noble society as well as other experts and friends of Harmonie, has the honor to advertise that he has decided to publish a collection of the best and newest operas and ballets, as well as original partitas for eight-voice Harmonie, in continuous yearly editions.[7]

The appearance of some copies in various European libraries indicates that Triebensee had at least some success in selling his series. One set is found in Vienna in the Österreichische Nationalbibliothek (Sm.3739) and carries this title written in his own hand.[8]

> Miscellannies de Musique … arranges pour Deux Hautbois, Deux Clarinettes, Deux Cors, Deux Bassoons … un grand Bassoon … par Joseph Triebensee, maitre de chapelle au service de son Altesse serenissime le Prince de Lictensten.

[6] It is my impression that most German-speaking, music-loving aristocrats at this time would have indeed been familiar with the partita as the wind band equivalent of the four-movement symphony for orchestra—the forms being the same. The reader should remember that during the Classical Period the titles were bound up with both form and medium, consequently Mozart would have been just as unlikely to compose a Partita for orchestra as he would have been to compose a Symphony for wind band.

[7] The original text reads,

> Da seit einiger Zeit mehrere Meisterstücke der berübmtesten Kompositeurs auf Harmonie gesetzt erschienen, bey welchen oft der Geist des Autors ganz verstümmelt, oft gar unkennbar war—ohne Rücksicht auf Instrumente—ihre Lage—ihre Anwendbarkeit—und dadurch die Freude der Künstler zur Produktion sich verlieren muss, von welchem allen die natürliche Folge ist, dass das erwartete Vergnügen des Zuhörers, wo nicht ganz vernichtet, doch wenigstens sehr geschmälert wird, so giebt sich Joseph Trübensee, der bereits, ohne ruhmredig zu seyn, schon lange das Glück genoss, dass die hohen Herrschaften sowohl, ala übrigen (P.T.) Kenner und Freunde der Harmonie seine Arbeiten mit ungetheiltem Beyfall belohnten, die Ehre, die Anzeige zu machen, er sey gesonnen seine Sammlung der besten und neusten Opern und Ballete, wie auch Originalparthieen für achtstimmige Harmonie in ununterbrochenen Jahrgängen mittelst Subscription herauszugeben.

To this he attached, with red sealing wax, a small printed form which represented his own personal attempt at 'copyrighting' his labor.[9]

> The present Harmonie-collection is my own work and was prepared by myself, authenticated by this sealed note; but at the same time I implore and rely on the justice and reasonableness of my respected and noble customer, that you reserve the use of this for yourself, and allow no unjust copying, allow me to emphasize it further, for through it I should earn my livelihood. Vienna.

Judging from the transcriptions of Triebensee I have studied, it does appear that he achieved somewhat higher musical results than some of his other contemporaries. On the other hand, I suspect I have only seen a small portion of his original works, in part because he almost never wrote his name on his scores and, consequently, it will be some time before his body of composition can be identified. I have performed a dozen or so of his ensemble *Variations* for *Harmoniemusik* and they often demonstrate considerable talent. His piano *Concerto* with *Harmoniemusik* is worthy of performance, if one leaves out the two Minuets and performs only the normal three-movement form.[10]

One of Triebensee's E♭ Partitas (Vienna, Gesellschaft der Musikfreunde in Wien, VIII 39986) is quite outstanding and the equal of any work in this genre, save the two by Mozart. The Allegro vivace is very lyric, harmonically interesting, and with florid passages for oboe, clarinet, and bassoon. The Andante is one of the most extraordinary movements of the *Harmoniemusik* literature. It begins almost as a hymn, but very heart-felt and lyric, in A♭ major. Suddenly the unaccompanied horn completely changes the mood to one of melancholy, with startling and abrupt modulations to several minor keys, all with interesting non-harmonic tones. Following the return of the 'hymn,' stated with interesting changes, the unaccompanied bassoons and contrabassoon conclude the work with a haunting augmentation of one of the basic motives. The Menuetto features the solo clarinet, while the Trio is scored for solo horns and bassoons. The concluding Rondo has an almost Mozartean character and ends, as very few final movements for any medium at this time do, softly. This *Partita* by Triebensee

---

[8] In an era when time still had little value, this was not uncommon. Vienna had two famous establishments at this time (Traeg and Lausch) who stocked great numbers of autographs and sold manuscript copies, priced by the page, to customers upon request. Both firms sold wind band music, together with music for all mediums.

[9] In his 1804 advertisement quoted above, Triebensee expressed similar concerns.

> Today one sees only too often in the field of music examples of forgery and other things of this sort.

[10] The first Beethoven sonata for piano also has a minuet and trio that no one plays today. This Concerto is also written with the expectation of the time that improvisation is expected in several obvious places. If this is not done then what remains is much like the fable of the 'Emperor without his clothes.'

was performed at the Vienna Music Festival in 1978 by Antonin Myslik and his colleagues from Prague to great applause. I believe it may have been the first wind ensemble work performed during this festival in modern times.

Some time between 1809 and 1812, Triebensee left the service of the Liechtenstein court and his exact whereabouts and duties remain somewhat unclear until he turns up in Prague in 1816, where he succeeded Carl Maria von Weber as director of the Prague Opera. It is only from this period that we have a personal description of the man by a contemporary. In 1827, a visiting Englishman, Edward Holmes, observed Triebensee at work.

> There was plenty of amusement at rehearsal, for the music-director and some women who were trying over songs for a new opera, seasoned their morning's work with a world of pleasantries.—The present maestro is a little wizened old man, remarkable for the quaint singularity of his dress, and his long hair, parted and streaming over his shoulders. Having found that his compositions will not do for the people of Prague, he ensconceth himself in his strong-hold as singing-master, in which capacity he is really excellent. With a counterfeit surliness in his voice and look, he sometimes sits in the orchestra eyeing a poor girl on the stage, and as she sings doubtingly, points to some particular inch of the throat from which the sound proceeds; but he does not quit his remarks nor renewed beginnings until the tone comes forth from the proper quarter.[11]

On 1 April 1812, Prince Liechtenstein reorganized his Harmoniemusik, now under the leadership of Wenzel Sedlak, who had served as second clarinetist in the Harmoniemusik under Triebensee.[12] The duties of the Harmoniemusik during the period of Sedlak no doubt remained in the past tradition.[13] In particular one reads of morning serenades (*musikalische Horgenunterhaltung*)[14] and of Sedlak's responsibility for the education of the noble children (*jungen Herrschaft*).[15]

The tradition in this court for operas transcribed for Harmoniemusik continued under Sedlak and from his pen one finds lengthy (sometimes twenty or more movements!) transcriptions of the most popular operas of his generation, including those of Rossini, Bellini, and Donizetti. One can not be sure how many of these extensive arrangements Sedlak

[11] Holmes, *A Ramble Among the Musicians of Germany*, 185ff.

[12] Stekl, 'Harmoniemusik und "türkische Banda," des Fürstenhauses Liechtenstein,' 168.

[13] Liechtenstein Hausarchiv, 3037 ex 1816, 15 June; 556 ex 1818, 30 4 January.

[14] Stekl, 'Harmoniemusik und "türkische Banda," des Fürstenhauses Liechtenstein,' 174, fn. 42.

[15] Liechtenstein Hausarchiv, ad 3659 ex 1826; and [no number], December 17, 1812.

made, but after the first twenty or so he sometimes numbered them. His arrangement of Rossini's *Semiramide*, Sedlak calls his '52nd Work.'

Although Sedlak did not seem to be a composer, he certainly had skill in transcribing and wrote well for the *Harmoniemusik* medium. Nothing demonstrates this better than his exceptional transcription of Beethoven's *Fidelio*, a transcription which was in fact published by Beethoven's publisher at that time, Artaria in Vienna. Beethoven himself placed an advertisement for the work in the *Wiener Zeitung* (July 1, 1814), which seems to suggest that this transcription was made from the autograph score with his complete approval.

> The undersigned, at the request of the Messrs. Artaria and Co., herewith declares that he has given the score of his opera *Fidelio* to the aforesaid publisher, for publication under his supervision in a complete piano score, quartets, or arrangements for Harmonie[musik].
>
> Vienna, June 28, 1814 Ludwig van Beethoven[16]

During his tenure as leader, Sedlak was paid 800 fl. per year, with the other members of the Harmoniemusik receiving from 300 to 600 fl.[17] They also received free uniforms and free housing, with a heating and lighting allowance. When the court was in Vienna the *Harmoniemusik* lived together in a house near the Liechtenstein Palace.

Prince Liechtenstein maintained a second wind band as well during this period, his 'türkischen Musik,' for Gardemusik. This wind band provided not only ceremonial music, but also played in church, in the theater, and for dancing and hunting.[18]

THE IMPERIAL *HARMONIEMUSIK*

After the retirement of Johann Wendt, the Kaiser's *Harmoniemusik* continued and included among its membership many of the leading wind players of this time in Vienna. It appears the leadership of the ensemble was taken over by someone who was not a composer, as the additions to their repertoire between 1800 and 1835 seem to consist entirely of music acquired from people outside the ensemble. The repertoire is, however, none the poorer.[19]

[16] The original text read,

> Der Endesunterzeichnete, aufgefordert von den Herrn Artaria und Comp., erklärt hier mit, dass er die Partitur seiner Oper: Fidelio gedachter Kunsthandlung überlassen habe, um unter seiner Leitung dieselbe im vollstandigen Clavier-Auszüge, Quartetien, oder für Harmonie arrangiert, herauszugeben.

[17] Stekl, 'Harmoniemusik und "türkische Banda," des Fürstenhauses Liechtenstein,' 171.

[18] Ibid., 168.

[19] Much of the repertoire of this Harmoniemusik can be identified from an official court catalog of the collection, made intermittently between 1826 and 1856. Another inventory was made in 1884, at which time some works were removed and a note was entered on page 110 of this catalog, reading, 'Those pieces of Harmoniemusik and current and obsolete concert music marked with a 'C' were transferred to the Conservatory on 29 January, 1884.' When I first read this note, in 1967, I immediately tried to find these works, but without success.

One large collection this *Harmoniemusik* acquired was the above mentioned 'Miscellannies de Musique' of Triebensee. On this set, Triebensee has added, in his own hand, a manuscript note reading, 'für der k.k. Hof Harmonie.'

Another extraordinary cycle of compositions first played by this ensemble was composed for the name-day celebration of Franz I and performed on 4 October 1805. These works consist of five independent compositions for *two Harmoniemusik* ensembles, by a well-known Viennese musician of that era, Ignaz von Seyfried.[20] First there is an opening March, for combined *Harmoniemusik*, based on a theme by Grétry. Next is a Divertimento, in two movements, for antiphonal *Harmoniemusik*. This is followed by a three-movement Cantata for STTB soli, SATB chorus, and both *Harmoniemusik*. The second movement of this work, a canon on a long subject, is quite beautiful. The next movement is an extraordinary Quodlibet, consisting of twenty-four 'movements.' Each movement is a brief excerpt from a then well-known opera or popular song. Some are quite funny in their abrupt endings, or in the manner in which they are followed by the next excerpt. Some vary in instrumentation, as for example one for bassoons only, and another which has an unaccompanied solo section for two contrabassoons! The first twenty-two movements are performed alternately by the two *Harmoniemusik* ensembles; the final two are scored for all eighteen players. The final movement, the Austrian National Hymn, and the following fifth composition, a haunting March based on a theme by Cherubini, both have a certain melancholic character. This is perhaps explained by the fact that even as this was being performed Napoleon was on his way to conquer Vienna, which he did a few weeks later, on 13 November.

Another possible indication of the activity of this Harmoniemusik can perhaps be seen in the fact that the imperial printing bureau (k.k. priv. Chemischen Druckerey) apparently printed a number of works for *Harmoniemusik*. Among these was a transcription for Harmoniemusik of one of Seyfried's 'biblical dramas,' for which he was locally famous, *Saul König in Israel*. In this case the composer himself made the *Harmoniemusik* version, which was part of a series of similar works published by this state printer. This issue carries an interesting note relative to this series.

[20] Seyfried (1776–1841) was an aristocrat who seems to have known everyone. He was a friend of both Mozart and Beethoven; a student of Haydn; and a teacher to Goethe and Franz von Suppé! He was well-known as a composer and conductor (first performance of *Fidelio*) during his life. Among his efforts are an additional movement, a 'Libera,' for Mozart's *Requiem* and his arrangement of Beethoven's three *Equale* (for trombones) as a *Trauer-Gesang* for TTBB for the funeral of Beethoven.

This journal follows in the sequence in which we have published, every two months since last May, 1810, of the invigorating operas, ballets, and other unique masterworks for either six or nine-part Harmonie. Our custom, as always with acknowledged and famous masters, is to work from autograph scores and with special diligence and exact knowledge of the characteristics of wind instruments.

The price [of this work] is the highest of the Harmonie works we have published, but in hindsight we will stand by this Harmonie publication before any other publication as the proof sheets have had special priority. No master of art has been so often consulted with each exact and painstaking correction. Only once have we permitted an embellishment to be undertaken, and that was determined by the master himself in his own authentic version. [This is necessary] since it can not be assumed that every manuscript is similar with regard to accuracy or requires the same diligence or effort.

Following this work is a list of other Harmonie pieces [published] by us. [This series] will be soon continued according to the wishes of the better k.k. regiments and other connoisseurs [of Harmoniemusik].[21]

The most valuable portion of the repertoire of this *Harmoniemusik* is the group of partitas (several are called Harmonie and dedicated to the emperor) by Franz Krommer,[22] the Viennese Court Chamber Composer. These works are quite above average in quality, some ranking with the very best of this genre. They represent an entirely new generation in the partita, for now the clarinet, rather than the oboe, is usually the chief soloist. They are also more advanced harmonically than the works of the late eighteenth century and can be said, I believe, to be a genuine harbinger of Romanticism. In addition, the Partitas of Krommer have much more advanced technical demands for each instrument, which offers a valuable insight, one which can not be found in the orchestral music of this period, namely that these players were of a technical level equal to the very best players today.

[21] A copy of this publication is in Vienna, Stadtbibliothek, Musiksammlung (M.24772/c). The list of additional publications listed are, with the exception of the Krommer, Beethoven, and Purcbl, lost. The full list read,

> [Anonymous], *Beliebter Marsch*
> Eppinger, *Marsch*
> Kanne, *Marsch*
> Krommer, 3 works for Franz I of Österreich, 8 works for Erzherzog, Joseph Palatinus, Ungarn
> Purcbl, 6 *Marsche*
> [Anonymous], Ballet *Figaro*
> Schiedermayer, 6 *Marsche*
> Weigl, *Marsch aus Waisenhaus*
>   *Marsch aus Hadrian*
> Beethoven, *Sonate Pathétique*
> Blumenthal, *Marsch aus Konig Lear*

[22] Krommer, who settled in Vienna in 1794, had previously worked for important courts in Western Hungary, in particular those of Counts Styrum-Limburg, Karolyi, and Grassalkowitz. In addition to a very large number of partitas for wind band, he has left works for military band, works with winds for church use and a political work, 'Gott erhalte Franz den Kaiser.'

13 Court Wind Bands in Germany

As in Austria, the aristocratic *Harmoniemusik* tradition continued in Germany for about the first third of the nineteenth century. One of the best-known of these served the Duke of Sondershausen from 1802 until 1835. In this court the twelve-member wind band was the only court ensemble, with the famous clarinetist, Simon Hermstedt, serving as Kapellmeister. Although Spohr referred to this ensemble in 1808 as a *Harmoniemusik*,[1] the duke himself used a version of the older baroque term, Hof-Obisten-Chor.[2]

An article by Gerber in the *Allgemeinen Musikalischen Zeitung* for 1809 provides some valuable information regarding the actual performances by this *Harmoniemusik*. Apparently the band played outdoors in a natural amphitheater near the duke's shooting arena during the Summer, in the shooting house hall during the Winter, in private concerts for the duke in his palace and in music festivals in other towns (Magdeburg in 1825 and Halberstadt in 1828). Gerber, who was present for one of the palace concerts, writes that the typical repertoire consisted of a 'grand partita in the manner and form of a Haydn Symphony,' followed by operas transcribed for *Harmoniemusik*.[3]

Another important *Harmoniemusik* was founded in 1801 by Duke Friedrich of Mechlenburg-Schwerin. At its birth, this *Harmoniemusik* consisted of nine members, but later a flute, trombone, alto clarinet and bass horn were added.[4] The ensemble wore green uniforms and for a time carried swords, however, the duke ended this practice after one of the hornists, Bode, in a drunken condition, struck his wife with his sword!

According to Meyer,[5] this ensemble was formed for the purpose of art music and performed with distinction, especially in the Summer to the delight of the guests at the baths at Doberan. The reader may perhaps recall that Mendelssohn was inspired to compose his *Notturno* for eleven winds (known today as the *Overture*, op. 24) for this band after hearing them perform in Doberan. Wilhelm Wieprecht also reported being impressed with hearing this 'so-called *Harmoniemusik*' perform there.[6]

---

[1] Spohr, *Autobiography*, 1:123.

[2] For further information, see Pamela Weston, *Clarinet Virtuosi of the Past* (London: Hale, 1971). The members of the wind band were Lundershause and Himmelstosse (oboe), Hermstedt and Georg Friedrich Heinrici (clarinet), Benleb and Friedrich Hermstedt (bassoon), Hartung and Seebach (horn), Hühne and Bartel (trumpet), Georg Heinrici (trombone), and Herrmann (bass horn).

[3] Hellyer, 'Harmoniemusik,' 232, cites an early print by Peters of Mozart Quartets arranged by Hermstedt for *Harmoniemusik*.

[4] Clemens Meyer, *Geschichte der Mecklenburg-Schweriner Hofkapelle* (Schwerin: i. M., L. Davids, 1913), 103. An article in the *Allgemeinen Musikalischen Zeitung* (1812, Nr. 30) listed the members of this *Harmoniemusik* as Hammerl and Stüber (clarinet), Haidner and Heller (bassoon), Bode and Theen (horn), Nicolai (oboe), Richter (flute), Winzer (trumpet), and Seipoldsdorf (serpent).

[5] Ibid.

[6] Quoted in Kalkbrenner, *Wilhelm Wieprecht*, 82.

> Ich selbst hörte noch diese sogenannte Harmoniemusik und zwar in Doberau von der Grossherzoglich Mecklenburg-Schweriuschen Hofkapelle in einer grossen Vollendung executiren.

The duke also had a military band, called Hautboisten, and one reads that during the period 1833–1835 the *Harmoniemusik* and the Hautboisten alternated playing concerts every other day.⁷

An issue of the *Allgemeinen Musikalischen Zeitung* (1811/18) provides some information on the *Harmoniemusik* founded in 1793 by Prince Ludwig Friedrich for his court at Rudolstadt. This report speaks of the high quality of the ensemble and of their usual court duties, which included playing music of all kinds, including dance music. The ensemble also played concerts, every Sunday and festival day, from 6:00 to 8:00 P.M., with the repertoire again given as partitas and opera transcriptions.⁸

The traveling Englishman, Holmes, whom I have quoted several times, heard in Munich what must have been an aristocratic *Harmoniemusik* in 1827. His touching account describes a concert in which it is evident the players were both excellent technically and sensitive.

> A friend invited me to an evening concert, in which were performed the overtures and various pieces from the Don Juan and Clemenza di Tito of Mozart, excellently arranged as sextetts for two clarionets, two bassoons, and two horns; there was not power enough for the full pieces, but the arias pleased me extremely, being blown with so subdued and mellow a tone as might have been borne in a small room. This *harmonie musik*, as it is termed, is a species entirely of German cultivation, and I suspect that the wrath of old Dominico Scarlatti against wind instruments might be appeased, were he to hear how skilfully they are tempered. One of the performers gratified me with a piece of sentiment which I did not expect from a person of his appearance; after playing a tender air from an opera of Mozart, he said, 'I think the composer means that the lady feels pain here,' placing his hand on his heart.⁹

The *Harmoniemusik* for the principal court in Munich, on the other hand, seems to have been primarily functional, if one can judge by the extant repertoire in the Bayerische Staatsbibliothek in Munich. A set of *Harmoniestücke* by Johann Poissl (1783–1865) carries a note, '*für die Harmonie der Königl Tafelmusik.*' More extraordinary by far is a complete library of *Harmoniemusik* from the first half of the nineteenth century, compiled by William LeGrand. Here (under *one* shelf-mark!) are five hundred and fifty-one individually numbered works

---

7 Meyer, *Geschichte der Mecklenburg-Schweriner Hofkapelle*, 118.

8 The members are given as Meyer and Junghaus (oboe), Müller and Flittner (clarinet), Wettich and Schöniger (bassoon), Sumner and Eschrich (horn), Buchmnn (flute), and Koch (contrabassoon, here 'quart-fagott').

9 Holmes, *A Ramble Among the Musicians of Germany*, 75–76.

for *Harmoniemusik*,[10] contained in leather-bound part-books. Looking at these volumes, one can almost hear the leader calling out to his colleagues, during perhaps an aristocratic banquet, 'Number eighty-six … Number three hundred and twelve.' This collection contains arrangements, of course, but also original works, among which is one for solo oboe, accompanied by the other eight members of the ensemble.

Holmes also reported hearing what must have been, in so early a date (1827), a *Harmoniemusik* concert in Dresden.

> The most noticeable music here given was some of the sinfonias of Beethoven and Haydn—The overtures to Fidelio and Anacreon, Mozart's finales to Don Juan and Figaro, ably adapted, and the voice parts taken in for a band by Meyer, brother of the celebrated composer of that name. I will not say that this music was so dashingly played as it might have been by our Philharmonic orchestra, but it was complete enough for those who enjoy the display of an author's mind more than the pride of perfect *fiddling*.[11]

It was for a *Harmoniemusik* in Dresden that Weber composed several works which accompany singers.

Court Wind Bands after the *Harmoniemusik* Period

While the financial demands of the Napoleonic Wars caused a retrenchment of such court luxuries as aristocratic *Harmoniemusik*, the general excitement and drama of the same wars played a part in making the larger military band a new status symbol. One can see this transition taking place in the cycle of band works by Paul Maschek, which have been discussed above, which were composed both during and to commemorate the Battle of Leipzig and the ensuing Winter Campaign of 1813–1814. Here the composer made two separate versions of the same music, one for large band, called 'Harmonie with turkish music,' and one for *Harmoniemusik*, as though he wanted to be prepared to sell copies according to the preference of the aristocratic customer.

As another illustration of this changing taste, I should like to quote two examples of wind bands used in a similar function—ceremonies in honor of an aristocrat. In the first, the

[10] Munich, Bayerische Staatsbibliothek (Mus.Ms.2316). These are scored for pairs of oboes, clarinets, horns, and bassoons.

[11] Holmes, *A Ramble Among the Musicians of Germany*, 203–204.

celebration of the birthday of the Grand Duke of Baden, in 1828, we see both the *Harmoniemusik* and the military band, türkishmusik, employed. Here, however, the *Harmoniemusik* still seems to have had the 'spotlight,' appearing in the central church ceremony, while the 'turkish music' was relegated to the street. The following court instructions[12] for the appropriate celebration of the grand duke's birthday may seem quite over done to the modern reader, but it must have been a scene played many times over before the twentieth century.

[12] Quoted in Suppan, *Blasmusik in Baden*, 238ff.

[1] A triple salute of all the firearms announces the birthday of Carl Friedrich on Saturday at 5:00 A.M. At 5:00 P.M. there will be an hour of bell-ringing, with a cannon salute every ten minutes, after which there will be a suitable song, accompanied by wind instruments, sung by the choir from the balcony of the church tower. At 6:00 P.M. there will be on the entire length of the district, and on the adjoining mountains …, fires of joy lit which will burn up until 10:00 P.M. The old castle, Windeck, will be especially lit and from here will be given the signals for the lighting of the other fires. The evening will be brought to a close by the turkish musik marching through the streets.

[2] Sunday will be announced by the ringing of all the bells, by the marching of the türkish musik, and by the salute of the cannon to announce the festive day.

[3] At 8:00 A.M. the civic bell will ring at which time the members of the various guilds will assemble at the communal hall and the school children will assemble in their school rooms. The guilds will march two by two behind their flags, followed by the children, to the city hall where the various national and local dignitaries will be located.

[4] The parade will begin from there in the following order:
   1. Die Musik
   2. A division of citizens militia
   3. Boys of the school
   4. Girls of the school
   5. Twelve girls dressed in white, with ribbons of the color of our Most Noble Princes House, leading three others in the middle, of which one carries the likeness of Carl Friedrich, while the other two hold a laurel wreath above the same.
   6. District officials, state officials and employees
   7. Deputies of all the communities in the district
   8. Community Court and Citizens Council
   9. Another division of citizens militia

[5] As soon as the above mentioned three girls with Carl Friedrich's picture appear in front of the official building, the other twelve will make a circle around these three; the civic militia present arms and the

flags should be dipped. Up till now the laurel wreath has been held above the likeness. Now the present assembly brings three cheers to the spirit of the unforgettable Carl Friedrich, following which the parade marches on toward the church, under the tolling of all the bells and firing of cannons.

[6] As soon as the parade begins, all the bells will ring and there will be rifle salutes every five minutes.

[7] After arriving in the church, the likeness of Carl Friedrich will be set up in the choir area, around which the twelve girls will make a circle. After this begins the festival service, with a sermon to be held in front of the church … following which the answer of Carl Friedrich to the letter of thanks of his subjects after the successful repeal of serfdom will be read. This is followed by High Mass, during which four church songs will be sung to the accompaniment of wind instruments. After the ending of the same, 'Herr Gott dich loben wir' will be sung, followed by the song mentioned above in [1]. 'Heil unserm Fursten, Heil!' will be sung by a four-voice choir, accompanied by wind instruments. After the church service so ends, the parade will return in the same order to the city hall where it will dissolve.

[8] The state officials will gather after this with the religious officials of the district, the deputies of the communities, the local court, and the Citizens Council, in the Gasthaus zum Raben, for a mid-day meal by which the following toasts will be brought (to Carl Friedrich, to his family, etc.).

[9] In the evening, the church tower, the city hall, and the main street will be illuminated.

[10] The day will end with a Ball in the above-named Gasthaus and with dances in all the other inns.

For the purpose of comparison, let me now mention a celebration given in honor of Queen Victoria of England in honor of her visit to Coblenz in 1845. Here, fewer than twenty years after the above ceremony in Baden, one sees no *Harmoniemusik* participation—not even for the dinner music, but only military bands. Wilhelm Wieprecht, who was invited to organize the music for these ceremonies, first describes rehearsals with one hundred and twenty men.[13] This was apparently a select ensemble, large as it was, for Wieprecht relates little difficulty in preparing the music, 'since they can read at sight even a difficult overture and with only a few comments the second time it goes with certainty.' But this was only the *dinner* music! The *pièce de résistance* was a great outdoor serenade by a massed band of five hundred and sixty military bandsmen, conducted by

[13] Letter from Wilhelm Wieprecht to Louis Schneider, quoted in Kalkbrenner, *Wilhelm Wieprecht*, 44ff.

Wieprecht, beneath the queen's window at the Bruhl Castle.[14] Wieprecht's description of the preparations for one of his celebrated massed band concerts is very interesting.

[14] An engraving of this serenade appeared in the *Illustrated London News* (September, 1845).

> Since my superior, Count Redern, left the instrumentation to me, I chose the instrumentation which I had suggested in my letters on Prussian military music. I had brought with me A♭ clarinets, cornets, and tenor horns, as well as my own music, and performed the music in the style of my great military concerts. On the 25th all the directors of the Rhein music choirs arrived for a conference with me. Here we fixed the program and the formation for the music of the reception which was demanded for Queen Victoria in the Castle Bruhl.
>
> Every director took it upon himself to have the parts copied and rehearsed with his band. By fixing the tempi in advance, it was thus possible to bring to life this performance of five hundred sixty players in only two rehearsals. The directors went back to their garrisons and I continued my rehearsals for the dinner music [the one hundred and twenty musicians mentioned above].
>
> On the 9th of August, from 8:00 until 12:00 in the morning, I had three rehearsals for the great evening concert, with small groups each consisting of four bands. On the same day at 4:00 in the afternoon we had the first full rehearsal.
>
> The success was so satisfying that I decided to do the performance with this single rehearsal. On the 10th I gave the bands a rest and on the 11th at 9:00 in the morning we had the dress rehearsal. The concert was at 8:00 that evening and the success I owe to the love and attention of the various directors and the bands working with them. This great mass of musicians I had placed in an open square, each band complete unto itself, and each with its own director. I took my place in the middle of the square. The front was occupied by the bands of the infantry, the right wing by the percussion, and the left wing by the cavalry bands …
>
> There were two hundred men with torches, formed in a large 'V' [for Victoria]; many thousands of listeners stood in astonishing quiet.
>
> The signal was given to begin and with this mass we played the folksong, 'God Save the King.' On the second, fourth, sixth, eighth, etc., measures I had arranged an accent with the rolling of tambours, with a diminuendo across the entire bar.
>
> The last roll was held in a long pianissimo, then very gradually increased until the beginning of my own composition, a Huldigungsmarsch, began. Then followed a fast march by Count Redern, the 'Wedding March' from Mendelssohn's *Mid-Summer Night's Dream*, the Overture and a march on the motives of the *Feldlager* by Meyerbeer, and a fast march by me. The final work in this serenade was *Rule Britannia*.
>
> Following the concert was the Zapfenstreich, a Retraite, and the Abendlied, after which this military scene was closed … The performance was perfect in spite of the difficult formation. We had neither music stands nor special persons to hold the music and in some areas there was too little illumination.

Wieprecht and his work with military bands in Prussia had contributed greatly to the popularity of the new large military bands in Germany, as I have detailed above. However, even before Wieprecht's rise to prominence, large military bands were popular with King Friedrich Wilhelm III in Berlin. Holmes reported observing this phenomenon there in 1827.

> Before the commencement of the opera the stage was crowded with a vast wind-instrument band and chorus (numbering about three hundred performers), which, with the assistance of the regular orchestra, Spontini at their head, gave a composition in honour of a court birthday. The ground-work of this music was 'God save the King,' but the simple tune was interlarded with long instrumental symphonies, which were quite irrelevant to its style and character. This noisy parade of loyalty was intended by Spontini to please the king of Prussia, whose ear is obtuse, except to an immense Crash.[15]

It is in this light that one can understand the existence of the functional works composed for the Berlin Court by Spontini and Meyerbeer for large bands.[16]

This predilection in Berlin for large military bands playing indoors for the aristocracy seems to have continued throughout the nineteenth century. The memoirs of one of the members of this court mentions a dinner given by Bismarck in 1873, in which the 'background' music was placed in a balcony, following a court tradition centuries old. In this case, however, a complete military band was placed there!

> All the big-wigs in Berlin were to be seen there. I sat between two court ladies. Conversation was out of the question, as the military band up in the gallery was making an infernal din. They began with the Overture to *Fidelio*, and I thought I was listening to massed bands on parade.[17]

This was a prince who appreciated music and once wrote, 'without music man is but half complete.'[18] If the reader gains the impression from the above quotation that this prince found a military band at dinner 'too much of a good thing,' imagine his reaction when, in 1890, he attended a dinner in Berlin which was accompanied by *two* military bands!

[15] Holmes, *A Ramble Among the Musicians of Germany*, 221.

[16] See volume nine of this series. The Spontini work referred to was the *Festmarsch*, which is extant. With regard to Meyerbeer, since all of his band manuscripts disappeared from Berlin during World War II, it is difficult to say with certainty what the nature of his output was. His surviving major band compositions all exist in arrangements by Wieprecht. These include the four works he composed for the weddings of members of the royal family, the famous *Fackeltänze* (composed 1842–1858) and a very interesting *Festival march* for two bands.

[17] *Memoirs of Prince Chlodwig of Bohenlohe-Schillingsfürst* (New York: Macmillan, 1906), 2:89.

[18] Ibid., 1:13.

> I sat opposite the Empress, and between Molke and Kameke. The former would have been very talkative, but was disturbed by the continual music, and was much annoyed therat. Two military bands were placed opposite one another, and when one stopped the other began to blare. It was scarcely bearable.[19]

This same prince, by the way, mentions the ancient tradition of German hunting music still being practiced late during the nineteenth century. In this case, he describes hunting on the private hunting grounds of the crown prince (six thousand acres, surrounded by a wall so the animals could not escape!).

> There was a good deal of game. But at first I shot badly, since I always attended more to the Crown Prince than the wild boars. Afterwards I lost my anxiety, and brought down five or six head, and fired at a good many animals that ran past. We returned to the Schloss after the shoot. Dinner at 3:30. A great stretch before the Schloss was illuminated by torches, and there was horn-blowing, etc.[20]

In Germany during the last half of the nineteenth century, these large military bands now replaced the ancient aristocratic trumpet choirs which for centuries had performed all important family ceremonies, from the oath-taking in the church[21] through funerals.[22] During the first half of the century an occasional reference to the ancient trumpet choir tradition can still be found. There were some works composed for massed trumpets by Weber, but perhaps the most extraordinary example is the reference Spohr makes[23] to his having composed music in 1824 for fifty-three trumpets! It is a work high on my list of compositions yet to be found!

> [For the celebration of the marriage of the Duke of Saxe-Meiningen] I had besides to compose a grand march with introduction of the melody of the old German ballad: 'Und als der Grossvater die Grossmutter nahm,' together with a torch-light-dance for fifty-three trumpeters, and two pair of kettle-drummers (for these were the numbers to be found in the music bands of the army of the Elector of Hesse); and as for the sake of the modulations I was obliged to take various tones of the trumpets, and the trumpeters of the bands not being very musical, I was obliged to practice them also beforehand in this torch-light-dance.

---

[19] Ibid., 2:422. The Baroness von Larish, in *Behind the Scenes with the Kaiser* (New York: Hertag, 1922), 52, tells of the Kaiser himself conducting some of the military band's marches during one of these dinner affairs.

[20] *Memoirs of Prince Chlodwig*, 2:240.

[21] See *William II, My Early Life* (New York: George H. Doran, 1926), 323.

[22] See Mason, *Musical Letters from Abroad*, 128–129.

[23] *Autobiography*, 2:155.

Before leaving this discussion of military bands in the Prussian Court, I must quote a newspaper item from 1881, relative to the court in Russia—which had, of course, been greatly influenced by Prussia since the time of Peter the Great. The implication of this extraordinary information, which some scholar must pursue, is that the aristocrats themselves performed in their own band!

> From St. Petersburg: The musical soirees for brass instruments, established by the Emperor Alexander III, when hereditary grand duke, are to take place again regularly every three weeks during the winter. The participants are the amateur grand dukes, the bandmasters of the regiments of the guard, and *dilettants* of the first families of the nobility, altogether about fifty persons.[24]

[24] *Boston Evening Transcript* (December 12, 1881), 7.

Although court composers in the eighteenth-century tradition no longer receive much space in music history texts in their discussions of nineteenth-century music, the libraries of Germany are filled with occasional works for aristocratic welcomes, birthdays, and marriages, etc., which remind us that there *were* still court composers. Therefore it is fitting that I close this chapter by mentioning that we sometimes forget that Wagner was once such a court composer.

In 1843 Wagner composed a *Weihegruss* for the unveiling of a statue of King Friedrich August I in Dresden. Wagner scored his work for male chorus, three trumpets, four horns, three trombones, and tuba. He also mentions, in his autobiography, a lost work by Mendelssohn which had been composed for the same ceremony.

> I had written a simple song for male voices [and brass] of modest design, whereas to Mendelssohn had been assigned the more complicated task of interweaving the National Anthem, 'Heil Dir im Rautenkrantz' ('God Save the King,' in English) into the male chorus he had to compose. This he had effected by an artistic work in counterpoint, so arranged that from the first eight beats of his original melody the brass instruments simultaneously played the Anglo-Saxon popular air … Mendelssohn's daring combination quite missed its effect, because no one could understand why the vocalists did not sing the same tune the wind instruments were playing.[25]

[25] Wagner, *My Life*, 312.

The following year Wagner composed another occasional court work, his *Greeting of Friedrich August the Beloved by his Faithful Subjects*. This work, now for male chorus with full band,[26] was performed upon the king's return from a visit to England. During the summer he composed this work, Wagner was working on *Tannhäuser* and at least one scholar believes this band piece, 'was the germ of the *Tannhäuser* march and chorus in praise of the Landgraf.'[27] Wagner himself describes the performance[28] as being given by a tremendous massed band.

> I had the entire song repeated, but, in accordance with the King's wish, only one verse was sung in our original crescent formation. At the beginning of the second verse I had my four hundred undisciplined bandsmen and singers file off in a march through the garden, which, as they gradually receded, was so arranged that the final notes could only reach the royal ear as an echoing dream-song.

The finest of Wagner's band works composed for the court is the *Huldigungsmarsch* of 1864, composed for the birthday of King Ludwig II, and after he had offered to rescue Wagner from his debts and to finance the first production of the *Ring of the Nibelungen*. Wagner himself conducted this work on several occasions, including a performance during the ceremonies for the laying of the cornerstone for his theater in Bayreuth (22 May 1872). Hans von Bülow described a surprise performance of this work he heard in Munich in 1865.

> Finally last night came the banquet: a big private concert in the Residenztheater with the house brilliantly illuminated, and no audience except His Majesty and between thirty and forty special Wagnerites. Wagner conducted.
> 1. Pilgrims' March from *Tannhäuser*, with a surprise: on the final E flat of the 'cellos, eighty military-band players struck up the *Huldigungs Marsch* behind the scenes. (You will know it by this time in my arrangement for pianoforte.) The effect was magnificent, the point of it all being the special relationship between the composer and the King.[29]

Finally, there are some scholars who believe the original version of the *Kaisermarsch* (1871) was for military band.[30]

---

[26] The band instrumentation calls for piccolo, E♭ flute, C flute, F, E♭, C, and B♭ clarinets, oboes, bassoons, F and B♭ horns, F and E♭ trumpets, six trombones, and tubas.

[27] Robert Gutman, *Richard Wagner, the Man, His Mind, and His Music* (New York: Harcourt, Brace & World, 1968), 99.

[28] Wagner, *My Life*, 334.

[29] Letter to Karl Klindworth, July 13, 1865, quoted in Richard, Count du Moulin Eckart, ed., *Letters of Hans von Bülow* (New York: Vienna House, 1972), 6.

[30] See Ernest Newman, *The Life of Richard Wagner* (New York: A. A. Knopf, 1937), 4:276; and Gutman, *Richard Wagner, the Man, His Mind, and His Music*, 312.

14 Court Wind Bands in Italy

Court *Harmoniemusik* in Italy seems to have vanished as the influence of Napoleon replaced that of Austria. The only reference I have found to a concert by an Italian *Harmoniemusik* is one heard by Spohr when he visited Naples in 1817, but these 'pièces d'harmonie' which the composer heard he noted were 'not of importance.'[1]

There was also a famous band in Naples early during the nineteenth century, the band of the Veliti del Regno di Napoli, belonging to the Grand Duke Leopoldo II. The band often played for the public in the gardens of the Boboli and for the duke and his family before his window in the Palazzo Pitti.[2] There is also an account of this band traveling to Modena to play for the visit of the pope.

> The Pope remained in Modena to the 28th when the celebrated military band of Velits Royaux Napolitains gave him an aubade.[3]

The leader of this band was a trumpeter named Brizzi, famous for the power and sweetness of his tone, who would lead the band by playing the solo parts standing in the middle of a circle of his players.

The long and extraordinary history of papal wind bands in Rome reaches its final chapter with the ensembles under Pope Pius VII. An eyewitness of his coronation in 1801 reports the papal bands spread around the Piazza S. Pietro with a concert by visiting bands from Frascati and Tivoli, together with the banda Tiburtini, playing 'all during the day triumphal symphonies.'[4]

In 1816 Pope Pius VII founded a military police unit, under the name Carabinieri Pontifici, which included sixteen trumpets. After the fall of the Republica Romana in 1849, this group was renamed the Reggimento dei Veliti Pontificci and a document of 1850 speaks of fourteen trumpets on horse and fourteen drums on foot.[5] Before this ensemble was disbanded in 1870, it reached a status, under the conductor Rolland, as the best of the papal military bands.

---

[1] Spohr, *Autobiography*, 2:23. Spohr also mentions seeing a 'Roman Festival' in Milan in 1816 which included a 'grand Triumphal-procession' with 'thirty to forty Hautboyists in the Roman costume with Turkish music!' (Ibid., 1:269)

[2] Vessella, *La Banda*, 160.

[3] Ibid., 161.

> Le Pape restait encore à Modene le 28 jour où la celèbre musique militaire des Vèlits Royaux, Napolitains, lui donna une aubade.

[4] Ibid., 175.

> ... in tutto quel giorno fecero delle trimoniose sinfonie.

[5] Ibid., 178.

Pope Pius VII also maintained trumpets and drums (i trombetti; i tamburi) for ceremonial use, and Vessella gives[6] a lengthy account of the uniforms, ordinances for marching, and training of these players.

Apparently the Church also employed military bands for entertainment purposes during the nineteenth century, for one account mentions hearing two bands playing waltzes in the Palazzo di Venezia in Rome during a reception for a new German cardinal (Cardinal Haulik of Agram) in 1851.[7]

Finally, there are two aristocratic occasions in Rome later during the nineteenth century for which there are reports of performances by massed bands. The first, a concert by three hundred players in the Palazzo Quirinale celebrated the safe return of Umberto I and Queen Margherita from Naples, where they had been the objects of an assassination attempt. This concert, given in 1878, included the first performance of Rossini's, *La Corona d'Italia* for band.[8]

The second performance, given in the same public square in 1896, celebrated the wedding of King Vittorio Emanuele III, who was then Prince of Napoli.[9] According to Veit, a march by Rossini was performed on this occasion, which was later published by Breitkopf & Härtel.[10]

[6] Ibid., 179ff.

[7] *Memoirs of Prince Chlodwig of Hohenlohe-Schillingsfürst*, 1:75.

[8] Weinstock, *Rossini*, 361.

[9] Vessella, *La Banda*, 149.

[10] Veit, *Die Blasmusik*, 49. Veit gives the instrumentation as piccolo in E♭, E♭ clarinet, 3 B♭ clarinets, bassoons, 4 trumpets (B♭, E♭, and A♭), 4 horns (E♭, A♭), 3 trombones, ophicleides, cornets in E♭ and A♭, with percussion.

15   *Court Wind Bands in France*

COURT WIND BANDS IN THE TRADITIONAL SENSE died in France with the Revolution of 1789. During the nineteenth century their functions, when required, were filled by military bands as in Germany. These pages, therefore, would be unnecessary but for the impossibility of passing by Napoleon without some comment on his relationship to wind band music.

To one interested in the history of wind band music, Napoleon represents the greatest of disappointments. He came into power following one of the finest moments in the history of the wind band, the period of absolute music for large bands during the revolutionary years. He employed as his official court composers two men who had been successful composers of band music, François Lesueur and Giovanni Paisiello. The other composers he was interested in had also been previously successful as band composers, among them Cherubini, Catel, and Méhul.[1] And yet, the fact that none of these composers produced a single important work for band, or any other significant court music, is an unfortunate reflection of the fact that Napoleon although so unusually interested in literature and painting, had no strong interest in absolute music.

He did surround himself with appropriate ceremonial music, but the music was never more than functional in nature. For his coronation, an eyewitness reported numerous military bands.

> Think of the number of the equipages and their richness, the beauty of the horses and the uniforms, of that multitude of musicians playing the coronation marches to the sound of bells and of cannon …
> ……
> The military bands were innumerable, and under the orders of M. Lesueur; these executed heroic marches, of which one, commanded by the Emperor from M. Lesueur for the army of the Boulogne, still ranks, in the judgment of connoisseurs, among the finest and most imposing of musical compositions. For my part, this music made me turn pale and tremble; I shuddered from head to foot in listening to it.[2]

[1] The emperor was particularly fond of Méhul's opera, *Les Bayadères*, and once made the bizarre request that the work be performed with all dynamic expression suppressed and all instruments muted! See Hubert Richardson, *A Dictionary of Napoleon and His Time* (Ann Arbor: Gryphon, 1971), 317.

[2] *Memoirs of Constant, First Valet de Chambre to the Emperor* (New York: Century, 1907), 2:30–32.

Military bands were also present for all important ceremonies of their own sphere, which, of course, enjoyed a central role in the court functions of Napoleon. The same eyewitness described a typical ceremony, one Napoleon organized to award medals to soldiers who participated in the Army of Boulogne.

> The Emperor wore the uniform of a colonel-general of foot-guards, and came at a gallop to the foot of the throne, admidst universal acclamations and the most frightful racket that could be made by drums, trumpets, and cannons, beating, soundings, and thundering together.
> ......
> Two pages ... took the decoration ... and handed it to His Majesty, who attached it himself to the hero's breast. As he did so, more than eight hundred drummers beat a roll, and when the decorated soldier came down from the throne by the staircase on the left, passing in front of the Emperor's brilliant staff, fanfares executed by more than twelve hundred musicians signalized the return of the legionary to his company.[3]

[3] Ibid., 1:232.

As in Germany, it was the military bands who played for state dinners.

> Toward the end of our stay, the generals gave a grand ball for the ladies of the city. The ball was magnificent; the Emperor was present at it. For this purpose a hall had been constructed in carpentry and joiner's work. It was decorated in perfectly good taste with garlands, flags, and trophies. General Bertrand was appointed master of ceremonies by his colleagues, and General Bisson took charge of the buffet. This employment perfectly suited General Bisson, the greatest gastronome in the camp, whose enormous paunch sometimes embarrassed him in marching. He required no less than from six to eight bottles with his dinner, which he never took alone; for it was a torment to him not to chatter while eating. He usually invited his aides-de-camp, whom, doubtless through love of mischief, he always selected from among the thinnest and frailest officers in the army. The buffet was worthy of him who had it in charge.
> The [music] was composed of the bands of twenty regiments, who played by turns. Only, at the commencement of the ball, they executed a triumphal march all together.[4]

[4] Ibid., 1:37.

I close with a particularly poignant recollection of an incident involving a 'serenade' played for Napoleon by some of his military musicians during the Siege of Moscow.

The Prince Neuchâtel, then Minister of War, seeing that no orders for departure came from the Emperor, and that the whole army was in despair at being kept in such a wretched position, collected some men from the bands under the Emperor's window, and told them to play the popular song, 'Où peut-on être mieux qu'au sein de sa famille?' They had scarcely begun, when the Emperor appeared on the balcony, and ordered them to play 'Veillons au salut de l'Empire!' The men were forced to play it as best they could, in spite of their pain, and immediately afterwards the order for departure on the next morning was given.[5]

[5] *Memoirs of Sergeant Bourgogne* [1812–1813] (London: P. Davies, 1926), 106–107.

16 Court Wind Bands in England

THE LAST IMPORTANT private English aristocratic wind band in the tradition which began during the Middle Ages belonged to George IV of England (1762–1830). Here was a noble with a strong natural talent for music and who was an active performer on the cello as a young man. An anonymous contemporary, writing in the *Quarterly Musical Magazine* (1818) credited him with 'a very extensive knowledge and a very sound taste.' George IV not only followed the rehearsals of his band in person, but when other aristocrats were visiting he often conducted transcribed symphonies of Mozart or Haydn himself. Another who knew him said, 'he was not only a musician among princes, but a prince among musicians.'[1]

He began his band when he was still Prince of Wales, sometime before 1811. Portions of the repertoire at this time are known from bills submitted by composers and arrangers.[2] Included here are indications of works prepared, between 1800–1802, by C. F. Eley, who had been an active composer for the English militia bands during the last twenty years of the eighteenth century. Eley's contribution to the Prince of Wales' library included transcriptions,[3] copies of his military marches, and a work called, *Volunt[ary]: March & Chorale St. Antoni*.

A much larger portion of the repertoire was provided by Henry Pick, between 1800–1805.[4] His contributions include numerous arrangements, including Overtures by Kozeluch, Haydn, Viotti, Stegman and Neubauer, as well as selections from operas. There were also copies of original works for wind band by Pleyel, Rosetti, Hobrecht, Jouve, Morris, Porter, Raimondi, Rogers and Mozart.[5] Especially interesting are some of the titles of works with larger instrumentation, including a *Divertimento* by Mozart and *The Creation Dr Haydn* for sixteen players, three collections of the music of Alday, Rosetti, Maschek and Viotti for fourteen instruments, a *Notturno* for sixteen players, and some marches for twenty instruments.

[1] Quoted in Adam Carse, 'The Prince Regent's Band,' *Music and Letters* 27, no. 3 (July, 1946): 147. The greater part of this material is based on this article.

[2] The titles, with these documents, can be found in the Archives at Windsor Castle.

[3] These included '2 Favorite Pieces' by Mozart, 'Dr Haydn's Surprise [Symphony] Compleate,' and works by Grétry, Cimador, Shield, and Bossi.

[4] Pick describes himself as a member 'of Her Majesty's [Queen Charlotte, Mother to George IV] Band' and living at 'No. 2 Carey street Lincoln's inn London.' In the British Museum there are significant collections of band music which were composed by Pick for the queen's band, among these are the volumes found under (R.M.21.b..16), a series of marches and a divertimento for 2 E♭ clarinets, 2 B♭ clarinets, pairs of horns, trumpets, bassoons, with a serpent, bass trombone, and small drum; two sets of part-books (R.M.21.c.32 and 21.d.2) containing opera arrangements, popular songs, chorales and an apparently original work by Sir William Herschel, the famous astronomer, for pairs of basset horns, oboes, horns, bassoons, and a serpent; and a volume (R.M.21.d.4) which contains an arrangement of J. C. Bach's Overture to *Lucio Silla*, for 3 clarinets, pairs of horns, bassoons, trumpets, trombones, with a serpent.

[5] Additional information regarding these titles can be found in Edward Croft-Murray, 'The Wind-Band in England, 1540–1840,' in *Music & Civilisation* (London: British Museum, 1980), 144–146.

The name of the band changed to the Prince Regent's Band between 1811–1820, to conform to the change in the title of the sponsor. The band is described during this period as being 'esteemed the finest in Europe' and as being housed in the Pavilion at Brighton.[6] One may assume the band had grown in size considerably during the period 1800–1820, for the instrumentation is given in the same source as,

[6] *Quarterly Musical Magazine* 1, no. 2 (1818): 158.

8 clarinets
2 oboes
3 flutes
4 bassoons
4 serpents (obbligato and 3 ripieno)
4 trombones (SATB)
4 horns
4 trumpets
timpani

This band was not attached to any military unit and indeed the prince seems to have relegated to the military bands the more mundane ceremonial duties.[7]

At some point during this period, or perhaps before, the distinguished German musician, Christian Kramer, joined the band as its leader. A review, from 1818, is very complementary of his abilities and, through its examples of the band's literature, gives additional hints that this band's primary role was in the performance of aesthetically fine music.

[7] For example John Ashton, in *Social England under The Regency* (London, 1899), 19, 32, quotes accounts of a military band playing 'God Save the King,' alternating with marches for five hours and of two other military bands playing 'various airs throughout the night' as part of the ceremonies related to the Prince of Wales taking the oath as Regent.

> From the most delicate song to the magnificent symphonies of Haydn, Mozart and Beethoven, and even the grandest of Handel choruses, he has preserved the bearing of each class throughout in their pristine beauty and design, and with so nice an attention to the particular cast of expression appertaining to each instrument, that he has left nothing to be desired. Those are the daily services rendered to the Prince and to music by Mr. Kramer.[8]

[8] *Quarterly Musical Magazine* 1, no. 2 (1818): 150.

One of Kramer's most important duties, of course, was to provide the music for the band. Judging by a comment in the *Brighton Gazette*,[9] this must have been a very extensive repertoire, for this paper mentions '300 books of parts' placed in boxes beside the music stands. Some of Kramer's arrangements were of full symphonies, including the Fifth of Beethoven and Mozart's 'Jupiter' and final E♭ Symphony. Another eye-

[9] Quoted in Carse, 'The Prince Regent's Band,' 151. The *Brighton Gazette* also mentioned that Kramer, like his king, suffered from gout.

witness reported that Kramer arranged complete symphonies by Mozart and Haydn for the band as well as overtures by Beethoven, Rossini and Cherubini and the entire opera, *Joseph*, by Méhul.

Kramer also had the responsibility of recruiting the best players possible for the band and for his personnel he apparently preferred German musicians, like himself. For this purpose he made frequent trips to Germany and even looked for his countrymen in French prisoner-of-war camps. The first clarinetist, Eisert, was in fact found in a prison.[10] It appears that this band included many famous instrumentalists of the day, including the famous elder Distin on Saxhorn[11] and a trumpet player, Schmidt, who some considered the finest player in Europe. An interesting comment associated with him reads, 'His flourish was the most terrific and appalling thing ever heard from a musical instrument.' Even the serpent player, a Frenchman named André, was often compared to the famous string bass player, Dragonetti, and was often featured in the performance of Corelli trios before visiting guests.

In Brighton the band rehearsed from 9:00 until 11:00 in the evening and were given supper and a pint of wine.[12] When the Regent was not in town, the band rehearsed from 11:00 to 1:00 in the morning. Their performances were given in a new music room, sixty-two by forty-two feet in size, which had been constructed in the Pavilion. It was here, after dinner, that the Regent would bring his guests to enjoy the performance of his band.

The coronation of George IV occurred in 1820 and then the band became known as the King's Household Band for ten years.[13] At this time the king moved the band to Windsor Castle, where they were housed in the conservatory. From this period accounts begin to speak of some functional music by the band, including playing in a boat while accompanying the king's fishing!

An article in the *Brighton Gazette*[14] gives the instrumentation for this period as being somewhat larger, with a stronger number of woodwinds relative to the brass.

12 clarinets
3 oboes
3 flutes

[10] Among the other German names in the band one recognizes the outstanding trumpeter, Johann Schmidt, the trombonists Albrecht, Schneider, and Behrens, the bassoonist J. G. Waetzig, the oboists Malsch and Spellerberg, the hornist Garmann, and another Waetzig, a trumpeter. The traveling Englishman, Holmes, describes meeting, in Dresden, in 1827, a former member of this band who had returned to Germany.

> I found here a man, named Stephan, a good trumpeter, who had lived for many years at Brighton in the private band of the Prince Regent, but who preferred Dresden in spite of more work and less pay. England he thought an expensive country, for, said he, 'I must pay six-and-tearty paunds a-year for my leetle hause.' Stephan said something more about his wife not liking our climate; but I saw plainly that he loved sociality, and thought our Sundays rather dull. (Holmes, *A Ramble Among the Musicians of Germany*, 205.)

[11] The famous key-bugle performer, John Distin, mentioned above, was also a member of this band until 1830.

[12] Once the Regent substituted ale for the wine and when detecting a consequent lack of enthusiasm in the playing of the band was informed by Kramer that it was because the wine had been withdrawn. The wine soon again replaced the ale!

[13] This band is not to be confused with the 'State' or 'King's Band,' which was only a nominal body consisting of honorary appointments given by the Lord Chamberlain. On official occasions when the band was expected to appear, non-member professionals were hired to replace the actual members, who were often persons with no playing ability at all!

4 bassoons
2 basset horns
4 horns
2 serpents
4 bass trombones
alto and tenor trombones
2 percussion

It is also from this period, 1820–1825, that a colored aquatint of the band was published, as part of John Nash's *Views of the Royal Pavilion*[15] (see picture opposite). Here one sees a somewhat smaller band of about twenty-five players, wearing uniforms with short blue coats, standing—although each player has a music stand, with the timpani placed in the front row center. The conductor, in evening dress, and his music stand face the audience, not the players, as was still the custom early during the nineteenth century.[16] The band is pictured standing at one end of the hall, roped off from the noble listeners, who are also standing.

A review of the band's performance in 1822 is again full of praise.

> It is impossible to exaggerate the perfection to which this band has been brought by the science and unremitting attention of Mr. Kramer. Their performance of arranged scores is inexpressibly fine, and their accompaniment is not less chaste, subdued and beautiful.[17]

The following year, Rossini visited the king at Brighton and heard the band play arrangements of his own Overture to *La gazza ladra* and selections from *Il barbiere*.[18]

A final review of the band is found in 1827:

> Mr. Christopher [sic] Kramer, the master of the King's most extraordinary and perfect band of wind instruments, in which office he has shewn talents of the highest order, both for arranging music for such an orchestra, and in directing the performance of it so as to produce effects unparalleled by any other military band.[19]

The band was dismissed soon after the death of George IV in 1830. Because of the recognized quality of the band there was wide concern in seeing its abrupt end. A typical comment was made by the Rev. George Croly expressing his hope that the new king, William IV, would have 'too much taste to dispense

[14] Quoted in Carse, 'The Prince Regent's Band,' 150.

[15] A reproduction can also be seen in J. B. Priestley, *The Prince of Pleasure* (New York: Harper & Row, 1969), facing 188.

[16] The reason for this was because court protocol prevented any servant from turning his back on this aristocratic lord.

[17] *Quarterly Musical Magazine* 4, no. 14 (1822): 240.

[18] At the wish of the king, Rossini accompanied himself at the piano while singing arias from *Otello* in his falsetto voice. The *Quarterly Musical Magazine* was scandalized, thinking Rossini was imitating one of the castrati, who had been 'banished from the stage for many years because they offended the humanity and modesty of the English.' (See Weinstock, *Rossini*, 136.)

[19] *Harmonicon* (December, 1827), 249.

Court Wind Bands in England   205

with a set of performers that would be an ornament to any court in Europe.'[20] The new king was more interested in sailing than music, but his queen, Queen Adelaide, reorganized the band.[21]

The band continued to exist under Queen Victoria, although beginning with her reign it was much smaller (seventeen players). Although there are records of performances of arrangements of music by Spohr, Meyerbeer, Weber, and Beethoven, the band members were now expected to be able to play strings as second instruments for use in dance music.[22] Early in 1840, Prince Albert reorganized the band into an orchestra[23] and from that date its character as a wind band ended, even though the archives continue to call it a 'band.'

[20] Quoted in Carse, 'The Prince Regent's Band,' 155.

[21] Grove 11:155.

[22] John Harley, 'Music at the English Court in the Eighteenth and Nineteenth Centuries,' *Music & Letters* 50, no. 3 (July, 1969): 334.

[23] Elizabeth Burton, *The Pageant of Early Victorian England* (New York: Scribner, 1972), 213, and Grove 11:155.

The Royal Band, from John Nash's *Views of the Royal Pavilion*.

PART 4
Wind Bands in the Church

17 *Wind Bands in the Church*

As the reader has seen in volume one of this series, the first appearances of wind bands in the church during the Middle Ages occurred as part of the retinue of aristocrats who celebrated family events there, such as coronations, marriages, and baptisms. These kinds of events continued, of course, throughout the nineteenth century and there are apparently even a few examples of church music for the old-fashioned aristocratic trumpet choir. I think, for example, of the Siegbert *Deutsche Messe* (ca. 1870) for SATB, seven trumpets, horn, trombone and bombard or the *Veni Sancte Spiritus* (1820) by Zweckstetter for SATB, eight trumpets, trombone, and timpani.

During the nineteenth century, however, it was more frequently the full military band who accompanied the noble to these family ceremonies in the church. One suspects something was lost in this substitution, or so it would seem by the comments of one prince who heard a military band welcome the emperor in the Strassburg Cathedral in 1886:

> Then we went over to the cathedral. In the aisle the good Stumpf had placed a brass band, which greeted us with diabolic music, so that one could not speak a word. I begged the Prebendary Straub, who was standing by me, to stop the fellows making such a noise, which he did.[1]

[1] *Memoirs of Prince Chlodwig of Hohenlohe-Schillingsfürst*, 2:358.

In volume four of this series I have discussed the fact that in Germany the historic Stadtpfeifer traditions had begun to die during the Classical Period and many of their functions were being taken over by the new civic militia bands. One of these functions was helping out in church by playing polyphonic music with the choir and this role is also taken over by the civic militia bands. Thus one finds references to this practice during the first half of the nineteenth century, such as one from Waldshut (Baden) in 1822–1823[2] or the recollection by a Benedictine Priest of his years in Hagnau,

[2] Suppan, *Blasmusik in Baden*, 139.
Wohl eine Vorläuferin jener Türkischen Musik, die 1822–23 neben der Kirchenmusik in Erscheinung trat, bei hohen geistlichen Festen aber die Kirchenmusik verstärkte, um 'figurierte Messen' aufführen zu können.

> ... a brilliant town band had existed there for a long time and in the church, even in my time [early nineteenth century] they still played the old 'winegrowers' *figurierte Mesen* with the sounds of horns and trumpets blaring.[3]

This being the practice, one finds references, which might otherwise seem startling, to the use of church funds to purchase band instruments, as for example in Onsbach, where in 1806 a calf-skin for the town drum was purchased, in 1812 a 'türkische Musik-Trommel' and a trumpet, and in following years even bells for the Schellenbaum![4]

The importance of this can be appreciated in reading a request in 1820 by the civic militia band of Oppenau for funds to purchase a new bass trombone.

> It has been already twenty to forty years since the public and the Church Music established a türkish band for the glorification and uplifting of the Services. During this period of time there have been only a few instruments purchased by the community. Now this necessary music is beginning to go down in flames, due to a lack of instruments and music, because no one has supported us for several years. We have played without profit, often paying for important necessities from our own pocket. Thus our request for support goes to a most honorable Oberamt in our new enthusiasm for music and especially for the glorification of God. Among our needs a bass trombone is most necessary as we have almost no bass instruments. Since it is the desire of the civic officials and the citizens that the band should again become active, thus we have been asked to request most obediently of the most honorable Oberamt to send us the allowance for the said bass trombone ... This will inspire new enthusiasm in our church music and bring us to a [new] degree of perfection.[5]

There was, however, an entirely new church festival which necessitated an appearance by the military bands of the nineteenth century and this new purpose resulted in an extraordinary body of original band literature, much of which is still extant in European libraries. An early example of the references to this new ceremony can be seen in the diary of Vincent Novello, who was touring the continent in 1829. During his visit to Antwerp, he made a notation which, at first glance, might seem rather enigmatic.

> Military Mass at 12. Overture Zauberflüte.[6]

[3] Quoted in ibid., 127.

[4] Ibid., 114.

[5] Quoted in ibid., 112–113.

[6] Novello, *A Mozart Pilgrimage*, 289.

In a Jesuits Church in Munich, Novello heard a similar service with a military band playing music even less traditional for a Catholic Church.

> The service began at half past Ten with the Sermon (which was a tedious affair) and at 11 the Band commenced the Salute with a crash of all the Instruments and a furious Roll on the Drums—the effect was very striking and novel to me in the Church.
>
> Next came a light Movement in B flat, quite in the Dance style and would have been very appropriate as Ballet music. The second piece was an melody in E flat followed by a Rondo and Polonaise—the whole was more like a Bravuro aria for the Prima Donna in an Opera than anything else.[7]

[7] Ibid., 298.

Bizarre as such an account reads, similar references can be found throughout the century. Nearly forty years after the Novello account, for example, the diary of the German prince quoted above mentions an identical practice.

> I forgot, by-the-way, to say that during the Mass a military band played the accompaniment to the religious ceremony. It began with the overture to one of Verdi's operas, I don't know whether it was Traviata or Trovatore. It was a mediocre performance, the sort of stuff you hear played at dinners.[8]

[8] *Memoirs of Prince Chlodwig*, 1:306.

Apparently throughout Europe, the Catholic Church, as one of its many colorful special festivals, began setting one Sunday each year aside for the purpose of the commemoration of the military. On such a day it was often a military band who played during the Service and sometimes provided the entire music of the Mass. There is no way of documenting how frequently such performances of operatic and ballet selections during the Mass by a military band, such as those quoted above, were heard. The extant music in European libraries suggests that more often the military band participated by playing music more in character with the occasion. In many cases composers wrote full length Masses with chorus for the military band to accompany. I think of the five movement *Mass* (1898) by Kempter, the truly distinguished *Mass* (published by Leuckart in 1897) by Rheinberger, or the *Deutsche Militar Messe* for TTBB and band by Späth. In addition, the German church-band repertoire includes numerous individual works, such as the *Motet* for SATB and band by Johann Böhner (1778–1860) or the *Te Deum* by J. F. Haue.

The military band also appeared in the Protestant Church in Germany during the nineteenth century, resulting in extant compositions ranging from the *Geistliche Gesänge für den militätrgottesdienst* (1847) by Zimmermann to the extraordinary body of works by Johann Christian Rinck (1770–1846) which are now housed in New Haven, Yale University Library. His body of works include at least six full Cantatas for voices and small band (usually flute, pairs of clarinets, bassoons, trumpets, horns, with contrabassoon and timpani), in addition to Chorales, settings of Psalms, and Motets.

Such wind band and wind ensemble music is confirmed in many extant records as well. For example, one reads of a wind ensemble playing chorales from a tower and of a military band playing during the Service for a Reform Church festival in Marburg in 1817.[9] The *Kreuzzeitung* (Ravensberg, 1877) even mentions an extraordinary Protestant 'Monster' concert performed by seven thousand singers and four hundred trombones![10]

Before the *Harmoniemusik* tradition died, this ensemble was found in German churches as well. Examples of extant repertoire used in the Catholic Service include the Heine *Salve Regina*, for soprano, with pairs of clarinets, horns, and bassoons; the *Harmoniemusik für Heil Comunion* by Kalliwoda, for pairs of clarinets, horns, and bassoons and the two *Masses* by Joseph Schnabel (1767–1831). *Harmoniemusik* was used in the Protestant Church as well, as one can see in the records of the Mecklenburg-Schwerin Court which mention pairs of clarinets, horns, and bassoons accompanying four-part chorales between 1826 and 1829.[11]

Representing the Austrian Empire there is a particularly rich repertoire of nineteenth-century works for voices and winds intended for use in the Catholic Mass. Again, these compositions come in all forms, from both minor and major composers alike. One composer who was particularly active in this field was the well-known Sigismund Neukomm (1778–1858). He composed six Masses for voices and band, mostly commissioned for services in France, but one for Rio de Janeiro. At the request of the widow of Michael Haydn, he also finished a

---

9 Heinz Oepen, *Beiträge zur Geschichte des Kölner Musiklebens* (Köln: Arno Volk-Verlag, 1955), 47.

> Am 30. Oktober 1817 fand des Reformationsfest statt. Zur Eröffnung wurde vom Schlossturm ein rührender Choral geblasen, in der Kirche des Vater Unser fon Fr. H. Himmel gesungen. Die hiesigen Musik-Kenner und -Liebhaber, Sänger und Sängerinnen, batten sich zu einem schönen Zweck vereinigt. Unter den Instrumentalisten wirken die Hoboisten des Regimntes Kurfürst aus Kassel mit … Eine Musik mit Pauken und Trompeten beschloss dieses akademische Feier.

10 Ehmann, *Tibilustrium*, 160.

11 Meyer, *Geschichte der Mecklenburg-Schweriner Hofkapelle*, 315ff.

Mass by Haydn for voices and winds. One of his works, which I have studied and found to be of considerable quality, is the *Missa pro defunctis ... Michael et Joseph Haydn*, which is scored for a very large wind orchestra. Neukomm also composed three full Requiems for chorus and band, an Oratorio for soli TB, chorus and brass band, and several smaller church works.

There are at least eight important compositions by Franz Liszt, including a *Requiem* and a *Te Deum*, scored for either band or brass ensemble accompaniment. And, let us not forget Anton Bruckner. Every musician knows his *E Minor Mass* for double chorus and band, but there are additional works which have never been published or made available in scholarly editions. These include three Cantatas: *Auf, Brüder auf*, for male soli, male chorus, SATB chorus, and band; a different work by the same title for SATTBB and six brass; and *Preiset den Herrn*, for male chorus and band. Two more works, *Lasst Jubeltöne laut erklingen* and *Das deutsche Lied* are for male chorus and brass. Especially interesting is his *Germanenzug*, which was published in Vienna in 1892. Here is a work scored for TTBB and a full military band, whose parts include two B♭ soprano cornets, euphonium, four trumpets, four horns, three trombones, and tuba!

One also finds *Harmoniemusik* for the Church in the Austrian Empire, including works by Vincent Maschek , Johann Baptist Schiedermayr, and others. Schiedermayr has also composed an interesting *Mass* (1815) for SATB, two basset horns, two bassoons, two horns, and organ.

Finally, I should mention that Holmes, another Englishman touring the continent, describes in his diary for 1827 hearing an ensemble of trombones in St. Stefan's Cathedral in Vienna.

> After the requiem was finished, a whole procession of priests and choir paraded the cathedral, at distant intervals chanting a Gregorian phrase, accompanied by four trombones, and I have heard nothing comparable to the delicious effect these instruments produce when heard at a distance in the cathedral; their tones are so softened in the space, and they join in the gradual swell of voices upon the silence with a sweet severity.[12]

[12] Holmes, *A Ramble Among the Musicians of Germany*, 140–141.

In England there seems to have been little activity of the nature I have been describing, although Harley mentions, 'Between 1821 and 1828 a military band attended and played when George IV went [to the Chapel] in his full military uniform.'[13]

The reader should also be reminded that until the period of the suppression of the organ ended in England (in someplaces as late as 1860), the so-called 'gallery' wind band continued to exist in many churches. Accordingly, in the records[14] for the Easton-on-the-Hill Church one finds between 1807 and 1847 various payments made for the purchase and repair of bassoons, clarinets, purchases of reeds, etc.

In France, on the other hand, there was enormous activity. Judging by the reaction of a somewhat baffled American visiting Paris in 1852, the military bands which appeared in the Catholic Service during the first half of the nineteenth century may have performed the same kind of popular music which earlier visitors had heard in Germany during the 1820s.

[13] Harley, 'Music at the English Court in the Eighteenth and Nineteenth Centuries,' 351.

[14] H. B. Sharp, 'Church Band, Dumb Organist, and Organ,' *The Galpin Society Journal* 14 (March, 1961): 38.

> The *religious* exercises commenced by a grand voluntary, by the military band in attendance, which was nothing more or less than the overture of the *Caliph of Bagdad*, by Boieldieu. The grand military mass now followed, and it consisted of a succession of popular operatic airs, played by the band, with an occasional roll of the small drum, an 'order,' or a 'present' by the old soldiers, and a pantomime by two or three ministers, bowing, kneeling, crossing, etc., etc., now here and now there. Words or thoughts are not necessary in such a worship as this, which seems to be designed for mere external sensuous impression—yet there were a few words chanted by the drummers, towards the close of the *solemnities*.
>
> 'It is a very solemn service,' said a young man, whom we happened to fall in with as we came away, and whom, from his speech, we supposed to be an American or an Englishman.[15]

[15] Mason, *Musical Letters from Abroad*, 156–157.

In any case, the second half of the nineteenth century was quite a different story! In Paris, in the Bibliothèque nationale, there are extant literally hundreds of *published* works for large band, with and without voices, composed for use in the church. Some individual composers contributed considerable numbers of works, among these are Abadie (twelve major works, including a *Messe Solennelle* for chorus and a large band which includes both a bass and a contrabass[!] saxophone part);

Blancheteau (twenty major works), Marie (eighteen major works), Migette (twelve major works), and Ziegler (seventeen major works).

One of the works I have looked at, the *3e Messe solennelle* by Lysias de Momigny, carries a dedication to Napoleon III, which perhaps expresses the intent of these special ceremonies intended to commemorate the military. This particular score, one which is ninety-five pages in length, was published between 1853–1858 in Paris for SATB, with large band accompaniment. The score says the work was 'composée expressement pour musique militaire,' and the dedication reads, in part,

> In the thought which inspired this work, Sir, you will find the echo of one of the greatest thoughts, the consecration of Military Glory by religious sentiment.

Another *Messe solennelle*, by Louis Welter, identifies the parts of the service where the military band played, thus giving us a valuable insight into how this large body of music was used. In this case, the five movements were performed as music for the,

1. Entrée (Tempo di Marcia)
2. Offertoire (Maestoso)
3. Élévation (Andante)
4. Communion (Moderato)
5. Sortie (Allegretto)

There are almost countless independent compositions for one or another of the above portions of the service and some are quite unusual. For example, an *Offertoire* by Perron is scored for large band, but with solo trombone. A *Morceau d'Élévation* by Douard, which I thought might be slow and reflective in character, turned out to be an Andantino of a rather florid style, with solos for flute and small clarinet.

Another work attracted my attention because of the internal variety of texture among its various movements. This is the *Stabat Mater* by Victor Buot, a work accompanied by a large band with saxophones, but without double reeds or tuba. The work consists of seven movements:

Stabat Mater	TTB Chorus and Band
Quis est Homo	Baritone solo with Band
Pro Peccatis	Tenor solo with Band
Sancta Mater	a capella
Virgo Virginum	Baritone, Tenor, Bass soli, with Band
Inflammatus et Accensus	Bass solo with Band
Finale	TTB Chorus with Band

The above discussion has been limited to the appearances of the military band and *Harmoniemusik* in the actual church service, but there are additional extant examples of repertoire which reflect the use of these mediums for other church ceremonies.

The reader may recall from volume one that one of the earliest occasions for which the Church itself employed wind players during the Middle Ages was the annual Corpus Christi procession, instituted by Pope Urban IV in 1264. This event frequently called upon wind instruments or wind bands during the following six centuries and the nineteenth century was no exception.[16] A large number of scores is extant in the German and Austrian libraries representing original music for voices and winds composed for these occasions, usually under the title 'Fronleichnamsfeier.'

Another occasion with which wind music has been historically associated is funerals, due, of course, to their outdoor environment. An account in the *Pressburger Zeitung* describes the performance of a Cantata for full chorus and winds performed during a Protestant funeral in 1816.[17] Hellyer cites a similar performance in Schwerin.[18] Again, the extant repertoire from Germany, Austria, and France is so large as to suggest this kind of music was common during the nineteenth century.

Finally, it is interesting to find that some monasteries continued to maintain their own wind bands and wind ensembles during the nineteenth century. Novello reported hearing such an ensemble during his tour of Germany in 1829.

> Tuesday, July 7th. Left Heilbronn at half past 7. In the morning we heard a very simple and melodious Chorale played by the small Band of wind Instruments which, as our Host afterwards informed us, belonged to a Monastery adjoining our Inn. It was tastefully played and well in tune.[19]

[16] Adam Gottron, *Mainzer Musikgeschichte von 1500 bis 1800* (Mainz: Auslieferung durch die Stadtbibliothek, 1959), 205, documents the participation of an eight-member *Harmoniemusik* in such a procession in Mainz in 1805.

[17] *Pressburger Zeitung* (May 31, 1816, Nr. 43).

[18] Hellyer, 'Harmoniemusik,' 364.

[19] Novello, *A Mozart Pilgrimage*, 45. In his diary, Novello partially notated this chorale.

The monastery at Melk apparently maintained a similar ensemble at about the same time, as is suggested by the repertoire housed there.

The most detailed study of one of these monastery wind bands has been done by Jirí Sehnal, the Director of the Music Division of the Moravian Museum in Brno, Czechoslavakia.[20] Dr. Sehnal reports that the school for choir boys at this monastery, which dates from 1648, began to emphasize the playing of wind instruments during the end of the eighteenth century. By about 1816 there appears to have been established, under the leadership of Father Cyril Napp (1792–1867), a regular *Harmoniemusik* of pairs of oboes, clarinets, horns, and bassoons played by these students.[21] In 1817, Napp was able to persuade the Abbot to buy a contrabassoon which the ensemble needed. Upon the long awaited arrival of this instrument, Napp wrote in his records that a new era in the monastery had begun and that the name of the Abbot would be forever remembered because of his help!

The selection of applicants for the boy's choir, judging by the results of examinations during 1816–1818, was closely related to the immediate needs for membership in the *Harmoniemusik*. The records of this period cite several examples of boys who were rejected not because of their musical abilities, or the success of their examinations, but because they had no ability on any of the four instruments used in the *Harmoniemusik*. If replacements could not be found when needed, other choir boys were ordered to begin practicing the necessary instrument immediately! In the case of some choir boys whose technical proficiency was not adequate, Napp arranged to have the boys take part in the rehearsals of the town regimental band for additional experience. Eventually, the artistic level of the ensemble was so high that its members were able to substitute for players in professional orchestras.

The *Harmoniemusik* had regular rehearsals, in addition to their rehearsals for church music, and when the occasion demanded special rehearsals were held. A case in point is the extra rehearsals held in 1817 to prepare the *Harmoniemusik* transcription of Rossini's *Tancred*, for performance at a banquet given by the Abbot. It is interesting to note that this perfor-

[20] Dr. Sehnal is one of the most distinguished musicologists in Central Europe and I am indebted to him for his kind help during my research trip to Brno in 1982. His study on the *Harmoniemusik* of the Augustian monastery in Brno has been published in the *Journal of Band Research* and I have made only a brief abstract of his findings here.

[21] As I have mentioned in volume four of this series, the monastery library inventories clearly indicate an ensemble of oboes, horns, and bassoons was active from at least the 1740s, but no information on its function is extant.

mance of *Tancred* by the *Harmoniemusik* occurred in Brno some three weeks before the first performance of the opera itself in that city.

How did the monastery acquire its repertoire of *Harmoniemusik*? In several cases it appears that the monastery was able to borrow *Harmoniemusik* in return for loaning works which they already possessed. In one such case, in 1816, they borrowed the transcriptions of *Don Giovanni* and *Titus* by Mozart from the conductor of the local regimental band, in return for a Partita by Krommer and a transcription of the ballet *Zephyren* by Duport. Once the music was in hand, it was the choir boys themselves who made copies for the monastery. The following year, this same military conductor proposed to Napp that he loan all new music he acquired to the monastery for copying, with the condition that his own son be given preferential consideration for admission to the school. The monastery records also indicate that on occasion they also purchased music for their *Harmoniemusik* as well.

As the reputation of the *Harmoniemusik* library at the monastery grew, requests began to come in from other *Harmoniemusik* ensembles who wished to borrow music. In one case, another similar *Harmoniemusik*, that of the Benedictine monastery in Rajhrad,[22] requested permission to borrow the transcriptions of *Tancred* and *Dichter und Tonsetzer*. Napp rejected the plea, criticizing that monastery for its too penurious attitudes and for its habit of trying to get everything without paying for it. Furthermore, Napp wrote, the monastery in question had never loaned anything itself and did not return things it had previously borrowed!

The general purpose of the Brno *Harmoniemusik* was to perform and uplift the usual music in the monastery church and to provide the opportunity for the monks, who were not allowed to frequent the theater, to hear whatever music was currently attracting the attention of the public. The *Harmoniemusik* also performed dinner music for the Abbot, especially when important visitors were present. Special concerts were sometimes given for visitors, in the refectory, the garden, or in the cloisters, who then were expected to make an appropriate donation to the ensemble. The *Harmoniemusik* also performed for occasions within the monastery, such as anniversaries, name-day celebrations, etc., for the members of the monas-

[22] Still another *Harmoniemusik* existed at the Premonstrates monastery in Hová Ríse.

tery; anniversaries for the reading of the first Mass by resident priests, or of their ordination, jubilees of appointments; and for New Year's Day. The *Harmoniemusik* also performed for funeral processions for the burial of monks or for their own relatives.

On less frequent occasions, the *Harmoniemusik* was allowed to perform outside the monastery. Such occasions included the weddings or private celebrations by relatives of one or another of the boys. In one rare case, the boys were allowed to perform a night serenade in a distant part of the town and were thus given permission to spend the night with trustworthy persons outside the monastery.

In addition to the *Harmoniemusik*, it must be mentioned that Napp also organized a Türkish Musik band from among his choir boys. As this kind of wind band required a larger number of players, the instrumentation had to be completed with players brought in from the outside. On occasion, when rehearsals continued late into the evening, these external musicians received permission to spend the night in the monastery.

The Turkish band also gave concerts, usually in the monastery garden or in the public square in front of the monastery. One of these concerts was an annual one on 1 May, beginning at 4:30 AM [!] and concluding at 5:30 AM. The morning of this concert in 1817 dawned with unusually cold weather. Therefore the musicians after a token appearance in the square were brought into the monastery and warmed up with two gallons of rose brandy and three loaves of bread by choirmaster Napp.

Bibliography

Bibliography

Allerhöchste Kabinetts-Order [November 8, 1810; August 10, 1813; March 13, 1816; May 14, 1816; January 15, 1817; January 28, 1817; February 10, 1817; October 16, 1820; January 1, 1821; January 14, 1823; January 17, 1825; March 21, 1825; March 15, 1830]. Berlin: Prussian State Library.

Allgemeinen Musikalische Zeitung (Vienna, 1812, Nr. 30) [On the Schwerin Harmoniemusik]; 1813; 1846.

Anonymous. Review of Wilhelm Wieprecht's 'Monster Concert,' of August 22, 1849. *Neuen Zeitschrift für Musik* (1849).

Armeemärsche Collection. Berlin: Schlesinger, 1817–1859.

Ashton, John. *Social England under The Regency*. London: Chatto & Windus, 1899.

Barzun, Jacques. *Berlioz and the Romantic Century*. Boston: Little, Brown, 1950.

———. *New Letters of Berlioz*. New York: Columbia University Press, 1954.

Bassetto, Corno di [George Bernard Shaw]. *London Music* (London, 1937).

Beeren, Major General von, letter to Major General von Hake, Nov. 1, 1810. Berlin, Secret State Archives, Acta betr. Die Musikchöre der Regimenter, He.A.Rep.4.Z.D.109.

Berlioz, Hector. 'Feuilleton.' *Journal des Débats* (April 1, 1945).

———. *Journal des Débats*. Paris (June 12, 1842).

———. *Memoirs of Hector Berlioz*. New York: A. A. Knopf, 1932.

———. *Mémoires*. Paris: Garnier-Flammarion, 1969.

———. *Treatise on Instrumentation*. New York: Kalmus, 1948.

Boston Evening Transcript (December 12, 1881).

Boulley, Aubéry du. *Des associations musicales en France et de la Société philharmonique de l'Eure, de l'Orne et d'Eure-et-Loir*. Verneuil, 1839.

Bourgogne, Adrien-Jean-Baptiste-François. *Memoirs of Sergeant Bourgogne [1812–1813]*. London: P. Davies, 1926.

Brixel, Eugen. 'Musikpapst und Blasmusik.' *Österreichische Blasmusik* (October, 1975).

———. *Das ist Österreiche Militär Musik*. Graz, 1982.

Bücker, F., 'Beim Generalkapellmeister Wieprecht.' *Der Bär* (1897), Jahrgang 23, Nr. 2.

Budden, Julian. *The Operas of Verdi*. New York: Praeger, 1973.

Bülow, Hans von, 'Zur preussischen Militärmusik.' *Neue Zeitschrift für Musik* (1846; 1858).

Burney, Charles. *The Present State of Music in Germany, The Netherlands, and United Provinces*. London, New York; Oxford University Press, 1959.

Burrell, Mary. *Letters of Richard Wagner*. New York: Macmillan, 1950.

Burton, Elizabeth. *The Pageant of Early Victorian England*. New York: Scribner, 1972.

Busby, Thomas. *Concert Room and Orchestra Anecdotes*. London: Clementi, 1825.

Buzzi, Gianfranco. *Cenni storici del Corpo di Musica Municipale di Milano*. Milan, 1894.

Carse, Adam. 'Adolphe Sax and the Distin Family.' The Music Review 6 (1945): 193–201.
———. 'The Prince Regent's Band.' *Music and Letters* 27, no. 3 (July, 1946): 147–155.
———. *Musical Wind Instruments*. New York: Da Capo Press, 1965.
Chlodwig, Karl Viktor. *Memoirs of Prince Chlodwig of Hohenlohe-Schillingsfürst*. New York: Macmillan, 1906.
Comettant, Oscar. *Histoire d'un inventeur au dix-neuvième siècle*. Paris: Pagnerre, 1960.
Croft-Murray, Edward. 'The Wind-Band in England, 1540–1840.' In *Music & Civilisation*. London: British Museum, 1980.
Degele, Ludwig. Die Militärmusik. Wolfenbüttel, 1937.
'Des regierenden Fürsten von Liechtenstein in Wien.' Vienna, National Library, Fasz. H-2, 159, 160 ex 1794, May 1.
Durant, Will & Ariel. *The Age of Napoleon*. New York: Simon and Schuster, 1975.
Dwight's Journal of Music (1852).
Eckart, Richard Count du Moulin, ed. *Letters of Hans von Bülow*. New York: Vienna House, 1972.
Ehmann, Wilhelm. *Tibilustrium*. Kassel: Bärenreiter, 1950.
Engel, Hans. *Die Musikpflege der Philipps-Universitäe zu Marburg seit 1527*. Marburg, 1957.
Fahrbach, Philipp. [On the band's instrumentation] *Allgemeinen Musik Zeitung* (Vienna, 1844).
Farmer, Henry George. *Handel's Kettledrums and other Papers on Military Music*. London: Hinrichsen, 1965.
———. *The Rise and Development of Military Music*. London: William Reeves, 1912.
Fox, Lilla M. *Instruments of Processional Music*. London: Lutterworth Press, 1967.
Galloway, William Johnson. *Musical England*. London: Christopher, 1910.
Goldman, Richard. *The Band's Music*. New York: Pitman Pub. Corp., 1938.
Gottron, Adam. *Mainzer Musikgeschichte von 1500 bis 1800*. Mainz: Auslieferung durch die Stadtbibliothek, 1959.
Grove, George. *The New Grove Dictionary of Music and Musicians*. Edited by Stanley Sadie. London: Macmillan, 1980.
Gumtau, Carl Friedrich. *Die Jäger und Schützen*. Berlin, 1834.
Gutman, Robert. *Richard Wagner, the Man, His Mind, and His Music*. New York: Harcourt, Brace & World, 1968.
Harley, John. 'Music at the English Court in the Eighteenth and Nineteenth Centuries.' *Music & Letters* 50, no. 3 (July, 1969): 332–351.
Harmonicon (December, 1827).
Hellyer, Roger. 'Harmoniemusik.' Dissertation, Oxford University, 1972.
Herbert, James W. 'Wind Bands of 19th Century Italy: A Short Sketch.' AD, 1984.
Holmes, Edward. *A Ramble Among the Musicians of Germany* [1827]. New York: Da Capo Press, 1969.
Hussey, Dyneley. *Verdi*. New York: Pellegrini and Cudahy, 1949.
Illustrated Leipzig Zeitung (May 20, 1893).
Kalkbrenner, A. *Wilhelm Wieprecht*. Berlin: E. Prager, 1882.

Kastner, Georges. *Manuel Général de Musique Militaire*. Paris: F. Didot frères, 1848.
La Capitale (August 14, 1878).
La Musica Popolare. Giornale mensile illustrato (Milano, February, 1884).
Larish, Baroness von. *Behind the Scenes with the Kaiser*. New York: Hertag, 1922.
'Liechtenstein Hausarchiv.' Vienna, National Library, Fasz. H-2, Nr. 27; 3037 ex 1816, 556 ex 1818; 3659 ex 1826.
Loesser, Arthur. *Men, Women & Pianos*. New York: Simon and Schuster, 1954.
Longyear, R. M., 'The "Banda sul Palco": Wind Bands in Nineteenth-Century Opera.' *Journal of Band Research* 13, no. 2 (Spring, 1978): 25–40.
Maréchal, Henri and Gabriel Parès. *Monographie Universalle de l'Orpheon*. Paris: Librairie Ch. Delagrave, 1910.
Mason, Lowell. *Musical Letters from Abroad*. Boston, 1854.
Max, Thomas. 'Heinrich August Neithardt.' Dissertation, Freien Universität, Berlin, 1959.
Meyer, Clemens. *Geschichte der Mecklenburg-Schweriner Hofkapelle*. Schwerin: i. M., L. Davids, 1913.
Morrocchi, Rinaldo. *La Musica in Siena*. Siena, 1886.
Murri, Alceste. *Sulle bande musicali: Pro-memoria*. N.p., 1888.
Neue Zeitschrift für Musik (July 1, 1858).
Neukomm, Edward. *Histoire de la musique militaire*. Paris, 1889.
Newman, Ernest. *The Life of Richard Wagner*. New York: A. A. Knopf, 1937.
Novello, Vincent. *A Mozart Pilgrimage*. London: Novello, 1955.
Oepen, Heinz. *Beiträge zur Geschichte des Kölner Musiklebens*. Köln: Arno Volk-Verlag, 1955.
Panoff, Peter. *Militärmusik in Geschichte und Gegenwart*. Berlin: K. Siegismund, 1938.
Parke, William Thomas. *Musical Memoirs*. New York: Da Capo Press, 1970.
Pressburger Zeitung (May 31, 1816).
Priestley, J. B. *The Prince of Pleasure*. New York: Harper & Row, 1969.
Quarterly Musical Magazine (1818; 1822; 1823).
Rasmussen, Mary, 'The First Performance of Mendelssohn's *Festgesang, An die Künstler*, Op. 68.' *Brass Quarterly* (Summer, 1961).
Reed, David, 'The Original Version of the *Overture for Wind Band* of Felix Mendelssohn-Bartholdy.' *Journal of Band Research* 18, no. 1 (Fall, 1982): 3–10.
Reicha, Anton. Autobiography, as *Notes sur Antoine Reicha*. Brno, 1970.
———. *Traité de haute composition musicale, faisant ssuite au Cours d'harmonie pratique et au Traité de mélodie*. Paris, 1824.
Reschke, Johannes. *Studie zur Geschichte der brandenburgisch-preussischen Herresmusik*. Berlin: VDI-Verlag, 1936.
Richardson, Hubert N. *A Dictionary of Napoleon and His Time*. Ann Arbor: Gryphon, 1971.
Rimsky-Korsakov, Nikolay. *My Musical Life*. New York: Tudor, 1936.
Rode, Theodore, 'Zur Geschichte der Kg. Preuss. Inf.- und Jäger-Musik.' *Neu Zeitschrift für Militärmusik* (1858) XLIX.
Russell, John F. and J. H. Elliot. *The Brass Band Movement*. London: J. M. Dent, 1936.

Sainsbury, John S. *A Dictionary of Musicians from the Earliest Times.* London, 1825.

Schrenk, Oswald. *Berlin und die Musik.* Berlin: E. Bote & G. Bock, 1940.

Sehnal, Jiri, 'Die Musikkapelle des Olmützer Erzbischofs Anton Theodor Colloredo-Waldsee 1777–1811.' *Das Haydn Jahrbuch,* volume 10 (Wien, 1978).

Sharp, H. B. 'Church Band, Dumb Organist, and Organ.' *The Galpin Society Journal* 14 (March, 1961): 37–40.

Shaw, George Bernard. *See* Bassetto, Corno di.

Spohr, Ludwig. *Louis Spohr's Autobiography.* London, 1865.

Stekl, Hannes, 'Harmoniemusik und "türkische Banda," des Fürstenhauses Liechtenstein.' *Das Haydn Jahrbuch,* vol. 10 (1978).

Stephan, Wilhelm, 'German Military Muisc: An Outline of its Development.' *Journal of Band Research* 9, no. 2 (1973): 10–21.

Sundelin, A. *Die Instrumentierung für Sämtliche Musikchöre.* Berlin, 1828.

Suppan, Wolfgang. *Blasmusik in Baden.* Freiburg: Musikverlag F. Schulz, 1983.

Szabolcsi, Bence. *A Concise History of Hungarian Music.* London: Barrie and Rockliff, 1964.

Tausch, Franz. [Discussion of possible employment] Berlin, Secret State Archives, Acta betr. Die Musikchöre der Regimenter, He.A.Rep.4.Z.D.469, I-II.

The Illustrated London News. London: 1845; 1846, IX.

Thomas, Max. 'Heinrich August Neithardt.' Dissertation, Freie Universität Berlin, 1959.

Vandam, Albert. *An Englishman in Paris.* New York: D. Appleton, 1892.

Veit, Gottfried. *Die Blasmusik.* Innsbruck: Ed. Helbling, 1972.

Vessella, Alessandro. *La Banda.* Milano: Istituto Editoriale Nazionale, 1935.

Wagner, Richard. *Mein Leben.* Munich: List, 1963.

———. *My Life.* New York: Dodd, Mead, 1911.

———. *Sämtliche Briefe.* Leipzig: VEB Deutscher Verlag für Musik, 1983.

Wairy, Louis Constant and Elizabeth Martin. *Memoirs of Constant, First Valet de Chambre to the Emperor.* New York: Century, 1907.

Watson, John F. *Annals of Philadelphia and Pennsylvania.* Revised by Willis P. Hazard. Philadelphia: Leary, Stuart Co., 1927.

Weinstock, Herbert. *Rossini.* New York: A. A. Knopf, 1968.

Weston, Pamela. *Clarinet Virtuosi of the Past.* London: Hale, 1971.

Whitwell, David. '19th Century Russian Composers: Their Music for Winds.' *The Instrumentalist* (February, 1968).

———. 'Beethoven's *Siegessinfonie* for Band.' *Journal of Band Research* 13, no. 1 (Fall, 1977): 3–6.

———. 'Concerning the Lost Versions of the Berlioz Symphony for Band.' *Journal of Band Research* 11, no. 2 (Spring, 1975): 5–11.

Wieprecht, Wilhelm, letter to Friedrich Wilhelm IV, April 4, 1853. Berlin: Secret State Archives, Acta generalia, Cap. 14, Tit. 7, Sect. 1, Nr. 4.

William II, Emperor of Germany. *My Early Life.* New York: George H. Doran, 1926.

Index

Index of Names

A

Abadie, Jacques, 19th-century composer for church music for choir and band, 214
Adam, Charles Adolphe, 1803–1856, French composer, 63, 66, 70
Adelaide, Queen of England, 205
Aiblinger, Johann Kaspar, 1779–1867, German composer, 18, fn. 56
Alabieff, A., 19th-century Russian composer, 86
Albert, Prince of England, 205
Alberto, Duke Carlo of Piedmont, 1831 ordinance on Italian bands, 88
Albrecht, Prince of Prussia, 25
Albrecht, trombonist in band of George IV, 203, fn. 10
Alday, composer in repertoire of band of George IV, 201
Alexander III, 1845–1894, Emperor of Russia [his wind band of nobles], 193
André, F., French serpent virtuoso in the Prince Regent band in London, 203
Auber, Daniel François Espirit, 1782–1871, French composer, 63, 70, 73, 134, 148

B

Barner, Major von, 19th-century cavalry leader in Berlin, 24
Barret, 19th-century oboist in London, 5
Bartel, trumpeter for Duke of Sondershausen, 185, fn. 2
Barth, leader of the Civic Band in Leipzig, 23
Barthe, Adrien, 1828–1898, composer, 153
Bauduin, ?, 1827–1835, director of civic band school in Douai, 148
Beethoven, Ludwig van, 6, 19 fn. 61, 34, 35, 41 fn. 3 [*Siegessinfonie*], 48, 81, 86 [Rimsky-Korsakov as arr.], 97, 108, 114, 132, 150, 153, 181, 183 fn. 21, 187, 202, 203, 205
Behrens, trombonist in band of George IV, 203, fn. 10
Bellini, 170, 180
Bender, conductor of the Guides, 73, fn. 24, 155
Benleb, bassoonist in the Duke of Sondershausen Harmoniemusik, 185, fn. 2
Berlioz, Hector, 1803–1869, 5, 7, 27ff, 37ff, 48 fn. 34, 66, 73, 86ff, 100, 109, 121, 138, 144ff, 164
Berr, Ennes, co-founder of the *Gymnase de Musique Mil.*, 62, 73
Beyle, Henri ([Pseud., Stendhal]), 1816 account of a band concert in Milan, 103
Bishop, Henry, 167

Bizet, Georges, 1838–1875, French composer, 156
Blancheteau, ?, 19th-century composer for church music for choir and band, 215
Blühmel, claimed to invent the valve for brass instruments in 1805, 4
Blumenthal, ?, 183, fn. 21
Bochsa, Charles Nicholas, 1781–1855, French composer and harpist, 143
Bode, hornist, court of Mechlenburg-Schwerin, 185, fn. 4
Boehm, Theobald, 1794–1881, developer of the modern flute, 7
Boettge, M., conductor of the Bayreuth military band, late 19th century, 38
Böhner, Johann, 1778–1860, German composer of a motet for band and choir, 212
Boieldieu, Françis-Adrien, 1775–1834, French composer, 148, 214
Boisdeffre, René, 1838–1906, French composer, 153
Boosé, Carl, conductor of the Scots Guards in 1845, 81
Booth, General, founder of the Salvation Army bands, 166
Bortniansky, Dimitri, 1751–1825, composer in Germany, 18, fn. 54
Boulley, Prudent-Louis du, 1796–1870, founder of civic bands near Paris, 149
Brahms, Johannes, 1833–1897, 131
Brépsant, Engebert, 19th-century French composer, 73
Brizzi, ?, famous 19th-century trumpeter in the Napoli band, 195
Bruckner, Anton, 1824–1896, his church works for choir and winds or band, 213
Brun-Lavainne, ?, conductor of Lille civic band in 1814, 148
Buchmann, flutist, court at Rudolstadt, 186, fn. 8
Buhl, David, 1781–1860, leader of the Versailles trumpet school, 57
Bülow, Hans von, 1830–1894, 22, 108 [reviews a band concert in 1858, conducted by Piefke], 114, 194
Buot, Victor, ?, 19th-century composer for church music for choir and band, 215
Bürgerl, ?, 19th-century Austrian civic militia composer, 126
Burney, Charles, 18th-century scholar, 13ff

C

Caccavajo, Salvatore, 19th-century civic band conductor in Naples, 157
Cambridge, Duke, creates Kneller Hall in 1856 in England, 83
Carafa, Michele, 1787–1872, co-founder of the Gymnase de Musique Mil., 62ff
Caravaglios, Raffaele, 1860–1929, civic band conductor in Napoli, 158
Carl Friedrich, Grand Duke of Baden, 188ff
Catel, Charles Simon, 1773–1830, French composer, 197
Cherubini, Luigi, 1760–1842, 182, 197, 203
Citizen Vivazza [Rossini], 87
Clagget, Charles, 19th-century London inventor, 4
Comettant, ?, 19th-century French reviewer of the Distin Quintet, 164
Compini, Leopoldo, Italian composer ca. 1850, 89
Coote, ?, editor of a 19th-century English band journal, 82
Cressonois, ?, conductor of a French band in the 1867 competition, 117
Czibulka, Alphons, 1842–1894, Austrian military band leader, 43

D

David, Felicien, 1810–1876, [judge of the 1867 world competition in Paris], 114
Delibes, Leo, 1836–1891, [judge of the 1867 world competition in Paris], 114
Distin, Henry, on visiting Sax in 1844, 82, 164
Distin, John, b. 1798, English brass player, 163
Distin, saxhornist, 203
Donizetti, Gaetano, 1797–1848, 170, 180
Donizetti, Giuseppe, 1788–1856, band director and brother to the famous brother, 89, fn. 6
Dörffeld, Anton, 19th-century director of the Russian Kaiser's Guard Corps, 17 fn. 48, 85, 117
Douard, ?, 19th-century composer for church music for choir and band, 215
Druschetzky [contemporary biographical notice], Georg, 1745–1819, [contemporary biographical notice], 101
Dubois, Theodore, 1837–1924, French composer, 153
Dunkler, ?, conductor of a Dutch band at the 1867 world competition, 117
Duport, Jean-Louis, 1749–1819, ballet, *Zephyren* arr. for winds, 218
Dürer, Albrecht, 1471–1528, 132
Dussek, Bohemian composer, 97

E

Eisenherdt, Mr., German band leader in England, 78
Eisert, ?, clarinetist in the Prince Regent's band in London, 203
Eley, C. F., 19th century leader of the Duke of York's Band in London, 201
Emanuel, Victor II, 1820–1878, 1st king of the united Italy, 90, 196
Eppinger, ?, 19th-century Austrian civic militia composer, 126
Eschrich, hornist, court at Rudolstadt, 186, fn. 8

F

Fabbrucci, Lorenzo, Italian composer ca. 1850, 89
Fahrbach, Philipp, Jr., 1843–1894, Austrian military band leader, 43, 177
Fahrbach, Philipp, Sr., 1815–1885, Austrian military band leader, 43, 45 fn. 28
Fessy, Alexandre, 1804–1856, 69 fn. 20, 70, 73
Fischer, C, German composer, early 19th century, 148
Flittner, clarinetist, court at Rudolstadt, 186, fn. 8
Flotow, 112
Formichi, Pietro, 19th-century civic band conductor in Siena, 157
Franz Joseph, Emperor of Austria-Hungary, 51
Frederick the Great, 9, 18, 26
Friederick Wilhelm I, 1744–1797, founds Prussian military music school in 1792, 16
Frederick William II, 1786–1797, 9, fn. 1
Frederick Wilhelm III, reigning 1797–1840, in Prussia, 109, 135, 159
Friedrich August I, 193
Friedrich of Mechlenburg-Schwerin, 185
Friedrich Wilhelm III, 1770–1840, 15ff, 18, 25ff, 191
Friedrich Wilhelm IV, 34
Fröhlich, 19th-century publisher in Berlin, 34
Fucik, Julius, b. 1872–1916, composer, Austrian military band leader, 43ff, 55

G

Gabetti, Giuseppe, b. 1796, famous band conductor in Piedmont, 77
Gansbacher, Johann Baptist, 1778–1844, Austrian composer, 126
Gatti, Domenico, 19th-century civic band conductor in Naples, 157
George IV, 1762–1830, King of England, 161, 201ff, 204
Gerber, 1812 publisher of an encyclopedia of music, 101 [article in 1809 in *Allgemenen Musikalischen Zeitung* on Harmoniemusik], 185
Girard, ?, 19th-century French composer, 75
Glinka, Mikhail, 1804–1857, 117, 121
Gluck, Christoph, 1714–1787, 35, [arr. by Wieprecht] 73, 132
Godfrey, Adolphus Frederick, 1837–1882, 81, fn. 14
Godfrey, Charles, 1790–1863, 81, fn. 14

Godfrey, Charles, Jr., 1839–1919, 81, fn. 14
Godfrey, Daniel, 1831–1903, 81 fn. 14, 84
Gounod, Charles, 1818–1893, 112, 147 fn. 2, 153, 156
Gouvy, Louis Theodore, 1819–1898, German composer, 153
Grell, Eduard, 1800–1886, composer for voices and band, 132
Grétry, André, 1741–1813, French composer, 182
Guarneri, Andrea, 19th-century civic band conductor in Milan, 156
Gungl, Josef, 1810–1889, Austrian military band leader, 43
Guttenberg, 132

H

Haberer, ?, 19th-century conductor in Sackingen, Germany, 129
Haidner, bassoonist, court of Mechlenburg-Schwerin, 185, fn. 4
Hainl, George of Lyon [letter from Berlioz], 146
Halévy, J.-F. Fromental, 1799–1862, French composer, 62ff, 73, 121
Hall, Richard, 19th-century organist, founder of a brass band contest in Hull, 167
Hallmayr, Victtorin, 19th-century Austrian band composer, 157
Hammerl, clarinetist, court of Mechlenburg-Schwerin, 185, fn. 4
Handel, George F., 1685–1759, German composer, 26, 35 [arrangements by Wieprecht], 73, 99, 168, 170ff, 202
Hanslick, Eduard, 1825–1904, Viennese critic, 99, 103, 114ff, 118, 149
Hartung, hornist in the Duke of Sondershausen Harmoniemusik, 185, fn. 2
Haydn, Josef, 1732–1809, Austrian composer, 107, 114, 170ff, 187, 201ff
Hegel, Georg, 1770–1831, German philosopher, 132
Heine, ?, 19th-century composer for voices and wind ensemble, 212
Heinrici, Georg, clarinetist in the Duke of Sondershausen Harmoniemusik, 185, fn. 2
Heinrici, trombonist for Duke of Sondershausen, 185, fn. 2
Heller, bassoonist, court of Mechlenburg-Schwerin, 185, fn. 4
Hemmerlé, ?, 19th-century French composer of band works, 151
Henning, Carl, civic music director in Zeitz, Germany in 1858, 17
Herbeck, Johann, 1831–1877, German composer, 133
Hermstedt, Friedrich, bassoonist in the Duke of Sondershausen Harmonie, 185, fn. 2
Hermstedt, Simon, leader Duke of Sondershausen Harmonie in Germany, 23, 185

Herrmann, bass hornist for Duke of Sondershausen, 185, fn. 2
Herschel, William, oboist and astronomer, 201, fn. 4
Himmelstosse, oboist in the Duke of Sondershausen Harmoniemusik, 185, fn. 2
Hobrecht, early 19th-century English composer, 201
Holmes, Edward [1829 account of band concerts in Munich & Berlin], 104ff, 133, 180, 186ff, 191, 213
Hühne, trumpeter for Duke of Sondershausen, 185, fn. 2
Hunten, 19th-century French composer, 73

I

d'Indy, 121, fn. 53

J

Jackson, Enderby, founder of the 1860 national brass band contest, 169ff
Jones, J. G., editor of a 19th-century English band journal, 82
Jouve, early 19th-century composer, 201
Junger, Oskar, military band arranger, 19th century, 123
Junghaus, oboist, court at Rudolstadt, 186, fn. 8

K

Kalkbrenner, Friedrich Wilhelm, 1785–1849, German composer, 20ff, 34
Kalliwoda, Johann, 1801–1866, Bohemian composer, 212
Kappey, J. A., editor of a 19th-century English military journal, 81
Karl von Mecklenburg-Strelitz, Duke, 19th century, 16
Kastner, Georges, 1810–1867, French army historian, 12ff 28, 30, 38, 42, 44, 47ff, 62ff, 85, 105 [as composer], 114
Kempter, ?, 19th-century composer of a Mass for band and choir, 211
Kerner, A. and I., inventors of 1806 trumpet valve, 4
Klosé, Hiacynthe, 1808–1880, French composer and educator, 62, 73
Koch, contrabassoonist, court at Rudolstadt, 186, fn. 8
Komzák, Karl, 1823–1893, Austrian military band leader, 43
Kozeluch, Leopold, 1747–1818, Bohemian composer, 201
Kramer, Christian, leader of the Prince Regent's band in London, 107, 202ff
Krommer, Franz, 1759–1831, Bohemian composer, 148, 183, 218
Küffner, Joseph, 1776–1856, German composer and arranger, 39, 73 fn. 24

L

Lamotte, Émile, 19th-century French composer, 75
Lanner, Josef, 1801–1843, 112, 136, 177

Lasek, ?, 19th-century German civic militia composer, 125
Lazzari, Sylvio, 1857–1944, French composer, 153
Lecomte, Pierre, conductor of the Douai civic band in 1827, 148
Lefranc, ?, 1837–1871, director of civic band school in Douai, 148
LeGrand, William, late 18th century vast collection of Harmonie music, 186
Leibl, Karl, 1784–1870, German composer, 133
Leonhardt, Andreas, 1800–1866, Bohemian figure in Austrian military music, 50
Leopoldo II, Grand Duke, 1797–1870, sponsors band in Napoli, 195
Lesueur, François, 1760–1837, wind composer for Napoleon, 197
Leuckart, 19th-century publisher in Breslau, 34
Leutner, band composer working in England, 82
Liechtenstein, Prince in Vienna, 1759–1805, 177ff
Lindpainter, 105
Liszt, Franz, 1811–1886, 22, 122, 213
Logier, 19th-century publisher in Berlin, 34
Louis XVI, 22, 143
Louise of Mecklenburg-Strelitz, 1776–1810, 9, fn. 2
Ludwig Friedrich, Prince of Rudolstadt sponsors Harmonie in 1793, 186
Ludwig II of Bavaria, 194
Lundershause, oboist in the Duke of Sondershausen Harmoniemusik, 185, fn. 2
Lwoff, Alexis Theodore, Russian composer of 1835 *Fantaisia militaire*, 86

M

Mabellini, ?, chairs Italian military band study in 1848, 89
Maelzel, 97ff
Maimo, ?, conductor of Spanish band in the 1867 world competition in Paris, 115
Mainberger, ?, Kapellmeister in Nürnberg in 1804, 113
Malsch, oboist in band of George IV, 203, fn. 10
Manfredi, Giuseppe, civic band director in Rome, 155
Maria-Amelia, Queen of France [letter from Berlioz], 1818–1857, 145
Marie Antoinette, 143
Marie, 19th-century composer for church music for choir and band, 215
Maschek, Paul, Viennese composer ca. 1813, 102, 187
Maschek, Vincent, 1755–1831, 201, 213
Mason, Lowell, 1792–1872, American educator, on bands in Germany in 1852, 107
Massenet, 150
Mattiozzi, Pietro, 19th-century civic band conductor in Florence, 157
Maximilian Josef, 19th-century King of Bavaria, 12

Méhul, Étienne, 1763–1817, 35 [arrangements by Wieprecht], 57, 197, 203
Mendelssohn, 1809–1847, 5, 22, 35 [Wieprecht arr.], 81, 105, 114, 132ff, 150, 170, 174, 185, 190, 193
Mercadantes, ?, chairs Italian military band study in 1865, 89
Meyer, leader of civic band in Dresden ('brother of the celebrated composer'), 187
Meyer, oboist, court at Rudolstadt, 186, fn. 8
Meyerbeer, Giacomo, 1791–1864, Italian composer in Berlin, 5, 22, 26, 28, 35, 73, 82, 86, 115, 120, 122, 148, 156, 190, 191, 205
Migette, E., 19th-century composer for church music for choir and band, 215
Mililotti, Giuseppe, 19th-century civic band conductor in Rome, 157
Mohr, J., 73, 81 fn. 15
Möllendorf, early 19th-century German composer, 26
Momigny, Lysias, ?, 19th-century composer for church for choir and band, 215
Moritz, J. G., co-inventor of the tuba, 25
Morris, composer in repertoire of band of George IV, 201
Mosell, Egisto, Italian military band conductor, 89
Mozart, Wolfgang, 1756–1791, 23, 36 [arrangements by Wieprecht], 81, 103, 105ff, 12, 114, 133ff, 153, 168, 174, 179, 186ff, 201ff, 217
Müller, clarinetist, court at Rudolstadt, 186, fn. 8

N

Napoleon, 1769–1821, 34, 57ff, 60, 77ff, 102, 113, 119, 138, 143, 182, 187, 195, 197ff
Napoleon III, 334, 119
Napp, Cyril, 1792–1867, leader of monastery Harmoniemusik, 217ff
Naue, J. F., 19th-century German composer for band and choir, 212
Neithardt, August, 1794–1861, German military band conductor, 19ff, 105
Netrefa, Cölestin, 19th-century Viennese trumpet professor, 52
Neubauer, early 19th-century composer, 201
Neukomm, Sigismund, 1778–1858, Austrian composer for choir and winds, 212
Nicholaus, Kaiser of Russia, 26ff
Nicolai, oboist, court of Mechlenburg-Schwerin, 185, fn. 4
Nicolas, M. L., 19th-century conductor of the Trélonnaise civic band in France, 151
Nicolini, 148
Noury, ?, 1835–1837, director of civic band school in Douai, 148
Novello, Vincent, 1781–1861, travels in Germany, 42, 106, 133, 210, 216

O

Onslow, Georges, 1784–1853, French composer, 63

P

Paisiello, Giovanni, 1740–1816, wind composer for Napoleon, 197
Paulus, ?, conductor of the French *Garde Républicaine* band in 1867, 117
Perron, Ed., 19th-century composer for church music for choir and band, 215
Pessard, Emile, 1843–1917, French composer, 153
Pezzini, ?, 19th-century civic band conductor in Rome in 1882, 158
Pick, Henry, English band composer, 1800–1805, 201
Piefke, Gottfried, 19th-century German military conductor, 19, 108
Pius IX, 1792–1878, Pope, 157
Pius VII, 1742–1823, Pope, his wind music, 195
Pleyel, Ignaz, 1757–1831, 97, 201
Poissl, Johann, 1783–1865, German composer, 186
Ponchielli, Amilcare, 1834–1886, Italian composer of many band works, 93, 156
Porter, composer in repertoire of band of George IV, 201
Printemps, J.-J., conductor of Lille civic band in 1817, 148
Purcbl, Joseph, 1768–1838, Austrian composer, 183, fn. 21
Puzzi, Giovanni, 1792–1876, established quintet concerts in London in 1817, 161

Q

Quantz, flutist and military leader under Frederick the Great, 26, fn. 91
Queisser, famous trombonist in Leipzig, 131, fn. 8

R

Raimondi, 201
Redern, Count of Berlin, 122
Reicha, Anton, 1770–1836, Bohemian composer, 58ff, 151ff
Reissiger, 19th-century German composer, 46
Rémusat, M. de, French minister who commissioned the Berlioz Symphony, 144
Rheinberger, Josef, 1839–1901, 211
Richter, flutist, court of Mechlenburg-Schwerin, 185, fn. 4
Righini, 36
Rimsky-Korsakov, Nikolai, 1844–1908, [as Inspector of Naval Bands], 7ff, 85ff, 121
Rinck, Johann Christian, 1770–1846, wrote many works for band and choir, 212
Rode, Johann Gottfried, 1797–1857, [regarding Jäger Battalions], 16, 21ff
Rogers, composer in repertoire of band of George IV, 201
Rolland, ?, late 19th-century conductor of the Pope's band in Rome, 195
Rosenkranz, Franz, 19th-century German composer for voices and band, 132
Rosetti, Antonio, 1750–1792, 201
Rossari, Gustavo, 1827–1881, civic band conductor in Milan, 156
Rossi, ?, 19th-century civic band conductor in Torino, 156
Rossini, Gioachino, 1792–1868, 36 [arrangements by Wieprecht], 73, 87, 90, 92, 103ff, 115, 119, 133, 148, 154, 156, 168, 170, 180ff, 196, 203f, 217
Rubinstein, Anton, 1829–1894, Russian composer, pianist composer, 153
Rumigny, Général de, friend of Sax and Berlioz, 6ff, 69

S

Sandow, trumpeter in the Berlin Guard Regiment in 1805, 15
Saro, Heinrich, 1827–1891, German military conductor, 19
Savoia, Paoalo, 19th-century civic band conductor in Naples, 157
Sawerthal, Joseph, 1819–1903, Austrian bandmaster, 45, 49
Sax, Adolph, 1814–1894, instrument maker and publisher, 37, 46, 62ff, 74, 90, 120, 164
Saxe-Meiningen, Duke of, 192
Schallehn, first leader of Kneller Hall in England, 83ff
Scharoch, band conductor of the Austrian IR 72 band, 111
Schick, Friedrich, 1822–1847, German military band conductor, 19ff, 105
Schiedermayr, Johann, 1779–1840, 183 fn. 21, 213
Schiller, Friedrich, 1759–1805, 19th-century German poet, 132
Schiltz, the best cornet player in Paris, according to Wagner, 147
Schlesinger, 19th-century publisher in Berlin, 34, 147
Schmidt, Johann, trumpeter in band of George IV, 203, fn. 10
Schnabel, Joseph, 1767–1831, composer of Masses for choir and winds, 242
Schneider, Georg Abraham, 1770–1839, head of Prussian military music, 19ff, 26
Schneider, trombonist in band of George IV, 203, fn. 10
Schöniger, bassoonist, court at Rudolstadt, 186, fn. 8
Schubert [Rimsky-Korsakov as arr.], 86
Schumann, Clara, 131
Schumann, Robert, 1810–1856, 5, 131
Sedlak, Wenzel, early 19th century arr. for Harmoniemusik in Vienna, 177ff, 180ff
Seebach, hornist in the Duke of Sondershausen Harmoniemusik, 185, fn. 2

Seidl, Anton, 1850–1898, protégée of Wagner, 123
Seipoldsdorf, serpentist, court of Mechlenburg-Schwerin, 185, fn. 4
Seyfried, Ignaz von, 1776–1841, Viennese composer, 182ff
Siebenkas, conductor of the Bavarian Infantry band at the 1867 competition, 115
Sieber, Ferdinand, Berlin music professor, 33
Siede, C., conductor of an Austrian band playing in Hamburg, 110
Siegbert, S., 19th-century composer for choir and brass, 209
Smyth, James, conductor of the Royal Artillery band, 83
Socrates, 54
Sondershausen, Duke of, 185
Sonntag, Gottfried, 123
Späth, German composer, 211
Spellerberg, oboist in band of George IV, 203, fn. 10
Spohr, Ludwig, 1784–1859, composer of the [*Notturno*, 1817], 102, 152ff, 156, 185, 192, 195, 205
Spontini, Gaspare, 1774–1851, Italian composer in Berlin, 22, 27, 30, 36 [arr. by Wieprecht], 61, 63, 73, 122, 148, 191
Stegman, composer in repertoire of band of George IV, 201
Steiner, Vienna, 101
Stephan, Wilhelm, successor to Wieprecht, 122
Stölzel, Heinrich, 1815 inventor of a modern valve for brass, 4
Strauss, Johann, Jr., 1825–1899, Viennese composer, 55, 111ff, 177
Strauss, Johann, Sr., 136
Strauss, Richard, 1864–1949, 132
Stüber, clarinetist, court of Mechlenburg-Schwerin, 185, fn. 4
Stumpf, band leader in Strassburg, 209
Stuntz, Joseph, 1793–1859, German civic militia composer, 125, 132
Sudre, Jean-François, 19th-century inventor of a language based on music, 58
Sumner, hornist, court at Rudolstadt, 186, fn. 8
Sydow, Herr von, 1804 announcement of a collection of military music, 101

T

Taffanel, Paul, 1844–1908, founder, chamber wind society in Paris, 153
Tausch, Franz, 19th-century German composer, 16, fn. 45
Tautwein, 19th-century publisher in Berlin, 34
Theen, hornist, court of Mechlenburg-Schwerin, 185, fn. 4
Thomas, A, composer, [judge of the 1867 world competition in Paris], 114
Ticci, Rinaldo, 19th-century civic band conductor in Siena, 157
Tillard, ?, 19th-century French composer of band works, 151
Triebensee, Josef, 1772–1846, Bohemian composer in Vienna, 177ff
Triébert, 19th-century double reed maker, 5

U

Umberto I, 1844–1900, of Italy, 196
Urban IV, Pope, 215
Urban, Emil, bandmaster of the IR 9th Regiment in Austria, 52

V

Verdi, Giuseppe, 1813–1901, 5, 121, 155 [as band conductor], 174, 211
Vessella, Alessandro, 1860–1929, Roman band conductor and historian, 155, 158
Victoria, Queen of England, 83, 189ff, 205
Vieuxtemps, 22
Viotti, composer in repertoire of band of George IV, 201
Vittorio Emanuele III, 1869–1947, of Italy, 196
Vogler, Abt, 36, 98

W

Waetzig, J. G., bassoonist in band of George IV, 203, fn. 10
Waetzig, trumpeter in band of George IV, 203, fn. 10
Wagenführ, 19th-century publisher in Berlin, 34
Wagner, Richard, 1813–1883, 5, 19 fn. 61, 26, 36 [Wieprecht as arr], 81, 86 [Rimsky-Korsakov as arr.], 108ff, 117, 121, 122ff, 145 [on the Berlioz *Symphony for Band*], 156, 172ff, 193ff, 236
Wagner, Joseph Franz, 19th century, Austrian military band leader, 453
Wallace, band composer working in England, 82
Weber, Carl Maria von, 1786–1826, German composer, 6, 23 fn. 84, 27, 36 [Wieprecht as arr.], 73 fn. 24, 82, 98, 107, 114, 118, 125, 134, 168, 192, 205
Welker, James, leader of the Wold Band of York, 168
Weller, Friedrick, German military conductor, 1840–1844, 19ff, 105
Welter, Louis, ?, 19th-century composer for church music for choir and band, 215
Wendt, Johann, 1745–1801, oboist, composer in Vienna, 181
Westmeyer, Wilhelm, 19th-century leader in Austrian band music, 52
Westmoreland, Earl of, composer of a Battle Symphony, 28
Wettge, Gustave, 19th century, conductor of the *Garde Républicaine* band, 75
Wettich, bassoonist, court at Rudolstadt, 186, fn. 8

Wieprecht, Wilhelm, 1802–1872, Head of Prussian bands, composer, 4ff, 17, 19ff, 23ff, 323ff, 38ff, 46ff, 51, 80, 108, 115, 118, 185, 189ff,
Wigglesworth, instrument maker at Otley, England, 168
William IV, 204
Winterhalter, Valentin, civic band conductor in Baden, 135
Winzer, trumpeter, court of Mechlenburg-Schwerin, 185, fn. 4
Witter, leader, military band in Munich, 107

Z

Ziegler, Johannes, 19th-century novelist, hears band concert in Vienna, 112
Zillmann, Kapellmeister in Dresden, 23
Zimmerman, Michael, b. 1833, Austrian military band leader, 43, 115
Zulehner, band conductor at Mainz, 46
Zulehner, Georg, 1770–1841, German composer, 133
Zweckstetter, Christoph, 1772–1836, composer for choir and brass, 209

About the Author

Dr. David Whitwell is a graduate ('with distinction') of the University of Michigan and the Catholic University of America, Washington DC (PhD, Musicology, Distinguished Alumni Award, 2000) and has studied conducting with Eugene Ormandy and at the Akademie fur Musik, Vienna. Prior to coming to Northridge, Dr. Whitwell participated in concerts throughout the United States and Asia as Associate First Horn in the USAF Band and Orchestra in Washington DC, and in recitals throughout South America in cooperation with the United States State Department.

At the California State University, Northridge, which is in Los Angeles, Dr. Whitwell developed the CSUN Wind Ensemble into an ensemble of international reputation, with international tours to Europe in 1981 and 1989 and to Japan in 1984. The CSUN Wind Ensemble has made professional studio recordings for BBC (London), the Koln Westdeutscher Rundfunk (Germany), NOS National Radio (The Netherlands), Zurich Radio (Switzerland), the Television Broadcasting System (Japan) as well as for the United States State Department for broadcast on its 'Voice of America' program. The CSUN Wind Ensemble's recording with the Mirecourt Trio in 1982 was named the 'Record of the Year' by The Village Voice. Composers who have guest conducted Whitwell's ensembles include Aaron Copland, Ernest Krenek, Alan Hovhaness, Morton Gould, Karel Husa, Frank Erickson and Vaclav Nelhybel.

Dr. Whitwell has been a guest professor in 100 different universities and conservatories throughout the United States and in 23 foreign countries (most recently in China, in an elite school housed in the Forbidden City). Guest conducting experiences have included the Philadelphia Orchestra, Seattle Symphony Orchestra, the Czech Radio Orchestras of Brno and Bratislava, The National Youth Orchestra of Israel, as well as resident wind ensembles in Russia, Israel, Austria, Switzerland, Germany, England, Wales, The Netherlands, Portugal, Peru, Korea, Japan, Taiwan, Canada and the United States.

He is a past president of the College Band Directors National Association, a member of the Prasidium of the International Society for the Promotion of Band Music, and was a member of the founding board of directors of the World Association for Symphonic Bands and Ensembles (WASBE). In 1964 he was made an honorary life member of Kappa Kappa Psi, a national professional music fraternity. In September, 2001, he was a delegate to the UNESCO Conference on Global Music in Tokyo. He has been knighted by sovereign organizations in France, Portugal and Scotland and has been awarded the gold medal of Kerkrade, The Netherlands, and the silver medal of Wangen, Germany, the highest honor given wind conductors in the United States, the medal of the Academy of Wind and Percussion Arts (National Band Association) and the highest honor given wind conductors in Austria, the gold medal of the Austrian Band Association. He is a member of the Hall of Fame of the California Music Educators Association.

Dr. Whitwell's publications include more than 127 articles on wind literature including publications in Music and Letters (London), the London Musical Times, the Mozart-Jahrbuch (Salzburg), and 39 books, among which is his 13-volume *History and Literature of the Wind Band and Wind Ensemble* and an 8-volume series on *Aesthetics in Music*. In addition to numerous modern editions of early wind band music his original compositions include 5 symphonies.

David Whitwell was named as one of six men who have determined the course of American bands during the second half of the 20th century, in the definitive history, *The Twentieth Century American Wind Band* (Meredith Music).

A doctoral dissertation by German Gonzales (2007, Arizona State University) is dedicated to the life and conducting career of David Whitwell through the year 1977. David Whitwell is one of nine men described by Paula A. Crider in *The Conductor's Legacy* (Chicago: GIA, 2010) as 'the legendary conductors' of the 20th century.

'I can't imagine the 2nd half of the 20th century—without David Whitwell and what he has given to all of the rest of us.' Frederick Fennell (1993)

www.ingramcontent.com/pod-product-compliance
Lightning Source LLC
Chambersburg PA
CBHW081349230426
43667CB00017B/2772